AUTOMOTIVE ELECTRICAL SYSTEMS

Third Edition

Walter E. Billiet, Ed. D., New Jersey Director, Office of Area Vocational Technical Schools, Formerly Coordinator of Automotive Training, Henry Ford Community College, Dearborn, Michigan.

Leslie F. Goings, M.Ed., Instructor, Automotive Technology, Henry Ford Community College, Dearborn, Michigan. Member, American Vocational Association.

American Technical Society Chicago 60637

PREFACE

The electrical system is a vital part of the modern automobile. It is involved in starting, operating, heating, lighting, ventilating, and signaling. The safety, dependability, comfort, and convenience of the car are dependent on the various electrical devices and equipment. This important system has undergone rapid changes in the last few years. New components have replaced older ones. Advances in electronic technology have caused changes in electrical theory and practice. That is the goal of this edition: to present the latest information on these changes and to explain the principles that underlie them so the automotive serviceman will be able to understand and service the newest electrical systems confidently and competently.

The text has been completely rewritten or revised to cover the latest trends and changes in the electrical system of the modern automobile.

A chapter on Automotive Electronics was written especially for this edition to clarify and explain the use of the new electrical and electronic devices and methods in the modern car. Diodes, transistors, zeners, and integrated circuits are some of the subjects in this important chapter.

Another change in the text includes a comprehensive treatment of alternators and their servicing. The Generators, still used on some types of vehicles, have been covered although the treatment has been altered to apply to units in present use and to delete obsolete material.

The relation of electrical equipment to emission control systems is included and will aid the mechanic to understand and service the various electrical means being used to assist in combating pollution on the highways.

The organization of the book has been completely changed and the importance of service work has been stressed by placing detailed testing and repair instructions in chapters separate from those covering principles, operation, and construction of the various electrical units.

The Publisher

CONTENTS

		PAGE
1	Principles of Automotive Electricity	1
2	The Storage Battery	32
3	Storage Battery Service	53
4	Cranking Motor System	78
5	Cranking Motor System Service	100
6	DC Charging Systems	123
7	DC Charging Systems Service	157
8	AC Charging Systems	191
9	AC Charging Systems Service	224
10	Ignition Systems	256
11	Ignition Systems Service	290
12	Automotive Electronics	318
13	Lights and Accessories Systems	332
14	Lights and Accessories Systems Service	354
15	Instruments and Gages	370
	Index	385

CHAPTER 1

PRINCIPLES OF AUTOMOTIVE ELECTRICITY

Any individual who wants to do electrical work for automotive vehicles should have a comprehensive knowledge of electricity and magnetism. Such knowledge is a distinct asset as electricity and magnetism play an important part in starting, lighting, ignition, and other operations. Without it he is, in many respects, no more than a "tinkerer"; an unskilled repairman. He has to follow a time-consuming process of trial and error, or elimination, until the correct solution is finally made, if at all. This chapter provides a groundwork for the student in understanding the various electrical systems and the principles that apply to them in the automotive field.

ELECTRICAL NATURE OF MATTER

To begin with, electricity and magnetism are closely related subjects. We cannot study one without the other. It is customary to take up electricity first, then magnetism, and then to combine the two. We shall follow that sequence.

The Electron Theory

All matter—automobiles, clothing, food, furniture, paper, metal—in fact everything about us, has weight, occupies space, and is composed of basic units, called molecules, that are so small they cannot be seen even with our most powerful microscopes. Each molecule can be divided into smaller particles called atoms.

An atom is composed of electrons, protons, and neutrons. The protons and neutrons are in the center of the atom in a group and form the nucleus (or core) while the electrons are in circles or paths revolving around the nucleus. These paths or orbits have been compared to the path of the earth around the sun. Fig. 1.

The protons have an attraction for the electrons that holds them

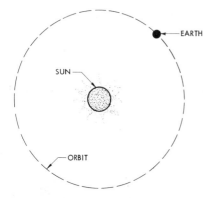

Fig. 1. A part of the solar system with the earth revolving around the sun.

in orbit. This attraction of the protons for the electrons is what we call electricity.

Every atom must have at least one proton and one electron. The hydrogen atom has one proton and one electron, Fig. 2. The electrons have a negative charge of electricity and the protons have a positive charge. Neutrons are neutral; that is they have no electrical charge. Each proton is balanced by an electron. There is an attraction between them that helps explain why the electrons stay in orbit around the nucleus. It should be noted that unlike electrical charges attract each other (positive attracts negative and vice versa) while similar charges repel each other.

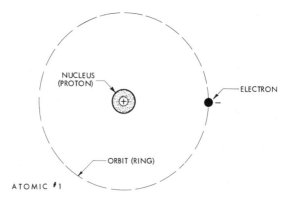

Fig. 2. An atom of hydrogen. One electron orbits the nucleus which has one proton. This is the simplest atom.

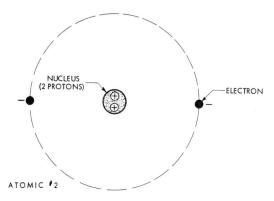

Fig. 3. An atom of helium has two electrons in a ring and two protons in its nucleus.

The electrons are arranged in rings or orbits around the nucleus. The first ring has a maximum of two electrons, the second ring has a maximum of eight. The element helium has two protons and two electrons and is in balance, Fig. 3.

The electrons in the outer rings are subjected to less attraction than the ones in the inner rings. Also any unfilled rings will affect the attraction between atoms. The element oxygen has eight protons and eight electrons. The first ring has its maximum of two electrons which leaves six for the second ring. Because there are an equal number of protons and electrons the atom is electrically in balance. The second ring, however, has only six electrons in it instead of the maximum of eight that it can accommodate. This is termed an incomplete ring. Fig. 4.

The number of electrons in the atom determines what characteristics it will have. A number of identical atoms in a group make up an element. There are 103 elements at the present time. Each element is distinctive and has certain characteristics due to the atoms that compose it. The elements are the building blocks of the universe. Alone or in combination with other elements they make up everything that we know. Water, for instance, is composed of two atoms of hydrogen and one of oxygen in each molecule. Chemists write this H_2O.

The number of electrons in an atom determines what element it is and also the number of rings or orbits. Each ring represents a

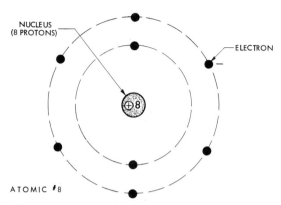

Fig. 4. An atom of oxygen. The inner ring is completely filled with two electrons. The outer ring has 6 electrons.

different energy level of the electrons. Each ring also has a definite path that is a fixed distance from the nucleus.

An atom of copper has 29 electrons and 29 protons: germanium has 32 of each; and uranium contains 92. A proton is believed to be 1836 times heavier than an electron.

Electron Flow and Potential

According to the electron theory electricity is the flow of electrons through a conductor. Let's see how this flow occurs.

An atom has an equal number of protons and electrons. The positively charged protons balance the negatively charged electrons and the atom is thus balanced and electrically neutral. The electrons orbit the nucleus at different levels. The first ring or level cannot hold more than two electrons. The second ring is completely filled when it has eight electrons. Each successive ring has a maximum number of electrons which it can hold. However, the total number of electrons belonging to the atom may be such that the outermost ring will contain only one, two, or three electrons after the other rings have been filled. The few electrons which make up the outermost, incomplete ring are not as stable or as closely held by attraction of the nucleus as the electrons which make up the completed inner rings. They have a tendency to leave the atom to which they belong and join the neighboring atoms. Such electrons are referred to as free electrons. Materials made up of atoms with incomplete outer rings are called *conductors* since electrons can be passed from atom to atom through them. Examples of good conductors are copper, silver, and aluminum. Liquids can also be good conductors and ones which conduct electron flow (electricity) are called electrolytes. Sulfuric acid is a good electrolyte.

Materials, on the other hand, which have complete outer rings and very stable electrons, since they are held to the nucleus very strongly, are very poor conductors and are called *insulators*. They have no tendency to give up electrons to neighboring atoms and the reverse may be true. They may have a tendency to attract free electrons.

Materials which are good insulators are mica (mineral silicates which separate in thin sheets), glass, paper, dry air, and distilled water.

Electron Flow

Just as water seeks its own level, the electron is attracted to whatever point will tend to neutralize its negative charge and restore the natural electrical balance. Conductors composed of atoms with a "free electron" structure provide a path along which the electrons can travel.

Electrons will travel from a point where they are concentrated to a point where they are less concentrated. In other words they go from a point of high potential (concentration of negative charge) to a point of lower potential (lower negative, or more positive, charge). The end of the path which is the source of the high negative charge is called the *negative terminal*. The point to which the current flows is called the *positive terminal*. Current will flow between these two points if a potential difference exists and if a path (or conductor) is provided.

The actual movement of electrons through the conductor is often compared to the old-fashion bucket line where buckets were passed one at a time from hand to hand from the well to the fire. The electrons pass from atom to atom from the high potential or negative terminal to the low potential or positive terminal.

Potential

To understand potential we must first define the electrical field. A field is a region, and an electrical field is a region in space sur-

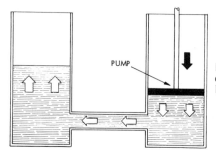

PUMP

Fig. 5. Water flows from a place of high pressure to a place of low pressure.

rounding a charged object. A charge in an electrical field possesses potential energy; that is, energy acquired by virtue of its position. Because of its potential energy water flows from high places downward. The potential of water is determined by measuring differences in height with the lower place being taken as zero. The higher the water above the low point the more potential it has. That is why high waterfalls such as Niagara Falls can be harnessed to generate large amounts of power.

In the case of electricity, potential is known as the amount of force required to move electrons in a circuit and cause current to flow. Potential difference is the difference in electrical pressure (voltage) between two points. It resembles pressure differences in liquids.

If a water tank is connected to a pipe and a pump is used, Fig. 5, a pressure difference exists between the ends of the pipe that forces the liquid to flow through it. The rate of flow is proportional to the amount of pressure exerted on the pump. The flow stops when the pressure difference vanishes.

Similarly, free electrons in a conductor will move from areas of concentration to areas of fewer electrons. Just as water in a higher tank will flow to the lower tank until both tanks reach the same level, so will electrons in a circuit go from the negative terminal to the positive terminal, Fig. 6, until the potentials of the two points are the same. The flow will continue until the potential difference between the two points vanishes.

Static Electricity

Static means "bodies or forces at rest or in equilibrium," that is the opposite to dynamic which means forces in motion. Static electricity is electrical energy at rest.

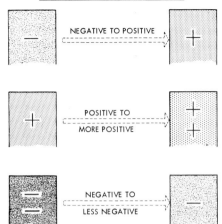

ELECTRONS WILL FLOW FROM

NEGATIVE TO POSITIVE

POSITIVE TO
MORE POSITIVE

NEGATIVE TO
LESS NEGATIVE

Fig. 6. Electrons flow from a point of higher potential to one of lower potential.

An example of the movement of electrons (electrical flow) can be illustrated by a simple experiment involving static electricity. Static electricity can be produced by friction, that is by rubbing unlike materials together. If a piece of amber, glass, or hard rubber is rubbed with a piece of silk, fur, or flannel, electrostatic energy is produced. This occurs quite often in very cold weather when the air is dry. Shoes or clothing will gather static electricity and produce a shock when a conducting surface is encountered. This may occur in a car or in a house. Some car owners attach a special strap to their cars which hangs to the ground and eliminates the possibility of shock due to static electricity. Gasoline tank trucks are also

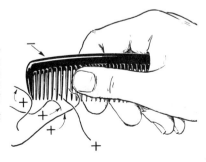

Fig. 7. A comb rubbed against hair collects a surplus of electrons. When brought near the hair the comb attracts the hair and it "stands up." Hair is positive and is marked "+" while the comb is negative and marked "—." This shows that unlike charges attract each other.

grounded for the same reason—to prevent sparks from static electricity causing an explosion or fire.

If you take a hard rubber comb and run it through your hair for a short time, you will notice that the hair nearest the comb will stand up when you place the comb just above your head. Fig. 7. If you take two combs and rub them against your hair and then bring them close together you will find that they will repel (push away from) each other. The combs had similar or like charges of static electricity that caused them to repel each other while the hair had a different charge and was attracted to the comb. Fig. 8.

In this case the combs attracted a large number of electrons from the hair and became negatively charged while the hair lost electrons and became positively charged. When a comb and the hair were close there was a mutual attraction that caused the hair to rise. When the two combs, both negatively charged, were brought together the negative charges repelled each other.

In order to test repulsion or attraction the objects must be brought close together. When the separation is great the force becomes so small it can no longer be detected.

Matter may be charged by gaining or losing electrons. Electrons can move from one atom to another. Protons do not move as they are stationary within the nucleus.

Basic Electrical Units

Electrical flow, unlike water, cannot be seen. However, to make practical use of electricity, a person must be able to determine the amount available, the amount needed, the amount lost, and to control the flow. Units of measurement have been established and meters have been devised to make accurate electrical measurements.

Fig. 8. Two combs, negatively charged by rubbing against hair, repel each other. This shows that like charges repel each other.

Ampere. The rate of current flow is measured in *amperes* (usually called *amps*). This is the quantity of electrons passing through a given point in one second. An instrument called an ammeter is used to measure the flow.

Volt. Electrical pressure or potential is measured in *volts*. A volt is defined as the amount of pressure required to send a current of one ampere through a resistance of one ohm. Voltage is measured by a voltmeter.

Ohm. All materials, whether conductors or insulators, offer some resistance to the flow of electricity. The resistance is measured in units of *ohms*. One ohm is equal to the resistance offered by a conductor in which one amp of current is produced by one volt.

The resistance of a conductor increases with its length and temperature. It decreases with an increase in the cross-section area (size) of the conductor. The longer the wire or the smaller the diameter the greater the resistance. If the temperature rises the resistance of the wire will also increase. Resistance varies with the material. Good conductors have less resistance than poor ones or insulators. In fact, insulators offer considerable resistance.

Wire thickness or diameter is measured by American Gage Standards. The AWG numbers are standardized and are used instead of actual thickness in inches. Standard wire gage tables usually give the dimensions and the resistances of each wire at various temperatures.

In the automobile different needs call for use of different size wire. The battery cables which connect with the starting system have to be thick because of the high current which they must carry at times. Smaller wires are used for lighting purposes.

Ohm's Law

Experiments have established that the flow of electricity is directly proportional to the voltage and is inversely proportional to the resistance. The relation between voltage, current, and resistance is summarized as follows: The current flowing in any circuit is equal to the voltage divided by the resistance of the circuit.

If I represents the amount of current in amps, E the electrical pressure in volts, and R the resistance in ohms, the relation may be expressed by the equations:

$$R = \frac{E}{I} \quad \text{or} \quad E = I \times R \quad \text{or} \quad I = \frac{E}{R}$$

These equations are simple, but most of the problems in electrical circuits may be solved by their application.

Ohm's law applies to direct current (DC) only. In alternating current (AC) other factors in addition to resistance must be considered to determine alternating current values.

In an automobile circuit trouble often reflects abnormal changes in the resistance of the circuit. Higher than normal resistance may be caused by frayed wires or cables, burned, pitted, or worn contacts and dirty or loose connections. Lower than normal resistance often indicates "shorted" wires or coils in the circuit. A circuit is shorted when the resistance is lowered to such an extent that it causes an abnormally large current to flow. Shorted wires cause overheating and create a fire hazard. Safety devices such as fuses and circuit breakers are placed in the electrical system to open or break the circuit in case of shorting and to prevent excessive current from flowing.

If, in a starting circuit, resistance is increased due to a dirty commutator (a device for changing the direction of an electric current) or some other cause, the fixed battery voltage and higher circuit resistance result in less current flowing through the circuit. Because of reduced current the starting motor cranks the motor at slower than normal speed.

Electrical Power

Electrical power is the rate of doing work by electricity. It is the product of voltage times current. The unit of power is the *watt* or *kilowatt* (kilo is a prefix that means 1000 so a kilowatt is 1000 watts).

When a current of 1 amp is maintained by an electromotive force of 1 volt work is being done at the rate of 1 watt. Electric bills are based on the number of watt-hours

Other prefixes frequently used in electrical measurements are *milli* (1/1,000), *micro* (1/1,000,000) and *mega* (multiplied by one million). For instance, one thousandth of an amp is called a milli-amp.

Sources of Voltage

Sources of voltage are called electromotive forces or *emf*. They are essential to the continuing flow of current in an electrical circuit.

In automotive systems there are two ways of generating voltage. One is by chemical action in the battery and the other is by electromagnetic induction in the alternator or generator and the induction coil.

Electrical Circuits

The flow of electricity is analogous to the flow of water, so suitable pathways must be provided to the various electrical devices. The paths are provided by the conductors or wires that carry the current from its source to the electrical device, and back to the source. When the path is completed it is known as an *electric circuit*. A simplified diagram showing the flow of electricity in a circuit is called *circuit diagram*. For the purpose of saving time and making circuit diagrams easy to understand and construct, a series of electrical symbols have been developed and are commonly used to describe electric circuits. Some of the common symbols used in a circuit diagram are shown at the end of this chapter. (Fig. 30)

If we trace the flow of electrons, we find that they flow out from the negative terminal of the source, through the load (resistance), and back to the positive terminal of the source. Circuits may be opened or closed by switches. Electrical circuits are of either the *series* or the *parallel* type.

Series Circuits. A series circuit is one in which electrical devices (or loads) are connected one after the other so that the same current will flow through each of them in succession, Fig. 9. A circuit is said to be in series when:

1. The current at every point of the circuit is the same.
2. The resistance of the circuit is equal to the sum of the individual resistances.
3. The voltage across the circuit is equal to the sum of the voltages across the separate resistances.

Using the resistance values of the light bulbs shown in Fig. 9 and applying Ohm's law, we have the following: The three resistances, 2 ohms, 1.5 ohms, and 2.5 ohms, add up to 6 ohms. The current through the circuit would therefore be

$$I = \frac{E}{R} = \frac{12 \text{ volts}}{6 \text{ ohms}} = 2 \text{ amperes.}$$

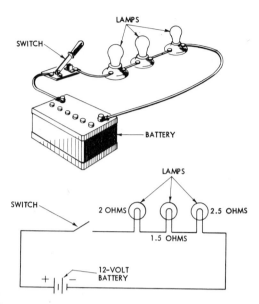

Fig. 9. A series circuit. Current from the battery flows to all three lamps (resistances) passing from end to end. A diagram of the circuit using symbols is shown below the drawing.

To find the voltage *across each resistance,* use the "voltage" varia-tion of the above formula with each resistance:

$$
\begin{aligned}
E = IR &= 2 \text{ amps} \times 2 \text{ ohms} &&= 4 \text{ volts across the 1st lamp;} \\
&= 2 \text{ amps} \times 1.5 \text{ ohms} &&= 3 \text{ volts across the 2nd lamp; and} \\
&= 2 \text{ amps} \times 2.5 \text{ ohms} &&= \underline{5} \text{ volts across the 3rd lamp.} \\
& &&= \overline{12} \text{ volts across the entire circuit.}
\end{aligned}
$$

It should be noted that the current flows through each of the devices in turn in a series circuit and if any one of the devices fails or is turned off the entire circuit is broken.

Parallel Circuits. A parallel circuit, Fig. 10, is one in which several electrical loads are connected to the main circuit so that the current flowing from the source is divided among them and re-turns to the source through a common return wire. A circuit is said to be in parallel when:

1. The voltage across the circuit is the same as the voltage across each branch.

2. The current in the circuit is the sum of the individual branch currents.

3. The reciprocal of the total resistance of the circuit is equal to the sum of the reciprocals of the branch resistances. In a parallel circuit, the resistance of the entire circuit is less than that of the smallest branch resistance.

A practical method of determining the total resistance of parallel circuits is to divide the product of the resistances in adjacent parallel circuits by the sum of the two resistances. If more than two parallel circuits are involved, the result obtained from the first calculation can be combined with a third parallel resistance, and so on, until the combined resistance of all the parallel circuits has been calculated. Thus, for the two parallel lamps nearest the battery in Fig. 10, the combined resistance is:

$$\frac{3 \times 6}{3 + 6} = \frac{18}{9} = 2 \text{ ohms.}$$

The combined resistance of the first two lamps is then used with the

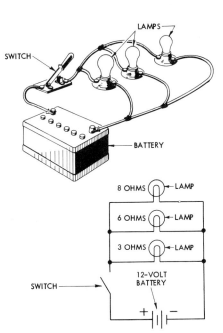

Fig. 10. A parallel circuit. The voltage to each lamp is identical. The total current from the battery divides into separate paths, one to each lamp.

resistance of the third lamp to find the total resistance of the three parallel branches:

$$\frac{2 \times 8}{2 + 8} = \frac{16}{10} = 1.6 \text{ ohms.}$$

The voltage across each of the branches is the same—12 volts. Since we know the voltage and the total resistance of the circuit, we can find the current being delivered by the battery using Ohm's law:

$$I = \frac{E}{R} = \frac{12}{1.6} = 7.5 \text{ amps.}$$

In parallel circuits each device is connected to the source of the current by a positive and a negative lead. Each device operates independently of the others.

Series-Parallel Circuits. Sometimes we find both series and parallel type connections in a single circuit. In this type of circuit the current passes through some units as in a series circuit, and the current is divided as it passes through other units as in a parallel circuit. In Fig. 11, all of the battery current flows through the 1 ohm resistor. The current divides, with some current flowing through each of the three lamps in parallel. All of the current then flows through the 0.4 ohm lamp, and finally back to the battery.

To find the current being delivered by the 12-volt battery, the

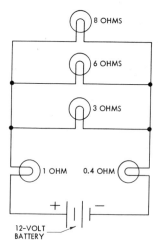

Fig. 11. A series-parallel circuit. This has some series connections and some parallel ones.

total resistance of the circuit must be found. Since the resistances in parallel in Fig. 11 are identical to the parallel resistance of Fig. 10, we are spared the calculation of the total resistance of the three lamps in parallel. Thus, the resistances in series, when added to the resistances in parallel, give the total circuit resistance:

$$R = 1 + 1.6 + 0.4 = 3 \text{ ohms total resistance.}$$

The current delivered by the battery is therefore:

$$I = E/R = 12/3 = 4 \text{ amperes.}$$

MAGNETISM

Magnetism is a force possessed by some materials which enables them to attract or repel certain other materials. Materials having magnetic properties fall into two broad categories, natural magnets and artificial magnets.

Natural magnets are found in an iron ore, magnetite or lodestone. Artificial magnets are metals that have been given magnetic properties by external means. Iron, steel, cobalt, nickel, and certain alloys are used for artificial magnets.

Artificial magnets may also be classed as permanent and temporary. A permanent magnet is made of steel or an alloy that is capable of retaining its magnetic properties for a long time. Magnets are made by being placed in a coil of wire in which a current is flowing. They may be demagnetized by heating or in other ways.

A temporary magnet is magnetic because it is in contact with another magnet. A steel bar after being rubbed by a magnet will be able to attract iron particles for a short time. It quickly loses its magnetic properties after the magnetizing force is removed.

Magnets are often made in two shapes, the bar and the horseshoe. A compass needle is a very light, thin bar magnet. Fig. 12 shows a horseshoe magnet.

Theory of Magnetism

Magnets have two poles, the north, or north-seeking, and the south, or south-seeking poles. The poles are located at the ends of the magnet where their strength is concentrated. This may be seen by dipping a magnet in iron filings. A large quantity will concentrate on the ends of the magnet.

When a bar magnet is cut in two parts each part becomes a

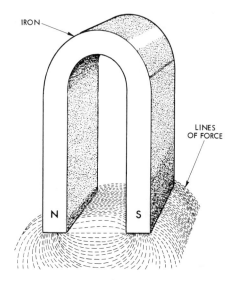

IRON

LINES
OF FORCE

N   S

Fig. 12. A horseshoe magnet. The lines of force flow from the north pole across the gap to the south pole and complete the circuit through the body of the magnet.

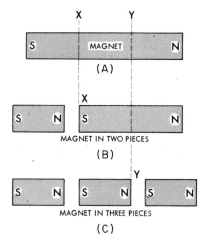

X   Y

S   MAGNET   N

(A)

X

S   N   S   N

MAGNET IN TWO PIECES

(B)

Y

S   N   S   N   S   N

MAGNET IN THREE PIECES

(C)

Fig. 13. Effect of dividing a bar magnet into pieces. Each piece becomes a separate magnet.

magnet with its own north and south poles, Fig. 13. It is believed that the molecules in a magnetic material are themselves miniature magnets. As in the case of electricity, unlike poles attract each other and like poles repel, Fig. 14. The force of attraction or repulsion is increased by making the magnets more magnetic. It is decreased by increasing the distance between the poles.

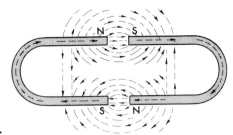

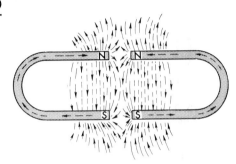

Fig. 14. Interaction of magnetic fields between unlike poles (top) and like (bottom) poles of horseshoe magnet.

In an unmagnetized piece of iron the molecules are disorganized so that the net effect is that they cancel each other's magnetic influences. Such a state is shown in Fig. 15 (top). When iron is magnetized the molecules rearrange themselves in an orderly manner so that the north pole of one magnet will attract the south pole of another and the magnetic influences of each molecule are added to those of the others, Fig. 15 (bottom). The result is that the magnets strengthen one another and cause the iron to exhibit magnetic properties.

Any magnetic material which has been magnetized will always retain some of its magnetism even though, in the case of temporary magnets, most of the magnetism is lost once the source of magnetism is removed. This is called residual magnetism and is important to the operation of generators.

The space about a magnet in which the magnetic force is exerted is called the magnetic field. This field is made up of lines of force which travel from the north to the south pole outside the magnet and from the south pole to the north pole within the magnet. The complete path in which these imaginary lines travel is known as the

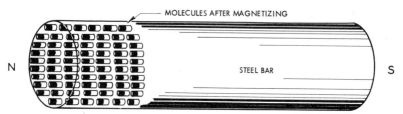

Fig. 15. Arrangement of molecules in a steel bar before (top) and after (bottom) being magnetized.

magnetic circuit. Notice the similarity between magnetic and electric circuits.

The line-of-force concept is used to aid in comprehending magnetic fields. The lines of force can be seen by placing a piece of paper over the magnet and sprinkling iron filings on the paper, as in Fig. 16.

The iron filings will arrange themselves in a pattern which follows the lines of force exerted by the magnet. The strength of a magnet varies with the number of lines of force per unit of pole area (usually in square inches); the greater the number of lines, the stronger the magnetic force exerted.

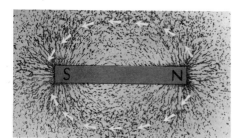

Fig. 16. Pattern of iron filings around a bar magnet.

Permeability

This is the ability of a substance to conduct magnetic lines of force. Non-magnetic materials such as air, wood, paper, and brass have a permeability of an arbitrarily assigned value of 1. Magnetic substances such as iron, steel, and nickel are capable of becoming magnetized and have a permeability many times greater than 1. It is possible to increase the permeability of some substances as high as several hundred times.

Magnetic Induction

When a piece of iron is brought close to a magnet the lines of force passing through the air are diverted and travel through the iron because of its greater permeability. The iron becomes a magnet itself by what is called magnetic induction. All artificial magnets are made by such induction.

ELECTROMAGNETISM

Electromagnetism is magnetism produced by electric current. When an electric current flows through a wire it creates a magnetic field around the wire. Fig. 17.

We may detect this electromagnetic effect by bringing a compass needle near a current-carrying wire. The needle will deflect as in a magnetic field. If we place a vertical wire through a horizontal piece

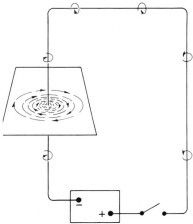

Fig. 17. A circular magnetic field is created when current flows through a wire.

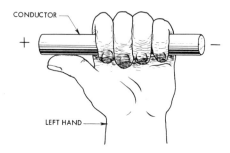

CONDUCTOR

+   —

LEFT HAND

Fig. 18, Left Hand Rule. With the thumb pointing in the direction of current flow, the curled fingers indicate the direction of the lines of force.

of cardboard and pass current through the wire we can observe the electromagnetic effect by sprinkling iron filings on the cardboard and tapping it lightly. The filings will form concentric rings around the wire. This shows the presence of magnetic lines of force.

The magnetic lines of force are at right angles to the wire and are distributed uniformly along its entire length.

Left Hand Rule

The strength of the magnetic field varies with the amount of current flowing through the wire. The direction of these lines of force is determined by the *Left Hand Rule*. Fig. 18.

The rule is: Grasp the wire with the left hand so that the thumb points in the direction of electron flow (from — to +). The fingers wrap around the conductor in the direction of the magnetic lines of force. If the direction of the lines of force is known, the direction of the flow of electrons can be determined by reversing the procedure.

If a wire carrying a current is twisted into a loop all of the lines of force traveling around the wire must pass through the loop, Fig. 19. On the outside of the loop the lines of force extend out into space. On the inside of the loop the lines of force are confined within the loop which increases the density or number of lines of force per

Fig. 19. Magnetic field around a coiled conductor. All lines of force pass through the inside of the loop.

square inch. The concentration of magnetic lines of force within the loop greatly increases the magnetic effect with the same amount of current flow. When checked with a compass a north magnetic pole will be found on one end of the loop and a south magnetic pole on the other end.

Magnetic Effect of Parallel Conductors

We have seen that a current flowing through a straight conductor creates a circular magnetic field around it. What happens to the magnetic field when two conductors lie side by side?

When the current flows in *opposite* directions in two conductors each conductor creates a circular magnetic field. But in one the field is clockwise and in the other it is counter-clockwise. This is shown in Fig. 20. The magnetic lines of force in the space between the two conductors are traveling toward each other strengthening the field while the ones on the outside are free to spread out. The crowding of the lines of force between the conductors causes the conductors to move away from each other (lines of force cannot overlap).

If the current flows in the *same* direction through the two parallel conductors the magnetic fields will travel around each conductor in the same direction. Fig. 21. When the two conductors are brought close together the lines of force in the space between the conductors oppose (tend to cancel) each other. Since the magnetic

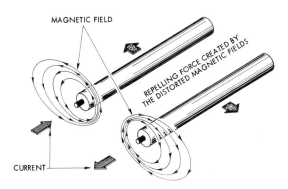

Fig. 20. When current flows in opposite directions in parallel conductors, the magnetic field between them is strengthened. The lines of force are compressed and act like springs to push the conductors away from each other.

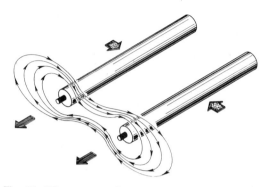

Fig. 21. When current flows in the same direction in parallel conductors, the magnetic field is weakened as the lines of force cancel each other between the conductors and the field encircles both conductors. The elongated field tends to shorten and pull the conductors toward each other.

fields are of the same strength the magnetic effect between the conductors is cancelled. Lines of force always form complete loops and never cross each other. As a result the lines of force take the long way around and encircle both conductors. Lines of force also act like stretched rubber bands and tend to shorten. This causes the two conductors to move closer together since conductor movement is always toward the weaker field. However, since the lines of force outside the two conductors are free to spread out this force is not great.

These figures, 20 and 21, illustrate the fact that there is a tendency for current-carrying conductors to move away from a stronger field and toward a weaker field. It is upon this principle that electric motors operate.

Coils

When a conductor is wound to form a coil the magnetic field around each loop of the coil has considerable effect upon adjacent loops. When the lines of force oppose each other they cancel out. When they travel in the same direction they reinforce each other. The outer and inner lines of force produce a field that forms continuous loops through and around the outside of the coil. Fig. 22. The inner lines of force are concentrated within the coil and the coil becomes strongly magnetic with north and south poles.

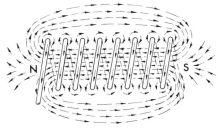

Fig. 22. The magnetic field produced by current flowing through a coil.

The polarity of the coil can be determined by use of the left-hand rule as applied to coils. Grasp the coil in the left hand with the fingers pointing in the direction of current flow. The thumb will point toward the north magnetic pole. Fig. 23.

Each loop of the coil contributes to the strength of the magnetic field. Consequently, the more loops in a coil the stronger the magnetic field will be. Also, the more current flowing through the coil, the stronger the field. So the total magnetic effect of a coil is proportional to (1) the number of turns of wire (loops) in the coil, and (2) the amount of current flowing through the coil. This is expressed as "ampere-turns."

Air is not a good conductor of magnetic lines of force. Nevertheless, air has been assigned a rating of one as a standard for measuring the conductivity (permeability) of other materials. When a coil is wound around a soft iron core, for instance, the lines of force increase over 300 times, creating a much more powerful magnet than

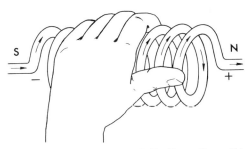

Fig. 23, Left Hand Rule for Coils. Grasp the coil in the left hand with the fingers curling in the direction of current flow. The thumb will point toward the north pole.

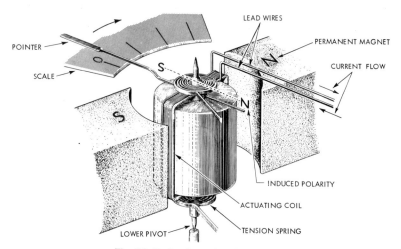

Fig. 24. Parts of an electrical meter.

the plain coil discussed earlier. Commercial electromagnets are composed of many turns of wire wrapped around a soft iron core.

The maximum strength of an electromagnet is reached when all the magnetic lines of force which the core can accommodate have entered the core. When this state is reached the core is said to be saturated.

ELECTRICAL MEASUREMENTS

Measuring electrical flow by meters is an important part of understanding and servicing the automotive electrical system. While there are many different makes and combinations of electrical test equipment on the market, the basic units that go to make up most test equipment are the ammeter and the voltmeter.

The basic principle of magnetic repulsion applies to the operation of electrical meters used to measure electrical flow (amperage) or pressure (voltage). Basically meters are made up of a movable coil of wire (armature) mounted in a magnetic field created by a permanent magnet. An indicating needle is attached to the movable coil. When current (electricity) passes through the movable coil one end of the coil becomes the north pole. The closeness of the north pole of the coil to the north pole of the permanent magnet exerts a repulsive force on the movable coil. Fig. 24.

A coil spring holds the coil in such a position that the indicating needle rests on zero, "0", when there is no electrical flow. When electricity passes through the coil magnetic repulsion forces the coil to pivot. However, the coil cannot swing freely since it must move against spring tension. With low electrical flow the coil will not move very far against the spring tension. The greater the electrical flow the farther the coil and indicating needle will move against the spring tension. The coil and needle movement is thus directly proportional to the electrical current flow through the meter coil.

Ammeters and Voltmeters

The major part of electrical trouble shooting as well as determining the need for preventive maintenance depends upon the ability to check for effective operation of the units.

Most of the electrical measurements are made with ammeters and voltmeters. It is important to understand the nature of these basic instruments, how to connect and use them, and how to evaluate the readings obtained. Likewise, it is necessary to appreciate what these instruments can do and also what their limitations are

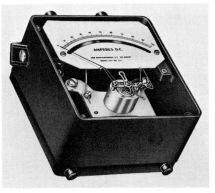

Fig. 25. Ammeter used to test automotive electrical units. The range of the readings can be changed by dialing shunts of varying resistance.

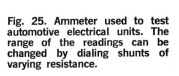

RESISTANCE OF SHUNT	RANGE OF METER AMPERES
no shunt	0.001
13.77777	0.01
0.04134	3.0
0.00413	30.0
0.00248	50.0
0.000413	300.0

as well. The basic construction of an ammeter and a voltmeter is the same; both operate by magnetic force created by an electrical flow through or past the meter.

For testing purposes an ammeter, Fig. 25, is used in a circuit differently than a voltmeter. Fig. 26. While the basic construction is the same for both a shunt is used in conjunction with an ammeter and a series resistance is used with a voltmeter. This means that care must be used to connect each meter correctly.

A *shunt* is a conducting element bridged across (parallel to) a circuit (in this case, across the meter winding) which establishes an auxiliary path for the current flow. See the diagram in Fig. 25. The capacity of the shunt that is used is determined by the amount of electricity that it is to carry. In an ammeter the shunt has less resistance than the wiring in the meter. Therefore, most of the electricity in the circuit being tested will flow through the shunt. The meter will carry only a small fraction of the total current in the circuit.

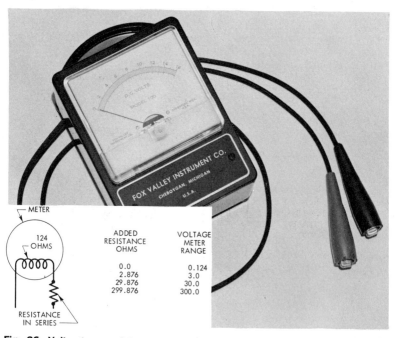

METER 124 OHMS	ADDED RESISTANCE OHMS	VOLTAGE METER RANGE
	0.0	0.124
	2.876	3.0
	29.876	30.0
	299.876	300.0

RESISTANCE
IN SERIES

Fig. 26. Voltmeter used in testing automobile electrical devices. Some meters can be dialed to change the range of the voltage readings. Fox Valley Instrument Co.

The flow through the shunt and meter is proportional to the flow in the circuit.

The voltmeter has a resistance unit in series with the meter coil. See the diagram in Fig. 26. The resistance unit creates an opposing force to the flow of electricity so only a small amount will flow through the meter. This flow will be proportional to the amount of electricity flowing in the entire circuit.

Although ammeters and voltmeters are usually built as separate instruments the two are sometimes combined in a single instrument. These meters contain both the parallel shunt and the series resistance with either a switching arrangement or a choice of terminals to permit using it either as an ammeter or a voltmeter.

Using an Ammeter

The ammeter is always connected in series in a circuit by disconnecting a wire of the circuit from its terminal and connecting the ammeter between the wire and the terminal. Fig. 27. The circuit involved and its relationship to other circuits must be understood to use an ammeter successfully.

Amperage is the measurement of the volume of flow so there must be a completed circuit and current flowing for a test. The circuit in Fig. 27 must have the switch closed before a reading can be taken.

Most automotive circuits have constant or near constant resistance peculiar to each circuit. The specifications from the manufacturers include this information for each electrical unit in the circuit. It is important to know the normal resistance when checking a device or unit.

When an ammeter is connected in series in a circuit it will show a higher than normal amperage if the resistance of the circuit is lower than normal with the voltage constant. If the current is being

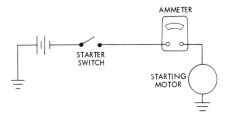

Fig. 27. An ammeter is always connected in series with the circuit to check current flow.

AMMETER

STARTER
SWITCH

STARTING
MOTOR

supplied by a battery of fairly constant voltage the assumption can be made that the resistance of the circuit is lower when the amperage is higher than normal.

The reverse is also true. If the amperage reading is lower than normal it can be assumed that the resistance of the circuit is higher than normal.

Using a Voltmeter

The voltmeter is installed parallel to a circuit or to any part of it. Fig. 28. When the voltmeter is parallel to the source of the current (with no current flowing) it indicates the open circuit voltage or pressure available as shown in Fig. 28A. Such readings usually have little significance.

A voltmeter installed parallel to any part of a circuit through which current is flowing can be used to determine the voltage within that part of the circuit. Any difference is referred to as voltage drop.

When current is being used in excess of the source's ability to

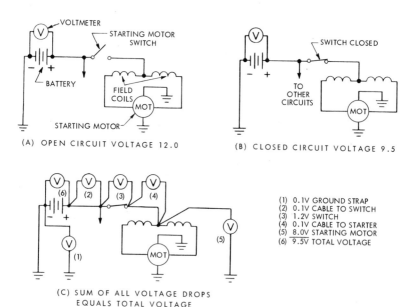

(A) OPEN CIRCUIT VOLTAGE 12.0

(B) CLOSED CIRCUIT VOLTAGE 9.5

(1) 0.1V GROUND STRAP
(2) 0.1V CABLE TO SWITCH
(3) 1.2V SWITCH
(4) 0.1V CABLE TO STARTER
(5) 8.0V STARTING MOTOR
(6) 9.5V TOTAL VOLTAGE

(C) SUM OF ALL VOLTAGE DROPS
EQUALS TOTAL VOLTAGE

Fig. 28. A voltmeter is always connected in parallel (across) the circuit being tested. Snap-On Tools Corp.

supply it the voltage at the source becomes less. When the starter switch in Fig. 28B is closed the battery voltage drops below the open circuit voltage.

The differences in voltage drops for individual parts of a closed circuit indicate the differences in resistance. This is illustrated in Fig. 28C where typical readings are shown with the voltmeter inserted parallel to different parts of the starting motor circuit. The sum of the individual voltage readings equals the total voltage available at the source. Thus $(1) + (2) + (3) + (4) + (5) = (6)$. Fig. 28C. In this illustration the figures are: $0.1 + 0.1 + 1.2 + 0.1 + 8.0 = 9.5$ volts.

Since parts of all circuits are shared by other circuits it is important that all circuits except the one being tested are turned off when checking specific voltage drop.

A possible source of trouble in any electrical circuit that is not operating properly can be located by checking the voltage drop in the circuit for each part of the circuit and comparing the voltage reading obtained with that of the manufacturer's specification for

Fig. 29. An ohmmeter is used to check the resistance of electrical units, make continuity tests, and to test components. Snap-on Tool Corp.

that particular part. In this way the exact point of trouble can be located quickly and corrected.

Ohmmeter

The ohmmeter is used to measure the resistance of various units in automobiles such as coils, wiring, resistors, transistors, diodes, rectifiers, alternators, and many other items. Fig. 29.

When trouble occurs and a unit is suspected its resistance should

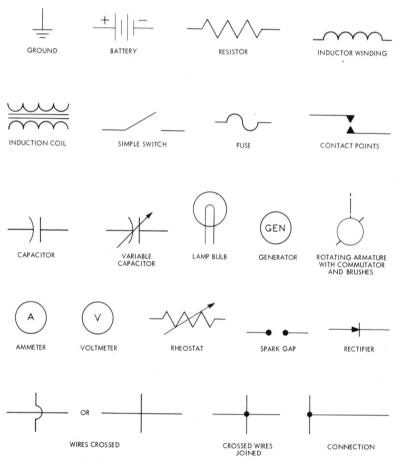

Fig. 30. Common symbols used in circuit diagrams.

be checked against specifications. Some ohmmeters have a test light on the panel for continuity tests to locate open circuits in components and wiring.

The scale on the ohmmeter is graduated to read in ohms and, through a switch on the panel, provides four ranges that permit measurements from 0.2 to 500,000 ohms. The meter's source of power is a single 1.5 volt flashlight cell in the case. A zero adjustment assures meter accuracy by compensating for variations in battery voltage.

TRADE COMPETENCY TEST

1. What are the subdivisions of all matter?
2. What is the central core of an atom called?
3. What is the polarity of an electron? Proton?
4. When is an atom electrically in balance?
5. What tends to hold the electron in its orbit?
6. What is the nature of an electric current?
7. What are free electrons?
8. What is a good conductor? Insulator?
9. In what direction does electricity flow?
10. The force that moves electrons is called what?
11. What is static electricity? How can it be generated?
12. What occurs when like charges of electricity are brought near each other.
13. What is the unit of measure for current flow?
14. What is the unit of measure for resistance?
15. What effect does heat have upon resistance?
16. What is Ohm's Law?
17. Name two ways of generating voltage in an automobile.
18. How does a series circuit differ from a parallel circuit?
19. What happens when unlike poles of a magnet are brought close to each other?
20. What is permeability?
21. Explain what is meant by magnetic induction.
22. What happens when a current flows through a wire?
23. What is an electromagnet? Describe how it operates.
24. How would you determine the north pole of a coil?
25. What is the purpose of a shunt in an ammeter?
26. How is an ammeter connected into a circuit?
27. What kind of a test is usually made to check for high resistance?
28. What electrical units are usually checked by an ohmmeter?

CHAPTER 2

THE STORAGE BATTERY

The storage battery and the generating system are the sources of all electrical current required by an automotive vehicle and become parts of every electrical circuit.

The storage battery is a group of connected electrochemical cells which convert chemical energy into electrical energy. Fig. 1. When the battery is connected to current-consuming devices such as lights, radio, or the cranking motor, chemical reactions take place between chemicals on the plates and the electrolyte. These chemical reactions cause electrons to flow from the battery as an electrical current when the circuit between the terminals is completed.

The capacity of a battery to produce current is limited depending mainly on the area of plate surface in contact with the electrolyte, the number of plates in a cell, and the concentration of sulphuric acid in electrolyte. After most of the plate surfaces have reacted with the acid the battery will no longer be able to produce current. The battery is *discharged*. Before it can be used again it must be *recharged*.

Recharging is accomplished by forcing current from an outside source through the battery in the opposite direction to the current flow during discharge. This reverses the chemical reactions in the battery so the battery restores its chemical contents.

Recharging takes place every time an auto engine is running unless there is trouble some place or too many accessories being operated.

In an automobile the storage battery may be considered the heart of the electrical system. It is used to provide a source of current for starting the engine, to furnish current for operating the electrical system of the car when the engine is not generating, and to furnish current when the electrical demands exceed the output of the generating system.

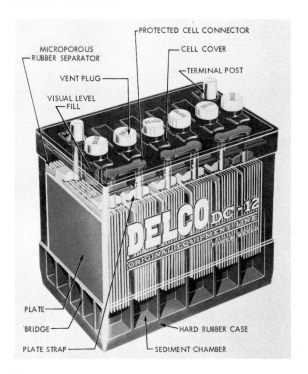

Fig. 1. Construction of a storage battery. The battery has six cells connected in series, producing 12 volts at the terminals. Delco-Remy Div.—General Motors Corp.

CONSTRUCTION OF A BATTERY

All automotive storage batteries are similar in construction and operation. The storage battery consists of a number of cells assembled in a battery case to produce the desired battery voltage.

The main differences between batteries are in the number of cells, the arrangement of the cells in the battery case, the number of plates in each cell, the size of the plates, thickness of the plates, and the type of separators used.

Cells

A battery cell, basically, consists of plates of two different materials immersed in an electrolytic solution that reacts with them chemically to produce an electrical pressure or voltage between the plates. The voltage depends upon the metals and the electrolyte.

In the storage battery each cell includes an element composed of interleaved positive and negative plates, separators to keep the plates apart, a case to hold the element, and an electrolyte. Fig. 1. Each case has a cover which includes a vent plug or filler cap with an air vent for releasing excess gases. Water is added to the battery through the vent plugs to keep the plates covered.

Several cells are generally connected in series to make up a battery of the required size. A fully charged cell will have about 2.1 volts. This is true regardless of the size of the cell or the electrolyte strength. By connecting three cells in series a 6-volt battery is made. When six cells are connected in series a 12-volt battery is the result.

Each battery has a positive and a negative connection. These are usually rather thick posts on each end of the battery. However, some batteries have lugs and some of the newest use a sealed terminal which has screw type connectors located on the side on the battery case.

The 6-volt battery was standard for many years and may still be found on some types of equipment or on older models. At present all new automotive vehicles are equipped with 12-volt batteries and electrical systems. Buses and other heavy duty vehicles may use from 24-32 volt systems.

Plates

The plates are the vital part of the storage battery since they store the active material which brings about the chemical reaction to produce electricity.

The basic structure of the plate is a grid framework cast from a lead alloy. Fig. 2. Positive plate grids are filled with a lead peroxide paste which is brownish when hardened. Negative plate grids are filled with a sponge lead which is gray in color. The lead pastes are called active materials and are submerged in the electrolyte. Both positive and negative plate active materials have a high degree of porosity that permits the electrolyte to penetrate the plate freely. Negative plates have expanders to keep the sponge lead from reverting to the solid inactive state.

Single positive and negative plates of the size used in automobiles will not create enough reaction to start an engine so a number of plates are connected together by their lug ends to form a plate group. Thus each cell is composed of a positive plate group and a

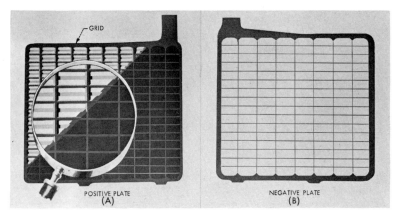

Fig. 2. The active materials of a battery are held in grids of lead alloy. The materials and grids permit penetration of electrolyte.

negative plate group. The plates in each group are connected by welding (sometimes called burning) the plate lugs to a post or connector strap. Fig. 3, top. The negative group always contains one more plate than the positive group so that there is always a negative plate on both sides of each positive plate.

Separators

The plates of a positive and a negative group are interleaved and separators are placed between each plate. Fig. 3, top. The separators insulate the plates electrically yet must be porous to permit free passage of electrolyte between them. One face of the separator is grooved vertically to allow for free circulation of electrolyte within the cell and to permit loose active material to fall to the sediment chambers in the bottom of the battery case.

Separators are made of materials that resist both heat and acid. Treated wood was used extensively in the past. Today, however, separators are usually of resin impregnated cellulose fiber types. Micro-porous rubber and plastics are used alone and in combination with glass fiber mats, and also flat glass fiber sheets with a micro-porous backing.

Elements

An element is formed by alternating positive and negative plate groups. Each plate has a separator on each side of it to insulate it from the adjacent plate. An assembled element is shown in Fig. 3, bottom, left. Each group of plates is held together by a connection at one side. These connections provide a means of holding the plates in place and for connecting the plates to other cells in making up a

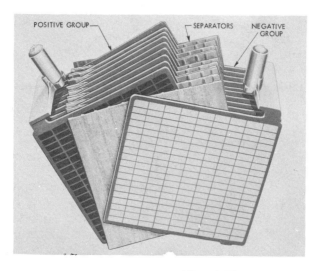

Fig. 3. A battery element. *Top*, partially disassembled to show positive and negative plate groups, connector straps, and separators. *Bottom*, left, an assembled element. *Right*, older design employs a separate cover for each cell. Delco-Remy Div.—General Motors Corp.

battery. The number and size of the plates used in an element will vary depending on the size and kind of battery needed.

Electrolyte

An electrolyte is used to cover the plates of the battery. In the automotive battery the electrolyte consists of a solution of sulphuric acid and distilled water. This is usually 38 percent sulphuric acid and 62 percent water by weight. The specific gravity (weight as compared with water) is approximately 1.260.

The electrolyte reacts chemically with the plates to produce electricity. The sulphuric acid combines with the active materials on the plates to form a new compound and to release electrons at the same time. This action is reversed when the battery is recharged.

Battery Case

A case is used to contain the battery. It is usually a one-piece molded hard rubber or plastic material. The case is not affected by acid or water and has as many compartments as there are cells in the battery. Fig. 1. There is a sediment chamber at the bottom of the case in each compartment to collect the materials that slowly wear away from the plates.

The case is covered in several ways. The old way was to cover each cell with rubber covers. Fig. 3, bottom, shows a single cell cover. A completely assembled battery using this type of construction is

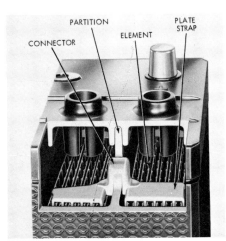

Fig. 4. Cutaway of a modern battery with a one piece, hard rubber top. Inter-cell connectors pass through cell partition instead of across top of the battery. Delco-Remy Div.—General Motors Corp.

shown in Fig. 1. The cells are connected electrically by metal straps that are welded to the positive and negative posts of the elements. A sealing compound is poured over the tops of the cell covers to seal the cover and the case. Each cover has a filler opening so that each cell can be serviced.

A later method is to cover the top of the battery with a single cover which fits over all the cells. The cover is cemented around the outside and across the partitions between the cells. Fig. 4. In this type of battery the cell connectors are located under the cover and pass through the cell partitions. This provides a shorter, protected path for the electrical current. A filler opening for each cell is molded into the cover.

Cell Arrangement

Storage batteries are made up of a number of cells. The number and dimensions of the cells depend on the service required from the battery. There are several arrangements of assembling the cells in a battery as illustrated in Fig. 5.

The cells are connected in series. The positive post of one cell is connected to the negative post of the adjacent cell. All the cells are connected in this way and a positive post and a negative one are left free for connecting to the battery cables.

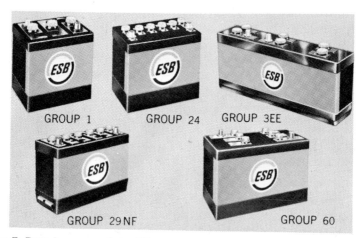

Fig. 5. Batteries are made in different physical and electrical sizes (capacities). Cells may also be variously arranged but are always connected in series.
ESB Brands, Inc.

THE STORAGE BATTERY

The voltage of a fully charged cell is about 2.1 volts. This is true regardless of the size of the cell since the voltage is a characteristic of the chemicals used. With the cells connected in series the total voltage is the sum of the voltages of the individual cells. A six cell battery will have a voltage of 12 volts.

Battery Sizes

Batteries are made in several physical and electrical sizes to meet the needs of the various vehicles.

The physical size (dimensions) of a battery is usually expressed by group numbers and letters established by national associations of engineers and manufacturers. Some are shown in Fig. 5.

The electrical size is expressed in volts and ampere-hour capacity, for example, 12 volt, 53 ampere hours; 12 volt, 70 ampere hours. The size has also been expressed as the number of plates in each cell or the total number in a battery such as 9, 13, 17 a cell or a total of 54, 66, and 78. No standards have ever been set for the size of battery plates so these ratings have no significance.

Warranty

All new batteries are sold with a warranty for a definite number of months. This is usually from 12 to 36 months depending on the capacity of the battery. If a battery proves defective within the warranty period credit is allowed toward the purchase of a new battery. As a result many vehicle owners, and many battery merchants, consider the battery as a consumable commodity such as tires. Some owners take advantage of the unexpired period of the warranty to buy a new battery at the approach of winter as a means of safeguarding against a battery failure in severe cold weather.

Owners have learned by experience that, from the first day of its use, battery capacity decreases just as the level of gasoline decreases with each mile of operation. New batteries, of course, have a wide margin of safety and more capacity than is ordinarily required. Due to the gradual but continual decrease in battery capacity few owners attempt to use the battery to the full extent of its useful life. The cost of one starting failure can well exceed the value remaining in a battery that has not been completely worn out.

Few repairs are made on the typical low cost automotive battery.

However, extremely large bus and coach and other heavy-duty batteries can be economically repaired in some instances.

OPERATING PRINCIPLES

The basic principle underlying the operation of a storage battery is that electrical energy is produced by chemical reaction between two unlike metals and an electrolyte. In an automotive battery the electrical energy is produced by chemical reaction between the active material of the plates and the sulphuric acid of the electrolyte.

While the battery operates as a result of chemical reactions you do not need to be a chemist to understand how the battery works.

The total amount of energy that can be delivered by a storage battery is controlled by the total quantity of active material in the plates. In other words, the three dimensions of the plate (height, width, and thickness) and the number of plates all have a bearing on the capacity of the battery. All of the active material is not in direct contact with the electrolyte and the reaction of some of the active material is retarded.

On discharge at high rates the amount of current is controlled by the amount of active material in direct contact with the electrolyte. The number of plates and their height and width (rather than thickness) are the factors that control the amount of current the battery can deliver at high rates as when cranking an engine.

Chemical Reactions on Discharge

When a battery is being discharged the active material in the positive plates (lead peroxide) and the active material in the negative plates (sponge lead) react with the sulphuric acid in the electrolyte to produce lead sulphate and water. Fig. 6. The sulphate is deposited in the form of a whitish scale on the plates. The electrolyte becomes weaker in concentration as the discharge proceeds. Hydrogen and oxygen are produced as gases and escape to the surface. Electrical energy is released during these chemical reactions. The reactions continue until practically all the active materials in both plates are converted into lead sulphate and the electrolyte is mostly water. The battery is then discharged.

Chemical Reactions on Charge

A discharged battery can be charged by restoring the plates and electrolyte to their original conditions. This is done by passing a

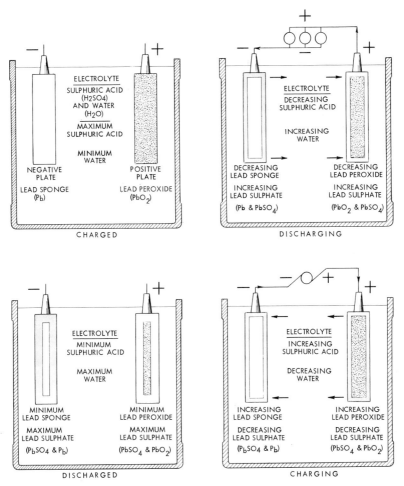

Fig. 6. Chemical reactions during charge and discharge. ESB Brands, Inc.

current through the battery in the opposite direction to the flow during discharge.

During charge the current flowing into the battery produces a chemical reaction in the battery that is opposite to that occurring on discharge. Fig. 6. The lead sulphate of the positive plates is converted to lead peroxide and the lead sulphate on the negative plate is reconverted to sponge lead. This releases sulphuric acid to the electrolyte. Hydrogen and oxygen gases are released during the reaction and escape. When all the lead sulphate has been reconverted to its original form the battery is fully charged.

Effects of Temperature

Temperature changes have a decided effect upon the rate of chemical activity within the battery. As the temperature increases the chemical reactions between the acid and the plates takes place more and more readily. When the temperature is lowered the chemical reactions become more and more sluggish. This has an effect on the ability of a battery to produce energy.

The individual cells, regardless of size, of a fully charged battery have an open circuit voltage of about 2.1 volts. However, when a battery is being discharged the voltage is influenced by the capacity of the cell, the state of charge, the rate of discharge, and the temperature.

When cranking an engine at 80° the voltage of a cell may drop to about 1.95 volts. At 0°F the voltage may be as low as 1.4 volts.

Cold weather causes the electrolyte to become more dense which slows down the diffusion of acid into the pores of the plates and through the separators. This slows down the rate of chemical activity, lowers cell voltage, and limits the output of the battery, especially at high currents.

Fig. 7 shows the effect of temperatures on the efficiency and cranking power of a fully charged battery. Note that only about two-fifths of the cranking power available at 80°F is available when the temperature drops to 0°F. The illustration also shows that the load is increased by stiff oil in the engine. It can be seen that at 0°F two and one-half times as much power is required to crank the engine

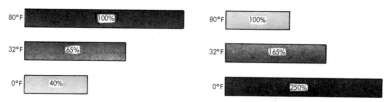

Fig. 7. Cranking power available and cranking power required at various temperatures. Fully charged battery and SAE 20 oil in engine.

than at 80°. The combined effects of zero cold in reducing battery capacity and the increase in cranking load due to stiff oil emphasize the need for keeping the battery in a well charged condition during cold weather.

Battery Self-Discharge

Batteries gradually lose their charge when standing idle even though no useful power is being used. The self-discharge or standing loss is due to a slow internal chemical action that takes place between the slight impurities in the battery materials and electrolyte. This is why so many batteries sold today are the "dry" charge type. This battery contains fully charged elements which are washed, dried, and sealed airtight. There is no electrolyte present so there is no discharge. When electrolyte is added at the time of purchase the battery becomes activated as a fully charged new battery.

The battery also loses some of its charge due to external current leakage. If the battery top is wet, dirty, or acid soaked there will be a slight loss of current between the battery terminal posts and from the ungrounded post and the nearest ground.

Temperature has a marked effect on self-discharge. The rate is higher when warm than when cold. A fully charged battery loses little of its charge at 0° while at 125°F it becomes discharged in a month.

This is the reason why batteries which are idle should be stored in a cool place, never in warm places or near radiators.

Battery Ratings

The amount of energy that a battery can deliver depends on the number and size of the plates used in a cell and the number of cells in the battery. The starting current of a fully charged battery is roughly proportional to the plate area. Consequently, automotive batteries are generally built with thin plates to provide a large area (by increasing the plates) so the acid can have access to as much active material as possible.

Batteries are rated according to the various kinds of service for which they are designed. Certain tests have been devised to serve as a guide in the selection of batteries. These are the S.A.E. twenty-hour rate test, the zero test, and the five-ten second voltage test.

S.A.E. Twenty-hour Rating. The S.A.E. twenty hour rate or ampere hour rating indicates the lasting power of a battery which is continuously discharging on a small load. The test gives an indication of the amount of active material in the plates. The battery is discharged for 20 hours at a rate equal to 1/20 of the published 20 hour capacity in ampere hours. As an example, a 12-volt battery rated by the manufacturer at 50 ampere-hour capacity would be discharged at 1/20 of 50 or at 2.5 amperes. The terminal voltage at the end of the test should be not lower than 10.5 volts. During the test the temperature of the battery should not vary more than 5° above or below 80°F. The same test can be used for 6-volt batteries. Terminal voltage at the end of the test for a 6-volt battery should be not lower than 5.25 volts.

The 20 hour rating indicates the capacity available for lighting, ignition, and electrical accessory loads. In comparing batteries of like quality, it is a major factor in determining storage battery life.

Zero Test. The zero or cranking ability test reveals the ability of a battery to operate under adverse temperature conditions at high discharge rates. Twelve-volt batteries of less than 90 ampere-hour capacity are discharged at 150 amperes while 12-volt batteries of 90 ampere-hour capacity or more and 6-volt batteries are discharged at 300 amperes at a temperature of 0°F.

The test indicates cranking ability at low temperatures. The purpose of the test is to find out how many minutes a battery can discharge continuously at its recommended rate before falling to a final over-all battery voltage of 3 volts for a 6-volt battery and 6 volts for a 12-volt battery.

Five-Ten Second Voltage Test. This test is made *during* the zero test described above and is the voltage of the battery five seconds (on 6-volt batteries, ten seconds on 12-volt batteries) after starting discharge at the rate indicated with an initial electrolyte temperature of 0°F. This rating furnishes a measure of the voltage available for ignition purposes when the battery is being discharged at a high rate. Sufficient voltage means a quick start with a minimum drain on the battery. As an example, on the zero test, a 12-volt battery would deliver 300 amperes for 1.2 minutes with a 10 second voltage of 6.8 volts.

Power Output of a Storage Battery

For many years, storage batteries used in automotive vehicles were of the 6-volt type and were compared by using the ampere-hour rating. Thus, one 100 ampere-hour battery would be similar in size and weight to another 100 ampere-hour battery, and a 120 ampere-hour battery would, naturally, be larger and heavier. However, the ampere-hour rating gives misleading information when used to compare 6-volt batteries with 12-volt batteries.

Let us consider a single cell of 11 plates. Connected in series, three of the cells will make up a 6-volt battery with a 70 ampere-hour rating. If six cells are connected together in series, we have a 12-volt battery, but the ampere-hour rating remains the same at 70 ampere-hours (because the cells in both batteries are of the same size). From this it can be seen that the 12-volt battery will weigh twice as much as the 6-volt battery. If the weight of the 6-volt battery were to be increased to equal that of the 12-volt battery, we would have to double the number of plates in each cell. This would still be a 6-volt battery, but now it would have a 140 ampere-hour rating. From this, it can be seen that the ampere-hour rating depends largely on the *number of plates per cell,* and that weight of battery materials cannot be a measure of comparison between batteries of different voltages.

A more practical unit of measure would measure the power output of the battery. Power output is measured in watts, the product of volts times amperes. As an example, a 6-volt battery is discharged at a 300-ampere rate when cranking a cold engine. The power output of the battery would be 6 volts × 300 amperes = 1800 watts. To produce the same number of watts, a 12-volt battery would have to be discharged at only a 150-ampere rate: 12 volts × 150 amperes = 1800 watts.

From this, it can be seen that each cell of a 12-volt battery can be smaller—about one-half the ampere-hour capacity of a 6-volt battery—to produce the same power to do the job. Although many 12-volt batteries are about the same in size and weight as 6-volt batteries, the trend is toward larger batteries to take care of the increased electrical loads.

ELECTROLYTE

The cells of a battery are filled with an electrolyte that covers the plates and separators. The electrolyte is usually kept at a level of $\frac{1}{4}$ to $\frac{1}{2}$ in. above the tops of the plates. The automotive storage battery uses an electrolyte that is a mixture of sulphuric acid and water.

Specific Gravity

The electrolyte used in the battery contains 38 percent sulphuric acid by weight or 25 percent by volume. The amount of acid in the electrolyte is generally measured by the specific gravity method. The specific gravity of the electrolyte changes as the battery is charged or discharged because the acid chemically combines with or is driven from the plates. Specific gravity readings which are based on the amount of sulphuric acid in the electrolyte can be used as the basis for indicating the state of charge of the battery.

Distilled water is used as the basis for determining specific gravity. It has a value of 1.000 and other substances are expressed in

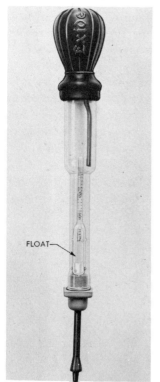

FLOAT

Fig. 8. Battery hydrometer. ESB Brands, Inc.

relation to it. The specific gravity of a substance is the percentage that the substance is heavier or lighter than an equal volume of water. Specific gravity is measured with an instrument called a hydrometer. Temperature also affects specific gravity and must be considered in making specific gravity readings.

Hydrometer. A hydrometer consists of a glass tube with a rubber bulb at the top and a short rubber hose at the bottom with a float inside the tube. The float is calibrated to read in specific gravity. Fig. 8.

Electrolyte is sucked up into the tube by the hydrometer and the float can be seen and read as it floats in the solution. The height of the float in the electrolyte indicates the relative density (weight) of the electrolyte as compared to water and indicates the specific gravity. The float rides high in the liquid if the specific gravity is high. It floats low in the liquid if the specific gravity is low. The readings are made on the float at the surface of the liquid. These readings

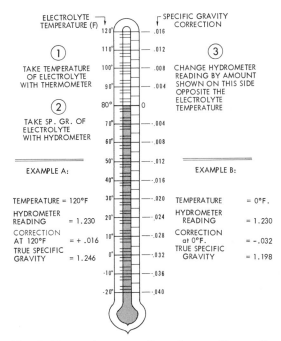

Fig. 9. Temperature corrections for specific gravity readings. Buick Div.—General Motors Corp.

are generally expressed to the third decimal place. In battery language the decimal point is usually ignored and the figure 1.280 is called "twelve eighty" or the figure 1.150 becomes "eleven fifty."

Temperature Correction. The specific gravity readings of the electrolyte vary with the amount of acid in the solution and they also vary with the temperature. As a result no hydrometer reading is strictly correct until the temperature has been checked and a correction applied. The hydrometer floats are calibrated at a specific temperature, usually 80°F. Temperature corrections are necessary for accurate readings because the electrolyte expands (becomes less dense) when it is heated and shrinks (becomes more dense) when it is cooled. Many hydrometers have a thermometer built in along with a scale to indicate the number of points to be added or subtracted for correct readings. Fig. 9.

The temperature correction is four points (0.004) specific gravity for each 10°F variation from the standard used for calibrating the hydrometer. The temperature correction is added to the specific gravity reading if the electrolyte temperature is above the standard (usually 80°F) and subtracted from the reading if the temperature is below.

Temperature corrections should be made whenever there is much difference between the electrolyte temperature and the standard. Two examples are given in Fig. 9 to show how misleading uncorrected readings can be at extremes of temperature.

State of Charge. Storage batteries can be fully charged and yet have different values of specific gravity depending upon the climate they are intended for.

Batteries used in cold climates have a normal specific gravity of 1.280 when fully charged. A reading of 1.180 indicates that the battery has only a half charge. Specific gravity of 1.080 shows a complete discharge.

Many battery manufacturers have reduced the specific gravity of the electrolyte from a reading of 1.280, containing 38 percent sulphuric acid, to 1.260, containing 35.6 percent sulphuric acid. The reason for this change was to provide a somewhat milder acid strength during the life of the battery. Since battery capacity is determined by the weight of positive active material, weight of negative active material, and weight of sulphuric acid, the capacity is retained by providing a larger volume of lower specific gravity.

TABLE 1. SPECIFIC GRAVITY OF BATTERIES USED IN
VARIOUS CLIMATES

State of Charge	Specific Gravity As Used in Cold Climates	Specific Gravity As Used in Temperate Climates	Specific Gravity As Used in Tropical Climates
Fully charged.....	1.280	1.260	1.225
75% charged	1.230	1.215	1.180
50% charged	1.180	1.170	1.135
25% charged	1.130	1.120	1.090
Discharged	1.080	1.070	1.045

Some batteries are made with an extra large space above the elements for water. These batteries have about three times the usual water reserve. Due to the extra water the specific gravity of the electrolyte is only 1.250 at 80°F. The vent plugs of such batteries are usually marked with this reading. Table 1.

All the cells of a fully charged battery in good condition should have approximately the same specific gravity. If the readings between cells differ it may indicate some trouble in the battery.

Tropical Climates. In tropical climates the electrolyte has increased chemical activity due to high temperatures. Batteries intended for such climates have an electrolyte with a 1.225 specific gravity. This is about 31 percent sulphuric acid by weight. A specific gravity of 1.135 indicates that the battery is half charged. In these climates batteries are considered discharged when the specific gravity reaches 1.045. The lower specific gravity reduces the chemical activity somewhat and prolongs the life of the battery plates and separators. It also slows the rate of self-discharge. Where freezing temperatures are not encountered there will be no danger from the lowered specific gravity.

Freezing of Electrolyte. In cold climates it is important that storage batteries be kept charged to avoid freezing of the electrolyte

TABLE 2. FREEZING POINTS OF
ELECTROLYTE AT VARIOUS
SPECIFIC GRAVITIES

Specific Gravity (Corrected to 80° F)	Freezing Temperature (Degrees Fahrenheit)
1.300....................	−95
1.280....................	−90
1.250....................	−62
1.200....................	−16
1.150....................	+ 5
1.100....................	+19

which might crack the container or damage the elements. In a discharged battery the electrolyte is composed mostly of water. Water, of course, freezes at 32°F. Table 2 shows the freezing points of electrolyte at various specific gravities. As you can see there is little danger that a fully charged battery will freeze although it could happen to a battery that is half charged or less than half charged in cold sections of the country.

Mixing Electrolyte

Electrolyte of the correct specific gravity is sometimes needed to fill new batteries shipped dry or to refill batteries that have lost some or all of the electrolyte. The electrolyte used in batteries is a mixture of sulphuric acid (H_2SO_4) and water (H_2O). The two are mixed together in the proper proportions to give electrolyte of the correct specific gravity.

Caution. Sulphuric acid must be handled with care. It will burn the skin and damage clothing. Wear rubber gloves, goggles, and a protective apron when mixing acid or handling acid. If any is splashed on the skin flush off with plenty of water. If there is any pain get medical attention. Acid splashed on clothing should be diluted with water at once and then neutralized with ammonia water or a baking soda solution.

Electrolyte is prepared by mixing battery grade sulphuric acid, either 1.835 or 1.400 specific gravity, with distilled or mineral free water. Table 3 gives the parts of water and acid by volume to be mixed to obtain electrolyte of the desired specific gravity. Always pour acid into the water, otherwise there will be a violent reaction and the acid may splatter. Stir continuously with a clean wooden stick while adding the acid to the water. Use only glass, earthenware, hard rubber, plastic, or lead-lined containers to mix or store electro-

TABLE 3. ACID MIXING-PARTS BY VOLUME

Specific Gravity	Parts Water	Parts 1.835 Acid	Specific Gravity	Parts Water	Parts 1.400 Acid
1.200	13	3	1.200	13	10
1.225	11	3	1.225	10	10
1.250	13	4	1.250	15	20
1.275	11	4	1.275	11	20
1.290	8	3	1.290	9	20
1.300	5	2	1.300	4	10
1.345	2	1	1.345	1	7
1.400	3	2			

lyte. If a glass container is used be careful. Considerable heat is developed when mixing acid and water and the heat may crack the glass.

Specific gravity readings should be made while mixing. Be sure to correct for temperature. Adjust to 1.300 after the electrolyte has cooled to room temperature. Always allow the electrolyte to cool to room temperature before putting it in a battery.

Adjusting the Electrolyte.

If the specific gravity of all cells in a fully charged battery is not within .015 of the specified full charge range (corrected for temperature) remove some of the electrolyte with a hydrometer and add a similar amount of water to reduce the gravity if it is too high, or add acid to raise the gravity if it is too low. Charge the battery for one hour after each adjustment to allow the electrolyte to mix and then make another reading. Continue this until the desired specific gravity is obtained.

Never adjust the specific gravity of any cell that does not gas freely while charging. Unless electrolyte has been lost through leaking or spilling it should not be necessary to add acid to a battery during its life.

If considerable acid has been lost from a battery correct as follows: Pour out all of the electrolyte in the battery. Fill with water and place on charge. This will drive the remaining acid in the elements into the water. Charge until the specific gravity of the water ceases to rise (usually not over an hour). Empty the battery again and then fill with full strength electrolyte.

This method may be used to get rid of dopes or high mineral content water that may have been added to the electrolyte. High mineral content water tends to neutralize the acid and should not be used.

Battery Dopes

Battery dopes are chemical compounds that are often sold with claims that their use will result in greater power from the battery or that they will restore life to a wornout battery. Such claims have been tested and found to be gross exaggerations. There is no satisfactory substitute for the simple mixture of sulphuric acid and water. Use of such "miracle" compounds may injure the battery and voids the manufacturer's guarantee.

TRADE COMPETENCY TEST

1. What is the voltage of a fully charged cell?
2. What active materials are used in the positive and negative plates?
3. What is the purpose of the separators?
4. What is the purpose of the vertical grooves in the separators?
5. What is a battery element composed of?
6. Why is the number of plates not a good yardstick for judging batteries.
7. Why do some owners replace their batteries before they are worn out?
8. Describe the chemical reactions that take place when a battery is being charged and discharged.
9. How does temperature affect the ability of a battery to deliver current?
10. What are the factors which affect battery self-discharge?
11. What tests have been devised to rate storage batteries?
12. How is the power output of a battery measured?
13. What is the composition of battery electrolyte?
14. What does the specific gravity reading of a battery indicate?
15. What effect does temperature have on specific gravity readings? How are specific gravity readings corrected for temperature?
16. What is the specific gravity reading of a fully charged battery? Of a discharged battery?
17. At what temperature will a discharged battery freeze?
18. When mixing acid for batteries, why should acid always be poured into the water rather than water poured into the acid?
19. What procedure should be followed to adjust the specific gravity of a battery that has lost electrolyte?

CHAPTER 3

STORAGE BATTERY SERVICE

TESTING

The automotive storage battery should be serviced at regular intervals to assure dependable service. This involves checking for exterior corrosion, foreign matter on the battery top, water level, cracked case or cover, and faulty or loose connections.

When necessary, battery tests are made to determine the state of charge and the serviceability of the battery under normal operating conditions. In most cases it will be necessary to determine the state of charge before deciding whether or not the battery is capable of performing at its rated capacity. An excessive load placed on a battery or a lower than normal charging rate may prevent a battery from operating effectively so it is important that a complete test be made of the charging circuit to locate any trouble before replacing the battery.

Battery tests are made to determine the state of charge and battery capacity (ability to deliver current). Battery state of charge tests are made with a hydrometer or open circuit voltage tester. Battery capacity is determined by a high rate discharge test.

State of Charge Test

The state of charge of a battery can be tested by measuring the specific gravity of the electrolyte or by checking the open circuit voltage of each cell with an expanded scale voltmeter.

The tests can also be used to determine the condition or serviceability of a battery. Differences in voltage develop between the battery cells as the battery approaches its failure point. These differences become apparent when the specific gravity or voltage readings are compared. When the cell differences reach .05 volts they indicate that the battery is not dependable and should be replaced. An additional test should also be made in determining the service-ability of a battery. This is a "capacity" or high rate discharge test.

Specific Gravity Test

A hydrometer is used to check the specific gravity of a battery. Never check the state of charge with a hydrometer immediately after adding water to the battery. It requires about thirty minutes of driving to thoroughly mix the water with the acid so the electrolyte above the plates will be representative of all the electrolyte in the cell.

The battery is checked by removing the vent plugs from the cells. The rubber tube of the hydrometer is inserted through the vent opening into the electrolyte. Fig. 1. Squeeze the bulb, then release it slowly until enough electrolyte is drawn into the tube to

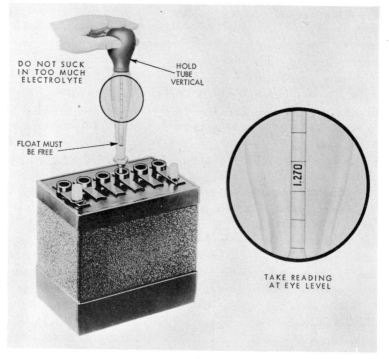

DO NOT SUCK IN TOO MUCH ELECTROLYTE

HOLD TUBE VERTICAL

FLOAT MUST BE FREE

1.270

TAKE READING AT EYE LEVEL

Fig. 1. Testing specific gravity with a hydrometer. Take reading where the scale is even with the electrolyte level and make necessary temperature correction. Chevrolet Div.—General Motors Corp.

cause the hydrometer float to rise and float freely. Be sure the float is not touching the tube at any place, especially the top or bottom. Hold the hydrometer at eye level and in a vertical position. Read the specific gravity on the scale of the hydrometer float at the surface level of the solution. Disregard the curve of the liquid against the glass of the float and the tube. This is caused by surface tension.

Note the temperature of the electrolyte on the thermometer in the hydrometer and the correction to be applied to the reading on the scale. Add or subtract the correction from the reading to obtain the correct specific gravity of the electrolyte.

Replace the tube of the hydrometer in the vent opening of the cell and squeeze the bulb, forcing the electrolyte into the cell. Test all cells in the same manner. Replace the vent plugs.

All cells of a battery should have the same specific gravity. Most fully charged batteries have a specific gravity of 1.260. In cold climates a gravity of 1.280 is used. Batteries that have a specific gravity above 1.235 can be considered as being in a satisfactory condition if the variation between cells is less than .05 points. If the variation is more than .05 the battery should be given a capacity test. If this test shows the battery to be in good condition, recharge it and adjust the specific gravity of the electrolyte as covered in Chapter 2.

Batteries that have a specific gravity of less than 1.235 should be recharged, especially in cold weather. After the battery is charged make a high rate discharge test to determine its condition and remaining useful life.

Open Circuit Voltage Test

The open circuit voltage test is an electrical way of testing the state of charge of a battery. The voltmeter used has an expanded scale to permit accurate readings. Fig. 2. An expanded scale voltmeter is one that does not start at zero reading or that has graduations that are expanded in the desired range. Expanded scale voltmeters are usually graduated in hundreths of a volt (0.01) and can be read to half this amount.

Batteries that have just been charging, as when a car comes in off the road, will have the voltage in the individual cells abnormally high due to what is termed a "surface charge." When making an open circuit voltage test it is recommended that the surface charge be dissipated to get accurate readings on the meter.

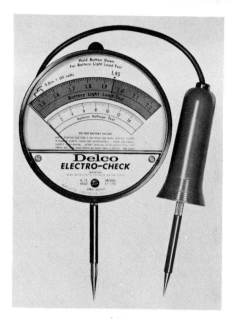

Fig. 2. Expanded scale voltmeter used in making open circuit voltage test of battery cells. Scale ranges from 1.45 to 2.25 volts. Delco-Remy Div. — General Motors Corp.

To remove the surface charge of a battery turn on the starting motor switch for about 3 seconds. Next turn on the headlight low beam and after one minute, with the lights still on, take the cell voltage readings.

The meter shown in Fig. 2 has the positive test prod attached to the meter and the negative prod on a flexible wire. Cell voltage readings are taken by pressing the prod points firmly into the battery posts or cell connectors across each cell and taking the voltage readings. *Caution:* The prod type voltmeter cannot be used on batteries with one piece molded covers.

In testing each cell be sure the positive prod is on the positive

TABLE 1. COMPARISON OF INDIVIDUAL CELL
VOLTAGE READINGS WITH BATTERY STATE
OF CHARGE

State of charge	Cell Voltage Readings
100%	2.10
75%	2.07
50%	2.04
25%	2.01

terminal of the cell and the negative one on the negative terminal. The comparison of cell voltages with the state of charge of the battery is shown in Table 1.

The condition of a battery is determined by noting the difference in the voltage readings between cells. Batteries in good condition and a satisfactory state of charge will show little differences in cell voltage readings between cells.

If all cells show a voltage of 1.95 or more and the difference between cells is less than 0.05 volts the battery is in good condition and state of charge. Fig. 3, top.

If the cell voltages are above and below 1.95 and the differences in cell voltages less than 0.05 the battery is in good condition but needs recharging. Fig. 3, bottom.

When all cell voltages are less than 1.95 volts the battery is too low for testing. Give the battery a booster charge at the fast charging rate for twenty to thirty minutes, depending on the size of the battery. Repeat the test and if the battery is found to be satisfactory recharge it. Fig. 4, top.

If only one or a few cells read 1.95 volts or more and the difference between cells is more than 0.05 volts the battery is defective and should be replaced. Fig. 4, bottom.

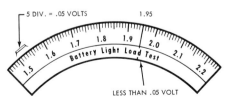

ALL CELLS READ 1.95 OR HIGHER

GOOD BATTERY—SUFFICIENTLY CHARGED

CELLS READ BOTH ABOVE AND BELOW 1.95

GOOD BATTERY—REQUIRES CHARGING

Fig. 3. Open circuit voltage test readings. Cell readings for a charged battery (top), and one needing to be charged (bottom). Delco-Remy Div. — General Motors Corp.

ALL CELLS READ LESS THAN 1.95

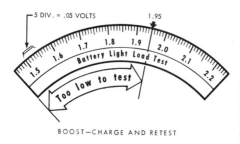

BOOST—CHARGE AND RETEST

Fig. 4. Open circuit voltage readings. Note difference between a battery that needs to be charged and retested (top) and one that needs to be replaced (bottom). Delco-Remy Div. — General Motors Corp.

ONE OR MORE CELLS READ 1.95 OR HIGHER

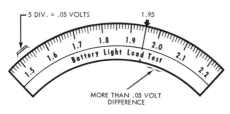

MORE THAN .05 VOLT DIFFERENCE

REPLACE BATTERY

A few batteries may have exposed cell covers and cell connectors while others will have both the cell covers and connectors covered with a sealing compound. On batteries with covered cell connectors the meter prods are pushed through the sealing compound to contact the connectors. After the test the pierced sealing compound is pressed back into place. Before testing such a battery be sure you locate the proper cell connectors since an error in making connections could damage the voltmeter.

Batteries with hard covers cannot be tested with a prod type voltmeter. To determine the state of charge of such batteries they must be tested by a hydrometer, a cadmium cell tester, or a high rate discharge test of the entire battery.

Cadmium Cell Probe Test

This is made with a cadmium cell tester shown in Fig. 5. This is an expanded scale type of voltmeter that has two cadmium metal probes or electrodes that are inserted in the electrolyte of adjacent cells. While this tester can be used on all types of batteries it is the only one that can be used on batteries with one piece hard covers.

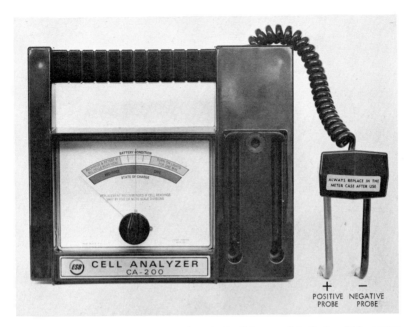

Fig. 5. Cadmium probe tester used to test all types of batteries. This tester uses probes immersed in the electrolyte instead of prods. ESB Brands, Inc.

Five separate readings are made with the cadmium probe. Each reading is a combination of the positive cadmium voltage of one cell and the negative cadmium voltage of the adjacent cell. The five readings cover all the voltages in all cells of a 12-volt battery.

In using the voltmeter the surface charge of the battery must be removed as described for using the prod type voltmeter, except headlights are turned off after one minute.

Remove the vent plugs and place the red probe in the vent opening of the cell containing the positive battery post. The probe should be in contact with the electrolyte. The black probe is placed in the adjacent cell. Fig. 6. Note the reading on the voltmeter.

Remove the probes and place the red probe in cell 2 and the black probe in cell 3. Observe the reading. Continue the tests on all the remaining cells and note the readings. These are interpreted to indicate battery state of charge and condition in the same manner as in the open circuit voltage tests.

Fig. 6. Using the cadmium probe tester. Left, place the red probe in the positive terminal cell and the black probe in the No. 2 cell. Note the reading. Right, next, move the red probe to No. 2 cell and the black probe to No. 3 cell. Note reading. Bottom, test all cells similarly. ESB Brands, Inc.

Capacity Test

A capacity or high rate discharge test gives additional information on the condition of a battery and its ability to deliver current under load. Satisfactory capacity tests can be made only when the battery equals or exceeds 1.220 specific gravity at 80°F. If the battery is below 1.220 it should be slow charged until fully charged in order to obtain accurate test results. The capacity test can be made quickly once the battery is suitably charged. In general, capacity testers consist of a voltmeter, ammeter, and a carbon pile rheostat. The rheostat (variable resistance) provides the means of establishing the required current load. Fig. 7.

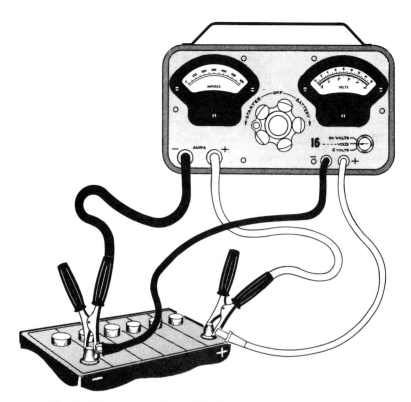

Fig. 7. Making a capacity or high rate discharge test on a battery.

To perform the capacity test make certain that the rheostat knob is in the "off" position. Turn the voltmeter selector switch to the proper voltage for the battery being tested (12-volt battery to 16 volt position). Connect the red voltmeter and ammeter leads to the positive battery post and the black voltmeter and ammeter leads to the negative post as shown in Fig. 7. Turn the rheostat knob until the discharge rate on the ammeter is equal to three times the ampere-hour rating of the battery (3 × 60 amp hr rating = 180 amps). Maintain the discharge load for 15 seconds and note the voltmeter reading. Turn the rheostat to the off position.

If the voltmeter reading is 9.6 volts or higher with the battery temperature at 80°F (4.8 volts for a 6-volt battery) the battery has a good output capacity and is in a satisfactory condition. If the voltage reading is less than 9.6 volts (4.8 for a 6-volt battery) the battery should be replaced.

If the proper test equipment is not available the load test can be made on a battery installed in the vehicle by using a low reading voltmeter while the engine is cranked. The voltmeter leads should make good contact with the battery terminals. To make this test the engine should be at normal operating temperature to assure a normal cranking load. The ignition switch should be in the "off" position. Where the ignition switch energizes the starter control circuit remove the high tension wire from the center of the distributor cap and ground it to the engine. This will guard against damage to the ignition coil and will prevent the engine from starting during the test.

With the voltmeter connected to the battery crank the engine with the starting motor. The battery can be considered in a satisfactory state of charge with reasonable capacity if the starter cranks the engine at a good speed for 15 seconds and the voltage does not drop below 9.6 volts (or 4.8 for 6-volt batteries).

The voltage readings obtained for this test may vary due to variables both within and outside the battery. These variables are the size, state of charge, and temperature of the battery, the engine size, temperature, and friction, and the resistance offered by the starting motor circuit. A dirty starting motor commutator or poor brush contact increases the resistance. Increased resistance affects both the current and voltage available at the starting motor. Do not crank the engine for more than 30 seconds without allowing the starting motor to cool. Otherwise it may be severely damaged.

421 Battery Test

The 421 battery tester, Fig. 8, will test all types of batteries regardless of their state of charge and even if the electrolyte level is below the tops of the plates.

The 421 tester consists of an expanded scale open circuit voltmeter, a rheostat that will permit discharging the battery at a 50 amp rate and, on some models, a 15-30 amp medium rate battery charger.

The test is based on two open circuit voltage readings. The first is taken after the battery has had the surface charge removed from the plates. Then the battery is discharged for 15 seconds at 50 amps.

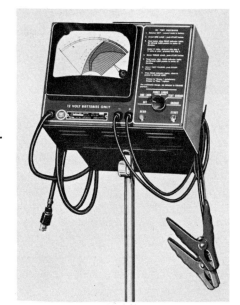

Fig. 8. The 421 battery tester. Sun Electric Corp.

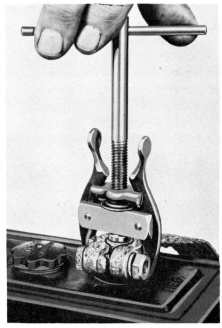

Fig. 9. Removing a bolt type terminal clamp from the battery post with a clamp puller.

After a 5 second wait the voltage is read. The battery is then charged for 45 seconds. After a 15 second wait the second reading is made. A comparison of the two readings indicate whether the battery is good or bad.

SERVICING THE BATTERY

Storage batteries must be properly installed and serviced if they are to deliver the expected performance and have a reasonably long life. When servicing the battery be sure to protect the car finish from the electrolyte by using a fender cover. If you are doing any work on a battery that is in a vehicle with an alternator always disconnect the ground cable from the battery to prevent damaging the alternator. This includes charging of the battery too.

Preventing Corrosion

Corrosion is formed by the action of acid on metal. If the top of the battery is dirty brush it thoroughly with an ammonia or soda solution to neutralize the acid. Be sure the vent covers are tight so that the ammonia or soda does not get into the battery and neutralize some of the electrolyte. Flush with clean water and dry.

If the battery cradle or hold down clamps are corroded remove the battery and clean the parts with ammonia or soda solution. Flush. Make certain that the cradle and clamps have not been so weakened that they cannot hold the battery securely. If necessary reinforce the cradle and clamps or replace them. Paint with acid-proof paint.

If the battery cable clamps are corroded loosen the nuts and remove the clamps from the battery posts. If the clamps are tight do not try to twist them off as this could break the posts at the strap. Instead, use a clamp puller. Fig. 9. Spring clamps are removed with a pliers. Fig. 10.

Clean the battery posts and the cable clamps with special wire brush tools designed for this purpose. Fig. 11. After installing the clamps apply a thin coat of grease (petroleum jelly) to the posts and clamps. Also oil the felt washer on each post. This will reduce corrosion.

Adding Water

There is a gradual loss of water from a storage battery when it

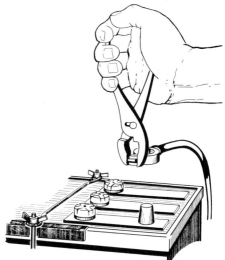

Fig. 10. Spring type terminal clamps are removed with pliers. Clamps should be flush or slightly below top of the post. Chevrolet Div.—General Motors Corp.

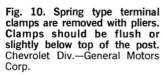

is in use. Some of the water loss from the electrolyte is the result of normal evaporation but the major loss is the result of the chemical action within the battery while it is beng charged. If the electrolyte level in the cells falls below the tops of the plates and separators the plates will be exposed to air and will be damaged. So it is necessary to check the level of the electrolyte at least every three months or 4,000 miles on batteries that have extra electrolyte capacity and to add water as needed to restore the level. Batteries with smaller liquid reserves will need to be checked more often. More water is lost in hot weather than in cold.

Most batteries have some type of mark or device that indicates the normal level of electrolyte. If no marks can be seen $3/8$ in. of water over the tops of the plates is a safe level. Do not overfill as the electroyte expands as the battery is charged and may spill out of the vent openings. The spilled acid will attack battery cables, hold down bolts, and other metal parts.

A number of present day batteries have a special vent cap in one or more cells. If the water level is low the center of the cap will glow. It may be necessary to wipe the top of the cap clear before checking for the glow effect. If the cap glows be sure to check the electrolyte level in all the cells. Fig. 12.

Ordinarily clear drinking water can be used in filling the bat-

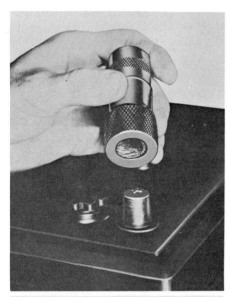

Fig. 11. Wire brushes designed to clean battery posts and terminal clamps. Buick Div.—General Motors Corp.

tery. However, if the water has a high mineral content, particularly iron, distilled or mineral-free water should be used.

In freezing weather water should be added to a battery just before the vehicle is used or the battery charged so the water will mix thoroughly with the electrolyte before it stands.

ONE PIECE
CELL COVER

DELCO EYE
ELECTROLYTE LEVEL
INDICATOR

VENT PLUG

HOLD-DOWN SLOT

Fig. 12. A hard top battery that features a vent plug which glows when the level of the electrolyte drops below a safe level. Delco-Remy Div.—General Motors Corp.

If it is found necessary to add water oftener than every three months or 4,000 miles check the setting of the voltage regulator and adjust it if necessary. Excessive water loss is an indication that the battery is being overcharged.

Replacing Battery Cables

Examine the battery cables. Replace them if the insulation is broken or if the clamps have been eaten away by acid. On cables with bolted clamps replace the bolt and nut if they are corroded.

When replacing cables clean and tighten the ground connection to the frame and the connections to the starting motor switch and starting motor. Oil the felt washer on the battery post. Tighten the clamps on the battery post after cleaning both and then apply a light coat of grease to the cable clamps and battery posts to reduce corrosion.

Changing the Battery

Always note the location of the positive terminal of the battery whenever you remove the battery or the cables. Be sure to install the replacement battery or cables with the positive terminal in the same position.

Remove the battery cables by loosening the nuts on bolt type clamps or by opening spring type clamps with pliers. If the clamps are stuck to the battery posts use a puller to remove them. Do not twist or pound them as this may break the battery post from the internal connections.

Remove the hold down bolts and lift the battery from the cradle. Examine the cradle for damage caused by acid. Clean the cradle, hold down bolts, and cable clamps. Reinforce or replace the cradle and hold down bolts if they are badly damaged. Paint with an acid resisting paint. Replace the cables if necessary.

Proper installation of the battery is the first step in correct maintenance. Be sure the positive terminal is in the correct place when replacing the battery. The battery should rest level and firm in the cradle and should be held firmly. The hold down bolts should be tightened evenly but not so tight that they squeeze or distort the battery case.

Be sure the cables are long enough to reach the battery posts without putting any strain on them which might cause them to become damaged or crack the sealing compound. Oil the felt washer on the posts and tighten the cable clamps securely. Be sure the clamps do not interfere with the vent plugs. Apply a coating of grease over the battery posts and cable clamps.

The job of installing a battery is not complete until the charging circuit has been checked for if the charging circuit is not operating properly the battery cannot give satisfactory service for very long. Check the generator output and the settings of the regulator to see that they meet specifications of the manufacturer for the vehicle.

The tests that have been described in this chapter allow the mechanic to determine the serviceability of the battery. If the battery proves defective it should be replaced. If, after charging, the battery tests O.K. it can be absolved of causing the electrical system trouble. Table 2 summarizes the results of the various tests, diagnoses the probable causes, and suggests the necessary corrections to be made.

TABLE 2. BATTERY TROUBLE-SHOOTING CHART

TYPE OF TEST WITH RESULTS	BATTERY CONDITION	PROCEDURE
HYDROMETER TEST (Corrected to 80° F)		
Specific gravity of all cells above 1.235.	Battery Charged. Most likely satisfactory	Make capacity or high rate discharge test. If voltage is 9.6 volts or higher (12 volt battery) battery is satisfactory. Less than 9.6 volts, replace battery.
Specific gravity of all cells less than 1.235.	Discharged	Recharge. Make capacity test.
Specific gravity of all cells above 1.235 but variation between cells is more than .050 points.	Short circuit in low cell, Loss of electrolyte. Old battery. Cracked cell.	Recharge battery; if variation still exists replace battery. If battery accepts recharge, make capacity test; if battery tests O.K., adjust gravity of all cells.
OPEN CIRCUIT TEST		
Variation between cells more than .05 volts.	Shorted cell. Sulfated cell.	Recharge battery. Retest, if recharging does not correct, replace battery.
CAPACITY TEST (High rate discharge test) .		
If the voltage is less than: 9.6 volts for 12-volt batt. 4.8 volts for 6-volt batt.	Discharged battery. Shorted battery.	Recharge battery. Repeat, if recharging does not correct, replace battery.

Battery Charging

The storage battery is recharged by a battery charger that delivers a direct current of the proper voltage. Since most commercially available electricity is alternating current (AC) the charger consists of a transformer to reduce the voltage to a usable value and a rectifier to change the alternating current to direct current. The charger usually has a control switch and ammeter so the charging rate can be adjusted. Battery chargers fall into two general classifications, the fast charger and the slow charger.

Preparing Battery for Charging

Before placing a storage battery on charge it is important that the battery be cleaned and conditioned. Wash all dirt from the battery and terminals and clean the terminal posts. Use ammonia or sal soda solution and follow with a thorough flushing with clear water. Inspect the case, cell covers, sealing compound, and vent plugs. Make any repairs that are practical.

Check the electrolyte level and make sure it is high enough. Do not overfill as it may bubble out of the vent openings during charging.

Caution: Hydrogen and oxygen gases are released by a battery when it is charging. These may explode and spray acid if they are ignited by a chance spark or flame brought too near them. Keep flames away from a battery and avoid causing sparks near the vent openings until the gases have been removed by gently blowing air into the cells.

When working on a battery assume that it has dangerous gases in the cells. Avoid sparks with tools. If the battery is being charged shut off the charger before disturbing the connections. If the vehicle has been driven in for battery service ground the bumper with a wire to prevent static electricity from igniting the gases while you are working on the battery.

Disconnect the ground cable from the battery on any vehicle equipped with an alternator before charging.

If electrolyte accidentally gets in the eyes wash it out with large quantities of cold water cupped in the hands. If discomfort continues seek prompt medical aid.

Fast Charging

The battery can usually be charged in one hour or less without removing it from the vehicle by using a fast charger. The time depends on the initial state of charge and the temperature.

Such chargers are usually constant potential machines with a high capacity so that initial charging rates of 80-100 amps for 6 volt batteries and 40-50 amps for 12 volt ones are common. These chargers maintain a constant voltage. Since the internal resistance of a battery increases as the battery becomes charged, the charging rate automatically tapers off. The charging rate can be varied through a control according to the state of the battery. The battery temperature should never exceed 125°F when using these chargers. Otherwise the battery may be severely damaged.

Most fast chargers have a time clock to shut them off after the allotted time. Twenty to thirty minutes of charging time will normally charge the battery so that the starting motor will crank the engine and the battery will not become overheated from the charging.

Fast chargers do not fully charge a battery in the time allotted for charging. The amount of charge the battery receives varies with the temperature to which the electrolyte rises while being charged. Batteries are 40-60 percent charged when the temperature reaches 110°F and about 90 percent at 125°F. Some fast chargers have controls for finishing the charging cycle at a low rate so the battery can be brought up to a full charge.

All batteries can be safely charged on a fast charger at a high rate provided that they will accept the charge without overheating. It is a good practice to place a thermometer in the vent opening of a center cell to check the electrolyte temperature.

Adjust the level of the electrolyte in the battery by adding water as explained earlier. Connect the battery charger positive lead to the battery positive post and the negative lead to the negative post. Be sure the ground cable is disconnected from the battery before connecting the leads. Connect the charger to a source of current as specified by the manufacturer of the equipment. Be sure all switches and accessories are turned off. Turn the battery charger on and ad-

 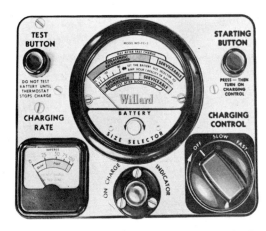

Fig. 13. A fast battery charger and a close-up of the dials. ESB Brands, Inc.

just to the recommended charging rate and time for the size and voltage of the battery being charged. Fig. 13.

Note: These instructions are general in nature because of the various makes of fast chargers available. Always follow the instructions of the manufacturer for the specific equipment you are using.

Upon completion of the charge remove the charging clips. Flush off any electrolyte that might have overflowed. Reconnect the ground cable.

Boost Charging

The fast chargers are also used to give the battery a boost for testing or emergency use. When the voltage in the cells is too low for an accurate open circuit voltage test the battery should be given a boost charge for twenty to thirty minutes at the normal fast charging rate. This builds the voltage up sufficiently for accurate testing.

The fast charger can also be used to give a battery an emergency boost when a customer is in a hurry or in some other emergency requiring quick service. The battery is charged at the normal fast charging rate (40-60 amps) for one-third to one-half the normal charging time. This puts back sufficient current for starting the engine. The vehicle should be operated for a long enough time so the car's generator or alternator can complete recharging the battery.

Slow Charging

Slow battery chargers operate at a low rate and take considerably longer to charge a battery. Fast chargers are identical in construction to slow chargers. The difference lies in their rate of charge and most commercial battery chargers are designed to deliver either fast or slow charges. Slow charging permits the battery to be completely charged.

To charge a battery connect the charger to a source of current. Connect the positive charger lead to the positive battery post and the negative lead to the negative post. Be sure to disconnect the ground lead from the battery if the car has an alternator.

If more than one battery is to be charged connect them in series, the positive post of one to the negative post of the next, and so on. This will leave one positive post and one negative post free to connect to the charger. Fig. 14.

Turn the control knob and adjust the charging rate to the cor-

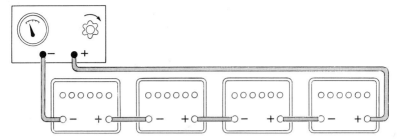

Fig. 14. The proper hook-up for simultaneously charging a number of batteries.

rect value. The rule for a conservative charging rate is one ampere for each positive plate in a cell. For example, a battery having nine plates would have four positive plates and should be charged at a rate of four amps. If the batteries are of various sizes the charging rate is determined by the smallest battery. The batteries may be safely charged at a higher rate if the battery temperatures are kept below 125°F. If it is necessary to leave the batteries on charge with no one in attendance reduce the charging rate by a half.

Sulphated batteries may overheat if charged at the normal slow rate. On such batteries reduce the charging rate to two or three amps for the period of time it takes to break up the sulphate.

In the conventional series circuit shown in Fig. 14 all batteries are charged at the same rate. This is satisfactory if the batteries are all in the same condition and size. If the full output of the charger is used all batteries in the circuit receive the full charging rate which may overheat and damage small and sulphated batteries. If the rate is reduced to avoid overheating these batteries the charging time for the large batteries and ones in good condition may be excessively long.

To recharge small and sulphated batteries at a low rate at the same time that larger batteries and batteries in good condition are being recharged at a higher rate the conventional series circuit is modified as shown in Fig. 15. In the modified circuit each battery in the series section receives the full amperage output of the charger. In the balance of the circuit the batteries are connected in parallel (lower row) so each group of batteries divides the ampere output of the charger.

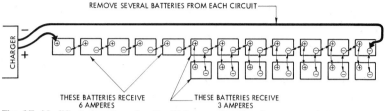

Fig. 15. Modified charging circuit which permits charging some of the batteries at a high rate and others at a lower one.

Check batteries several times during the first few hours of charging to make sure they are not overheating or gassing so much the electrolyte bubbles over. If they feel hot or are gassing excessively lower the charging rate or discontinue charging until the battery cools.

Hydrometer readings should be taken after the battery has been on slow charge for about 10 hours. Batteries in good condition can be fully charged in 12 to 16 hours at normal rates. At lower rates the time will be longer. Sulphated batteries may require 24 hours or longer. A battery is considered fully charged when the hydrometer readings (corrected for temperature) do not rise in three successive readings taken one hour apart. This is with the battery gassing and the charger at the normal setting.

The specific gravity for a fully charged battery should be from 1.260 to 1.280. If there is more than fifteen points (0.015) in the specific gravity readings between the cells of the battery after it has been fully charged adjust the electrolyte by removing some and adding acid or water to correct the specific gravity. Charge for one hour after adjusting the electrolyte to mix the materials.

Overcharging

When a battery is completely charged further charging is no longer useful. It only converts water into hydrogen and oxygen gases which bubble out of the electrolyte. Gassing is normal as a battery nears its charged state if the charging rate is not excessive. Otherwise high temperatures and violent gassing may cause particles of active materials to break loose from the plates. The hot acid also attacks the plates and separators and shortens their life.

Overheating distorts the plates and separators and causes them to warp. Warped plates will cut through the separators and short circuit the cells.

Batteries that are regularly overcharged require frequent amounts of water. A high loss of water indicates that the battery is being overcharged.

Sulphation

Active material in the plates is converted into lead sulphate during discharge and this lead sulphate is changed back into the active material of the plates during recharge. This is a normal cycle that is continually repeated in the battery. However, if a battery is operated for a long time in a low state of charge or stands in a low charge or discharged condition it becomes sulphated.

In a sulphated battery the lead sulphate becomes hard and crystalline. This is very difficult to convert back into active plate material by ordinary charging methods. Such batteries are usually placed on a slow charge, about half the normal rate. Sometimes it is necessary to cycle the battery in bad cases of sulphation. That is the battery is repeatedly charged and discharged to break up the sulphation. Batteries that are heavily sulphated generally cannot be restored to a serviceable condition.

Dry Charge Batteries

Dry charge batteries are manufactured and distributed with fully charged plates but no electrolyte in the cells. Vent seals in the filler opening effectively seal the cells so no moisture or air can enter the cells. As long as the cells remain dry no chemical action can take place. This allows the battery to retain a charge for a long time.

To activate the battery the seals are removed and the cells filled with electrolyte of the proper strength. The electrolyte comes along with the battery in a plastic container. After five minutes the battery should produce its rated voltage. If it is found that the electrolyte shows more than thirty points (0.030) drop from the specific gravity of the electrolyte used in filling the battery the battery should be recharged.

Wet Charge Batteries

New wet charge batteries are fully charged with the electrolyte installed at the time of manufacture.

A wet charge battery is constantly losing some of its charge due to chemical reactions. This "self-discharge" occurs faster at higher temperatures so wet charge batteries should be stored as cool as possible and checked for state of charge every 30 days. Recharge if they show an appreciable loss.

Battery Defects

Most battery manufacturers warrant their batteries for a period of 90 days after purchase against defective materials and workmanship. After that many warrant their batteries for 12 to 48 months on a prorated agreement. This provides for replacement of the battery with the user paying only for the months he used the battery.

Except for minor repairs there is no justification for extensive work on batteries. The cost of a new battery, especially those covered by replacement warranties, is usually considerably lower than the labor and parts needed to repair the original battery.

TRADE COMPETENCY TEST

1. What are the two preferred methods of testing batteries?
2. What is the specific gravity of a fully charged battery?
3. What is the condition of a battery whose specific gravity is above 1.235 with more than .050 points difference between cells?
4. How does the open circuit voltmeter differ from other voltmeters?
5. What is meant by the term "surface charge"?
6. When making an open circuit voltage test, what does a reading in all cells of 1.95 volts with less than .05 volts difference between cells indicate?
7. Can an open circuit voltage test be made on a battery with a one-piece battery cover?
8. How does the cadmium cell tester work?
9. What should the specific gravity of a battery be before an accurate capacity test can be made?
10. At what rate should a battery be discharged when making a capacity test?
11. How can a battery be tested under load when no capacity tester is available?
12. When should water be added to a battery during freezing weather?
13. Name several methods of recharging batteries.
14. When working on a battery, what precautions should be taken to avoid an explosion?
15. What is the maximum permissible temperature when charging a battery with a fast charger?

16. To what rate in amperes is the initial charging rate adjusted on fast chargers when charging a 12-volt battery.

17. What is the charging rate when charging normal batteries on a slow charger?

18. How should sulphated batteries be charged?

19. What are the effects of overcharging?

20. What is a dry-charged battery? A wet charged battery?

CHAPTER 4

CRANKING MOTOR
SYSTEM

The automotive cranking motor circuit includes the starting motor, the storage battery, the starter switch, the cables to connect the motor and switch to the battery, and the ground return circuit.

STARTING MOTOR

The starting motor is a low voltage, direct current motor which converts electrical energy from the storage battery into mechanical energy. The starting motor is referred to as a cranking motor by some manufacturers. The starting motor cranks the engine at speeds sufficient to cause starting when the circuit between the starting motor and the storage battery is completed by the starting switch.

Starting Motor Construction

Starting motors used in automotive vehicles are similar in construction and operation although they vary in size, voltage, number of poles, and number of brushes. They consist of a housing, field coils, pole shoes, armature, brushes, commutator, the drive, and drive housing. Fig. 1. Starting motors are either 6 or 12 volts, and, while similar in construction, are not interchangeable.

Starter Housing. The starter housing is a heavy cylindrical machined case that holds the starting motor assembly. Steel pole shoes (bottom, Fig. 1) are securely attached to the inner surface by screws. The pole shoes hold the field coils in place inside the housing. The field coils are connected to a terminal and are insulated from the housing.

Field Coils. The field coils are made of heavy, flat, copper strips to carry the heavy current needed for starting purposes. Fig. 2. Current flowing through the field coils magnetizes the pole shoes and creates a strong magnetic field across them. Fig. 3, left. The coils on

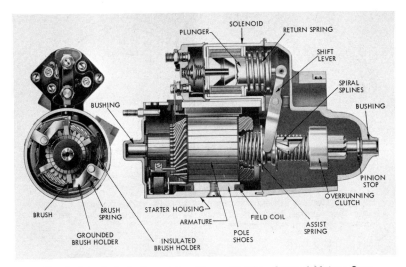

Fig. 1. A typical starting motor. Chevrolet Div.—General Motors Corp.

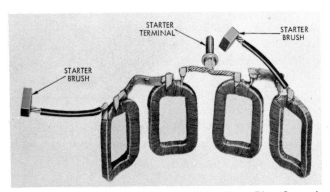

Fig. 2. Field coils connected in series. Delco-Remy Div.—General Motors Corp.

adjacent pole shoes are wound in opposite directions which gives their respective pole shoes a north and a south magnetic polarity. The housing acts as a return circuit for the magnetic lines of force, Fig. 3, right.

The coils are connected in series with the armature windings through the starter brushes. This permits all of the current flowing

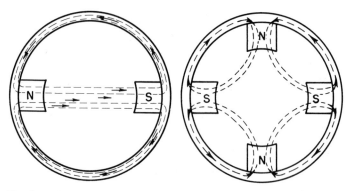

Fig. 3. A. Current in field coils magnetizes pole shoes creating a magnetic field across them. B. Circuits in a four pole starting motor. Housing acts as a return circuit.

through the field coil circuit to flow through the armature windings also. Depending on design, either two, four, or more field coils may be used. Fig. 3 illustrates the magnetic circuits of two and four pole starting motors.

Armature. The armature consists of a slotted iron core, shaft, commutator, and armature windings. Fig. 4. The armature revolves between the pole shoes in bushings mounted at each end of the motor assembly. The iron core of the armature completes the magnetic circuit between the pole shoes. To reduce loss of magnetic lines of force as they flow from the pole shoes to core, the core is designed to fit between the pole shoes with a minimum of clearance.

The commutator is pressed on the armature shaft and is com-

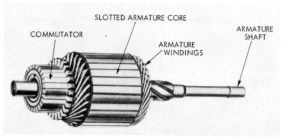

Fig. 4. Parts of the armature. Oldsmobile Div. General Motors Corp.

posed of copper segments separated from each other and the armature shaft by insulation.

The armature windings are made of a heavy, flat copper strip instead of wire or cable to carry the heavy current that passes through them. The windings consist of a number of coils of a single loop each. The sides of the coils fit into slots of the armature core and are insulated from it. Each slot contains the sides of two coils. The coils are connected to the commutator so that the current from the field coils flows through all the coils at the same time. This creates a magnetic field around each conductor, resulting in a repulsion force all around the armature.

Brushes. The brushes in a starting motor are formed under high pressure from a mixture of powdered carbon and copper. The brushes usually have one or more heavy pigtails of flexible copper wire securely fastened to the brush. The opposite end of the pigtail is either soldered to its connection or is provided with a terminal to permit attachment by means of screws. Starting motors usually have four brushes.

The brushes are mounted in a holder within the starting motor (Fig. 1), although on many motors still in use they will be found mounted on the end frame. The brush holders support the starting motor brushes in position and have flat or coil springs to hold the brushes against the commutator with the correct pressure. Alternate brush holders are insulated from the housing or end frame while those in between are grounded to the housing.

Commutator End Frame. The commutator end frame on present starting motors consists of a metal plate that bolts to the commutator end of the housing and supports the commutator end of the armature in a bushing. On many starting motors still in use the commutator end frame also supports the brushes. The end frame is positioned on the starter housing by a dowel pin to insure proper alignment.

Drive Housing. The drive housing supports the driving end of the armature shaft and also contains the mounting flange by which the starting motor is attached to the engine. It is also positioned on the starter housing by a dowel to insure correct alignment.

Operating Principles

A starting motor operates on the principle that unlike magnetic fields attract each other and like magnetic fields repel each other. Let us recall several basic facts about magnetism to understand how a starting motor operates.

When current flows through a conductor a circular magnetic field is created around the conductor. The strength of the field depends on the amount of current flowing through the conductor. The direction in which the field moves depends on the direction of the current in the conductor. The direction of the magnetic field around the conductor can be determined by the left-hand rule. Fig. 5.

Left-Hand Rule. With the left hand grasped around the conductor and the thumb extending along the conductor pointing in the direction the electrons flow (toward positive) the fingers indicate the direction of the magnetic field around the wire.

Another fact to remember is that two magnetic fields traveling in different directions cannot exist in the same place. If only the magnetic lines of force from the permanent magnets were present the magnetic lines of force would be in straight line, left, Fig. 6. If only the effect of current in the length of wire were present the lines of force would be in a circle around the wire. However, the two magnetic fields cannot simultaneously exist as shown in Fig. 6, left.

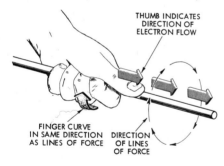

THUMB INDICATES
DIRECTION OF
ELECTRON FLOW

FINGER CURVE
IN SAME DIRECTION
AS LINES OF FORCE

DIRECTION
OF LINES
OF FORCE

Fig. 5. The Left-hand rule demonstrated.

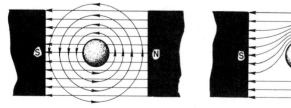

Fig. 6. Distortion of magnetic lines of force by opposing fields.

Below the wire the lines of force from the two sources (the magnets and the wire or coil) are traveling in opposite directions. This is an impossibility. What happens is that the lines of force underneath the wire cancel or neutralize each other (weakening the field), while those above the wire combine with or strengthen each other resulting in a magnetic field that is bent or distorted. Fig. 6, right.

Bent or distorted lines of force act somewhat like stretched rubber bands. They try to shorten and the magnetic effect shown in Fig. 6, right, is the result. A force is exerted on the wire moving it in a downward direction. It is this repulsion force that causes the motor armature to revolve.

A simple series electric motor with only one loop of wire is shown in Fig. 7. The armature and field coils are connected together in series so that current flowing through one must flow through the other before returning to the battery. With the starting switch closed current flows from the battery into the armature coil through the brush and commutator bar attached to one end of the coil, leaving the coil by the other commutator bar and brush. Leaving the armature the current flows through the field coils and returns to the battery.

The current sets up a strong circular magnetic field when flowing through the armature coil wire. The current flows in opposite directions in the two sides of the loop of the coil. This results in circular magnetic fields traveling in opposite directions. Fig. 7. The same current flowing through the field coils makes electromagnets of the two pole shoes creating a strong magnetic field between them.

Fig. 7. A simplified series type motor showing magnetic field.

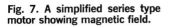

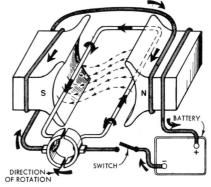

The field coils are wound so that one has the inner face a north magnetic pole and the other one has a south magnetic pole. The polarity of the pole shoes can be determined by the left hand rule.

The reaction between the two magnetic fields (the armature coil and the pole shoes) causes the main magnetic field across the pole shoes to become distorted or bent. The strongest part of the field passes over one side of the coil and under the other. Bent magnetic lines of force tend to straighten so they exert a force on the armature coil which causes it to rotate.

The single coil in Fig. 7 would only revolve clockwise to an upright position and then stop as the tendency of the coil to rotate will occur only when it is moving across the lines of force of the main field.

The commutator bars are arranged on the coil to cause a reversal in the direction of current flow through the coil. The reversal of the current in the coil continues the flow in one direction so it rotates another half turn. To have continuous rotation the starting motor armature has numerous coils spaced around the circumference.

The greater the current flowing through the armature and field coils the greater the repulsion force exerted on the armature.

The strength of the magnetic field can be raised by increasing the number of turns in the coils. Starting motors are usually wound so the current flows through the field coils before entering the armature coils. The current leaves the armature coils through brushes grounded to the frame of the starter.

The current flows in opposite directions in the two sides of the armature coils so the brushes must be located to change the direction of flow in the coils at the proper time as the armature coils rotate.

If the flow of current reverses too soon or too late the coils will tend to retard the motor instead of making it revolve. The proper location for the brushes is on the neutral point. The neutral point is the point where the coils of the commutator have the least effect on rotation. In Fig. 7 the armature coil is least affected by the main field when it rotates to an upright position. This is a point that is midway between a north and a south pole and where the armature coil is moving parallel or nearly parallel with the lines of force of the main magnetic field.

The neutral point would be at right angles to the lines of force if they went straight across between the pole shoes as in Fig. 8. However, the current flowing through the armature wires produces a magnetic field within the armature, Fig. 9. The field produced by the armature is termed armature reaction or cross magnetization. When combined with the field produced by the pole shoes it causes a shifting of the lines of force as shown in Fig. 10. The positive (+) current is flowing away from the viewer while the negative (−) current is flowing toward him.

With the field shifted by the armature reaction the brush shown in solid lines is no longer properly placed and must be shifted to the dotted position to be at the neutral point.

Fig. 8. The magnetic field produced by current flowing through field coils.

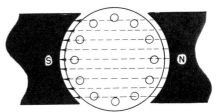

Fig. 9. Magnetic field produced by current flowing through the armature wires.

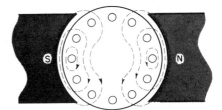

Fig. 10. Shifting (twisting) of magnetic field due to armature reaction. Current marked with a plus (+) is flowing away from the viewer. Current marked with a minus (−) is flowing toward the viewer.

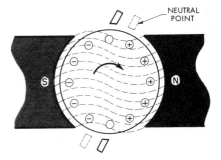

Internal Motor Circuits

The field windings and armature are normally connected so the current entering the motor flows through both the field windings and the armature. The motors are series wound; the field coils and the armature are connected in series. Fig. 11 shows typical starting motor circuits.

A four pole, four brush starting motor with two field coils is shown in Fig. 11A. The field coils are wound in the same direction making their shoes of the same polarity. The starter housing return circuit causes the pole shoes without coils to have an opposite polarity. The current entering the motor divides at the terminal with half passing through each field coil to the insulated brushes. The current enters the armature windings from the insulated brushes and leaves through the grounded brushes. The insulated brushes are generally connected with a jumper lead which acts to equalize the voltage at the brushes.

A four pole, four brush motor with four field coils is illustrated in Fig. 11B. The adjacent field coils are wound in opposite directions making their pole shoes of north and south magnetic polarity. The field windings are connected in series and current flows through all the field coils to the insulated brushes. A jumper lead equalizes the voltage at the brushes. The current from the armature returns to the battery through the two grounded brushes.

A series-shunt type of winding is shown in Fig. 11C. Three of the field coils are connected in series with the insulated terminal and

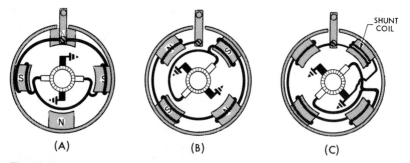

(A)   (B)   (C)

Fig. 11. Some typical starting motor circuits. A. Four pole, four brush starting motor with two field coils. B. Four pole, four brush type with four field coils. C. Series-shunt type winding with three field coils in series with insulated terminal and brushes and fourth (shunt) coil connected from insulated terminal to ground at grounded brush.

brushes. The fourth, or shunt, coil is connected from the insulated terminal to ground at the grounded brush. The addition of another series winding serves to increase the magnetic strength and torque output of the motor.

Fig. 12 is a starting motor circuit which has one of the pole shoes designed to move so that it will shift the starter drive mechanism into mesh with the flywheel. During operation the starter is a series motor with the current dividing at the terminal with half going to each pair of field coils to the insulated brushes. A jumper equalizes the voltage at the brushes.

When the starter is not in use one of the field coils is connected directly to ground through a set of externally mounted contact points. Fig. 12. When the ignition switch is turned to "start" current flows through the grounded field coil. The magnetism created by the field coil pulls the movable pole shoe, which is attached to a lever, downward to its seat. This moves the shift lever which moves the drive mechanism into engagement with the flywheel.

When the pole shoe seats it opens the grounded contact points and the starter operates normally. A hold-in coil wound integrally with the field coil holds the pole shoe and starter drive in the en-

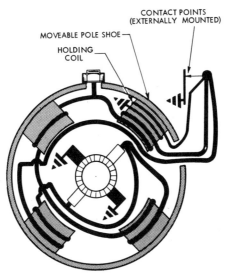

Fig. 12. A starting motor circuit with a movable pole shoe.

gaged position while the motor is turning the engine. Fig. 13 is a disassembled motor of this type.

Motor Characteristics

The starting motor draws considerable current from the battery in cranking the engine. The current required varies from 150 to 300 amps or more depending on the speed of the starting motor. The faster the motor runs the higher its resistance and the less current it uses. Anything that reduces starting motor speed lowers the operating resistance of the motor and causes an increase in the current used. Twelve volt motors are wound with slightly smaller wires and operate at slightly higher speeds than six volt motors.

The starting motor is designed to produce high power for its size. To do this a high current must flow through it which generates considerable heat. These motors are not designed for continuous use and long cranking periods may cause overheating and seriously damage them. Starting motors should not be operated for more than 30 seconds at a time without pausing for two minutes to allow the motor to cool.

A starting motor uses current from the battery at a faster rate than it can be supplied. This lowers the voltage of the battery. Motors that are cranking an engine at slow speeds may lower the voltage so much the ignition system may not receive enough current for efficient operation and the engine is difficult to start.

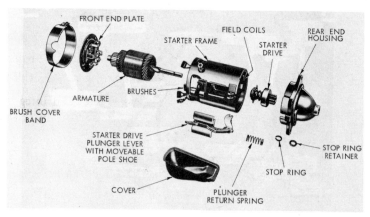

Fig. 13. Disassembled view of starting motor diagrammed in Fig. 12.
Ford Div.—Ford Motor Co.

The power developed by a starting motor is measured as torque or the ability to turn. It is measured in pounds-feet. The "stall" torque of most starting motors varies between 8½ and 48 lbs/ft depending on design and requirements.

STARTING MOTOR DRIVES

Starting motors are usually mounted on the side of the engine by a flange bolted to the flywheel housing. The starting motor cranks the engine through a drive mounted on the end of the armature shaft. Motors that have the drive attached directly to the shaft are classed as direct drive motors. Some motors have a gear reduction system in the drive end to increase the cranking torque. Gear reduction motors Fig. 14, have the drive mounted on a separate shaft which is driven by the armature shaft through reduction gears.

The starting motor drive transmits the torque developed by the motor to the engine flywheel which cranks the engine. The drive is usually connected and disconnected to the engine flywheel automatically.

The drive gear has few gear teeth compared with the number of teeth on the flywheel. This provides a gear reduction that enables

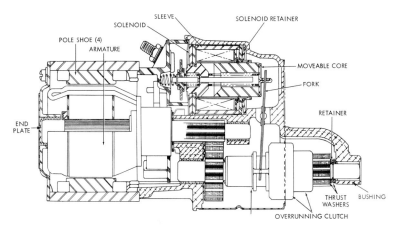

Fig. 14. Gear reduction type of motor. Plymouth Div.—Chrysler Corp.

the torque of the starting motor to turn the engine over at cranking speeds. The gear ratios vary but an average is about 12 to 1 (12 revolutions of the drive gear to 1 of the flywheel). Thus, to turn an engine over at 125 rpm the drive gear must revolve at 1,500 rpm.

Once the engine starts its speed may be greatly increased. If the drive gear remained in mesh with the flywheel and transmitted its speed to the starting motor the armature would revolve several thousand rpm. The great centrifugal force developed by such speeds could result in the armature coils being thrown out of their slots and wrecking the motor. The drive mechanism has provisions which either disengage it from the flywheel or from the armature shaft immediately when the engine starts to prevent this occurring. Two common types of drive mechanisms are the overrunning clutch and the Bendix.

Overrunning Clutch Drive

The overrunning clutch has a lever to shift the drive pinion and clutch on the armature shaft in and out of mesh with the flywheel. The shift lever is usually operated by a solenoid switch automatically.

The overrunning clutch (also called a one-way clutch) is located directly behind the drive pinion. Fig. 15. This clutch transmits the torque of the armature shaft to the drive pinion in one direction

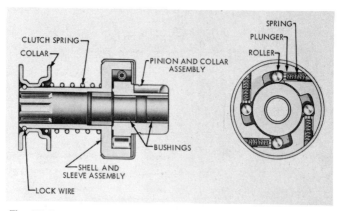

Fig. 15. Overrunning type of clutch drive. Delco-Remy Div.—General Motors Corp.

but permits the pinion to revolve freely in the opposite direction. This prevents the engine from driving the armature.

The clutch assembly consists of a shell and a sleeve. The sleeve is splined to the armature shaft. The drive pinion and collar fit into the shell. The shell has four tapered notches which contain hardened steel rollers. In the position shown, Fig. 15, the rollers have room and the collar can turn freely.

When the starting motor begins to rotate, the notched shell begins to turn also. The rollers in the shell roll away from the springs and move into the tapered ends of the notches where they wedge (or jam) against the collar. When the rollers are wedged between the shell and the collar the whole assembly turns as a unit.

As the engine starts the flywheel drives the pinion faster than the armature rotates. The collar runs faster than the shell and sleeve. This spins the rollers out of the tapered ends of the notches and back against the springs where there is ample room for them. This allows the pinion to turn freely without speeding up the armature.

Bendix Drive

The Bendix drive has been manufactured in a number of forms. Basically, all operate by a combination of screw action and inertia to mesh the drive gear with the flywheel. Fig. 16.

The standard Bendix drive is no longer used on new cars but may be found on old models. It has a drive gear or pinion mounted on

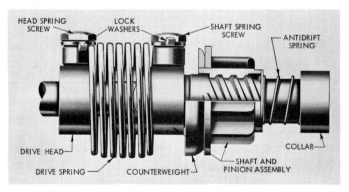

Fig. 16. A standard type Bendix drive. Electric Auto-Lite Co.

a threaded sleeve. The threads of the sleeve and the internal threads of the pinion mate with a loose fit. When the starter switch is closed the armature begins to revolve. The inertia of the pinion momentarily prevents it from turning. The screw action of threaded shaft forces the drive pinion forward along the drive shaft and into mesh with the flywheel. The shock of the meshing gears is absorbed by the spring. As the pinion reaches the end of the shaft it turns with the shaft and drives the flywheel.

When the engine starts the flywheel starts to turn faster than the drive pinion. This would speed up the starting motor and could damage it. However, the pinion threads back along the shaft and out of mesh with the flywheel. An antidrift spring on the shaft and pinion keeps the pinion retracted except when the starting motor is operating. A number of adaptations of this have been used.

The Folo-Thru drive is a variation of the Bendix drive. It has spiral threads on a shaft with matching threads in the pinion barrel. It also has a spring to take the shock of starting. A feature of the Folo-Thru drive is a locking pin in the pinion barrel which rides on top of the threads as the pinion moves. The pin drops into a detent in the threads when the pinion is fully extended. This locking pin holds the pinion in mesh with the flywheel until a certain speed is reached by the flywheel. Then the greatly increased centrifugal force overcomes the spring pressure on the locking pin and permits the pinion to thread back along the shaft. The locking feature prevents premature demeshing of the pinion if the engine fails to continue running after one or two firings. The screw shaft is in two sections connected by a dentil clutch which acts as an additional safety device to prevent overspeeding before the pinion disengages. Fig. 17.

STARTING MOTOR SWITCHES AND CIRCUITS

The starting motor switch operates the starting motor by making or breaking the circuit between the storage battery and the starting motor. The switch is designed to carry the high current needed by the starting motor and to make and break the circuit with a positive action to reduce arcing at the contacts.

Many different types of starting motor switches have been used over the years from the simple hand or foot operated ones to switches that automatically control the opening and closing of the starting motor circuit. Most engines are started now by turning the

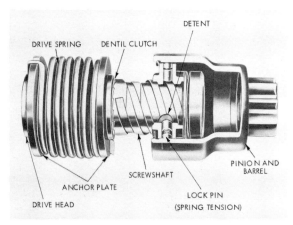

Fig. 17. Folo-Thru variation of the Bendix drive. Delco-Remy Div.—General Motors Corp.

ignition switch to the start position where contacts complete a circuit to a solenoid switch.

Solenoids

A solenoid is simply a coil of many turns of wire. When current flows through the coil the solenoid becomes an electromagnet. A moveable iron core is placed just inside the coil. When the current is applied the core is drawn further inside the coil. Fig. 18 shows this effect. The permeability of the core diverts the magnetic field as shown. The lines of force flow through the core and magnetize it. The south pole of the core is then attracted to the north pole of the coil. So the core is made to move into the coil by passing a current through the coil. This is a solenoid.

Solenoid Switches. There are two types of solenoid switches used to operate a starting motor. In one type the solenoid operates only as a magnetically operated switch (called a relay). This type only closes the starting motor contacts when a remote switch is closed to activate the coil.

The other type of solenoid in addition to closing the starting motor contacts mechanically engages the starting motor drive pinion to the flywheel before the starting motor begins to crank the engine. This type is usually referred to as a solenoid switch.

The solenoid switch is mounted on the starting motor housing.

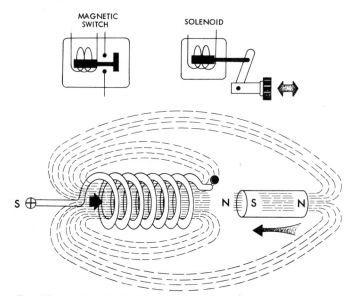

Fig. 18. A solenoid showing method of operation and use in a switch and a starter.

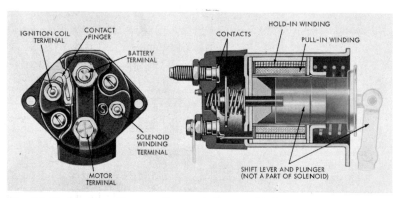

Fig. 19. Starter solenoid connections and disassembled parts. Delco-Remy Div. —General Motors Corp.

Fig. 19. This switch has two windings in the solenoid, a pull-in and a hold-in coil. It also has a large plunger and a small plunger and contact disk. Fig. 20.

When the ignition switch is turned to "start" current flows to both windings of the solenoid. This creates a magnetic field strong

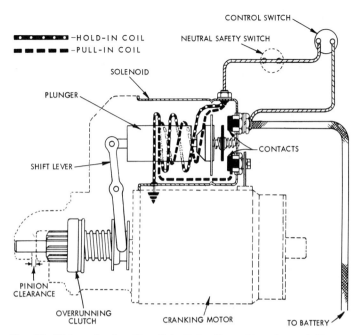

Fig. 20. Wiring of solenoid switch. Delco-Remy Div.—General Motors Corp.

enough to pull in the large plunger which shifts the overrunning clutch and drive pinion into mesh with the flywheel. As the large plunger nears bottom it strikes the small plunger and contact disk and forces the disk against the contacts of the starting motor switch. This completes the circuit and the starting motor operates.

When the main switch closes the pull-in winding loses its effect due to the voltage being equal at both ends of the winding. The hold-in coil continues to hold the plunger in the closed position and reduces the current needed by the solenoid. When the ignition switch is released the current to the solenoid stops. The springs within the solenoid open the starting motor circuit contacts and shift the clutch and pinion assembly to the at-rest position.

Relay Switch. A starting motor switch used with a Bendix drive is shown in Fig. 21. Such switches are controlled by the ignition switch although push button or vacuum switches operated by the accelerator have been used in the past.

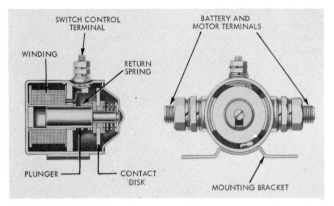

Fig. 21. Starting motor switch for Bendix drive. Delco-Remy Div.—General Motors Corp.

The starting motor switch is a relay which consists of a solenoid winding, a plunger to which a contact disk is attached, battery and starting motor terminals and a switch terminal.

The complete circuit is shown in Fig. 22. When the ignition switch completes the circuit current flows through the coil winding. The magnetic field in the coil pulls on the plunger. The plunger moves the contact disk against the contacts. When the ignition switch is released the springs pull the plunger against the residual magnetism of the coil and make a quick break of the switch contacts.

Ignition Resistor

The ignition has a resistor connected in series in the primary circuit between the coil and the battery. The resistor is either con-

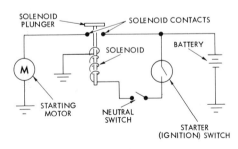

Fig. 22. Complete circuit of starting motor switch shown in Fig. 21.

tained in the primary wire to the coil or is mounted separately. The resistor protects the distributor points from excessive current by limiting the flow in the primary circuit at low speeds when the current is high. However, when the starter is cranking the engine the resistor is by-passed permitting the available current to flow to the coil for starting. Since current is simultaneously being used by the starter there is no danger of damaging the distributor contacts. The direct circuit to the ignition coil is completed either in the solenoid starter switch or by contacts in the ignition switch.

Neutral Safety Switch

A vehicle equipped with an automatic transmission has a neutral safety switch in the starting motor control circuit which prevents starting the engine except when the transmission is in the "neutral" or "park" position. Fig. 23. The neutral safety switch is connected in series with the starting motor control circuit and is operated by the transmission control lever.

Other Starting Circuit Controls

At times various methods were used to control the operation of the starting motor. Some solenoid switches had a control relay be-

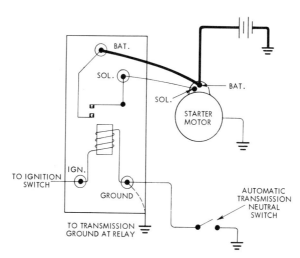

Fig. 23. Neutral switch is in series with starting motor circuit.

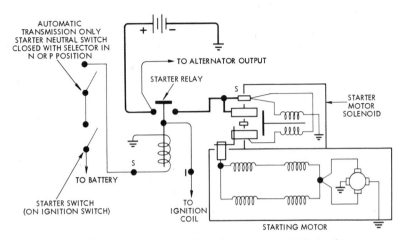

Fig. 24. Another variation of starting motor control circuit.

tween the battery and the solenoid. The starting switch closed the relay which created a connection between the battery and the solenoid and caused the starting motor to operate.

Others used a vacuum switch mounted on the carburetor to control the operation of a solenoid switch. Contact points were normally closed in the switch when the engine was not running. To start, the ignition switch was turned on and the accelerator depressed. This caused the vacuum switch to connect the solenoid to the battery and the starter to crank the engine. When the engine started the vacuum in the carburetor caused the contacts to open and break the circuit. As long as the engine was running it was impossible to accidentally operate the starter. Variations of these starter controls are shown in Figs. 23 and 24.

TRADE COMPETENCY TEST

1. What is the function of the field coils in a starting motor?
2. What type of winding is used in the field coils and armature?
3. Of what materials are starting motor brushes made?
4. How many insulated and how many grounded brushes are there in a four-brush starting motor?
5. Can you describe how a starting motor operates?
6. Why is it important that the starting motor brushes be located at the neutral point?

7. Trace the flow of current through the starting motor.

8. What effect does the speed at which a starting motor operates have on the amount of current required to operate the motor?

9. What types of drives are employed on starting motors?

10. On what principle does the Bendix drive operate?

11. How does the overrunning clutch drive differ in operation from the Bendix drive?

12. What is the purpose of the lockpin on the Folo-Thru type of starter drive?

13. Can you explain how the simple magnetic type switch used on Bendix drive starting motors operates?

14. How does the solenoid switch differ in construction from a simple relay type switch?

15. What is the function of the relay on starting motor switches equipped with such relays? How does it operate?

16. What is the purpose of the neutral safety switch employed on some vehicles?

17. What is the purpose of the vacuum switch employed in the starting motor control circuit on some vehicles?

CHAPTER 5

CRANKING MOTOR SYSTEMS SERVICE

The starting motor has proved to be extremely reliable in operation over long periods of time. Occasionally trouble does develop in the starting motor or the cranking motor circuit. It is to your advantage to be able to locate the trouble quickly and make the necessary repairs to restore the starting motor and circuit to an operating condition.

Diagnostic procedures for locating starting motor and circuit troubles are given in this chapter as well as tests for determining the condition of the components and their repair.

PRELIMINARY TEST

Normally the starting motor will operate satisfactorily without attention throughout the life of the engine. Cleaning the outside of the motor and checking for loose cable connections and mounting bolts are the only things that can be done to a starting motor when it is on the vehicle because of its location and construction. However, dirt, dust, water, frequent starting, and excessively long cranking periods, may cause rapid wear and make an overhaul necessary. If trouble develops in a starting motor it should be completely overhauled.

Do not remove a starting motor for an overhaul unless you are quite sure it requires attention. Test the motor on the vehicle according to the trouble shooting procedures in this chapter. If it is found to be defective remove it for an overhaul.

A number of tests can be made on a starting motor to determine whether or not it is functioning properly. Manufacturer's testing recommendations vary and consequently their specifications will be based on the tests they advocate. Always check manufacturer's specifications before making any of the tests.

TABLE 1. TROUBLE-SHOOTING GUIDE

CONDITION	PROBABLE CAUSE	CORRECTION
STARTING MOTOR DOES NOT OPERATE.	1. DISCHARGED BATTERY, ONE OR MORE DEAD CELLS IN BATTERY.	1. TEST SPECIFIC GRAVITY. RECHARGE OR REPLACE BATTERY AS NECESSARY.
	2. CORRODED OR POOR ELEC-TRICAL CONNECTION AT BATTERY CLAMPS OR CABLE TERMINALS.	2. CHECK VOLTAGE DROP TO DETERMINE RESISTANCE OF CIRCUIT. CLEAN AND TIGHTEN BATTERY AND CABLE TERMINALS.
	3. FAULTY STARTER (IGNITION) SWITCH.	3. TEST SWITCH AND REPLACE IF NECESSARY.
	4. FAULTY NEUTRAL STARTER SWITCH.	4. TEST AND ADJUST SWITCH LINKAGE. REPLACE SWITCH IF NECESSARY.
	5. OPEN OR SHORT CIRCUIT IN STARTER CONTROL CIRCUIT WIRING (BETWEEN STARTER IGNITION SWITCH, NEU-TRAL SWITCH, AND SOLENOID SWITCH).	5. INSPECT AND TEST ALL WIRING.
	6. FAULTY STARTING MOTOR.	6. REMOVE AND TEST STARTER. REPAIR AS NECESSARY.
	7. DEFECTIVE SOLENOID OR MAGNETIC SWITCH.	7. TEST AND REPLACE IF NECESSARY.
STARTING MOTOR ENGAGES BUT DOES NOT CRANK ENGINE.	1. PARTIALLY DISCHARGED BATTERY. DEAD CELL IN BATTERY.	1. TEST SPECIFIC GRAVITY AND RECHARGE BATTERY IF NECES-SARY. REPLACE BATTERY IF DEFECTIVE.
	2. STARTER CLUTCH SLIPS.	2. REPLACE STARTER CLUTCH.
	3. SOLENOID CHATTERS; FAILS TO HOLD STARTER DRIVE IN THE ENGAGED POSITION.	3. CHECK SOLENOID HOLD-IN WINDING.
	4. DEFECTIVE ARMATURE WIND-INGS OR FIELD COILS, BENT ARMATURE SHAFT.	4. REPAIR STARTING MOTOR.
STARTER CRANKS ENGINE SLOWLY	1. PARTIALLY DISCHARGED BATTERY. FAULTY BATTERY CELL.	1. TEST SPECIFIC GRAVITY RECHARGE OR REPLACE BATTERY AS NECESSARY.
	2. LOOSE OR CORRODED BATTERY OR CABLE TERMINALS.	2. CHECK VOLTAGE DROP IN STARTER CIRCUIT. CLEAN AND TIGHTEN BATTERY AND CABLE TERMINALS.
	3. UNDERSIZE CABLES BETWEEN BATTERY AND STARTING MOTOR.	3. REPLACE CABLES.
	4. HIGH INTERNAL RESISTANCE IN STARTING MOTOR.	4. REPAIR STARTING MOTOR.
	5. EXCESSIVE ENGINE DRAG, HEAVY OIL, TIGHT BEAR-ING, ETC.	5. MAKE NECESSARY COR-RECTIONS TO ENGINE TO ELIMINATE EXCESSIVE DRAG.
	6. HIGH RESISTANCE IN SOLENOID SWITCH CON-TACTS.	6. CHECK VOLTAGE DROP ACROSS TERMINALS. RE-PAIR OR REPLACE SWITCH.
	7. HIGH RESISTANCE IN MAGNETIC SWITCH CON-TACTS (WHERE APPLICABLE).	7. CHECK VOLTAGE DROP ACROSS TERMINALS. REPAIR OR REPLACE SWITCH.

All manufacturers will recommend an initial amperage draw test while cranking the engine. This is also called the starter load test and the result of this test will determine whether the starting motor should be removed from the engine. It is generally safe to assume that if the starting motor operates within specifications during the starter load test it will function in a normal manner. The Trouble Shooting Guide, Table 1, indicates the troubles that may occur in the cranking motor circuit.

Starter Load Test

A starting motor should be tested on the automobile to determine if the voltage and current required to crank the engine are within specifications. The test equipment consists of a high reading ammeter, a voltmeter, and a heavy duty carbon pile resistance connected into the cranking circuit as shown in Fig. 1.

Make certain the control knob on the carbon pile is turned to maximum resistance so that no current is flowing through the ammeter and carbon pile resistance. Remove the high tension wire from the center of the distributor cap and ground it against the engine. Connect a jumper switch between the battery terminal of the starter relay and the ignition switch terminal of the solenoid. The jumper switch closes the circuit to the starting motor and permits cranking the motor while taking the voltage. Close the switch to crank the engine. Crank it only long enough to obtain an exact

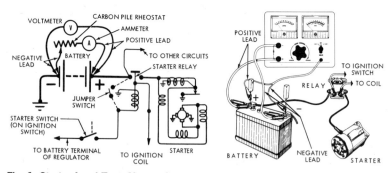

Fig. 1. Starter Load Test. Note voltage across the battery while cranking engine. Open the cranking circuit jumper switch. Turn the variable resistance until the voltmeter reading duplicates the reading obtained while cranking the engine. Compare the ammeter reading (which indicates the starting motor current draw) to the manufacturer's specification for this test. Ford Div.—Ford Motor Co.

reading of the voltmeter. Observe whether cranking speed is normal during the test to eliminate engine mechanical problems.

Now turn the carbon pile resistance control until the voltmeter indicates the same voltage reading when the engine was being cranked. The ammeter will indicate the starting motor current draw that was required to crank the engine. If the current draw is not within specifications for the motor being tested remove it for repairs.

STARTING MOTOR TESTS

Starting motors that are removed from the engine should be tested on a test bench. Details will be listed for a no-load test and a stall test. If the starting motor meets specifications for these two tests it should function properly when reinstalled. Overhauled motors should be given these tests before being reinstalled. Starting motors should be checked when removed from the engine to see that the locked resistance test meets specifications. This test indicates internal troubles in the motor.

No Load Test

The starting motor terminal is readily accessible on most starting motors and permits the motor to be connected for testing purposes without including the relay or solenoid switch in the test circuit. On others the test is made with the solenoid in place. The battery used for the tests should be of the proper voltage and fully charged.

Connect a cable from one battery post to the starting motor terminal and a second cable from the other battery post to the starting motor frame. Be sure the polarity is right. If this test is being made after working on the motor be sure to operate it for 30 seconds to seat the brushes. Blow out all dirt with compressed air and allow to cool to room temperature. Never operate a starting motor for more than 30 seconds at a time while testing it without allowing it to cool. Overheating can seriously damage the motor.

To make the no load test connect a high reading ammeter and carbon pile resistance in series with the starting motor terminal and a battery. Fig. 2. The ammeter should be capable of reading several hundred amperes so that it will not be damaged if the armature does not turn freely. Connect one lead of the voltmeter to the starting motor terminal and ground the other voltmeter lead on the starting motor frame at a place free of grease and paint.

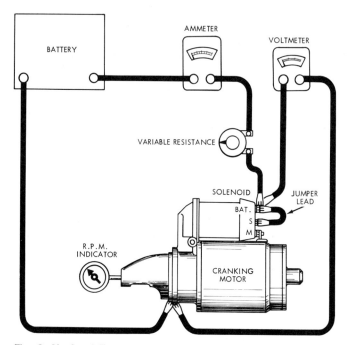

Fig. 2. No Load Test. To make test, gradually turn the variable resistance until the voltage rises to the value specified by the manufacturer. Now compare the ammeter reading and cranking speed to specifications. The starting motor shown is being tested with the solenoid in place. The test leads are therefore connected to the BAT terminal of the solenoid instead of directly to the cranking motor (M) terminal. Delco-Remy Div.—General Motors Corp.

It should be noted that some starting motors of the Bendix type may have only one terminal through which they can be wired to the circuit. Most present motors have attached solenoids which shift the drive pinion into position and close the contacts to the motor. It is possible to by-pass the solenoid completely to test the starting motor by connecting the test leads directly to the motor terminal (M) Fig. 2. The solenoid is usually included in the test circuit and a jumper is inserted between the battery terminal (Bat) of the solenoid and the ignition switch terminal (S). The jumper activates the solenoid which holds the drive pinion shift in drive and closes the contacts to the starting motor.

Before closing the test circuit make certain that the carbon pile resistance (or other type being used) is set to maximum resistance. Ground the battery cable to the starting motor frame to close the circuit. At this time there is no current flow through the circuit due to the high resistance. Both the ammeter and the voltmeter read zero.

Adjust (decrease) the carbon pile resistance until the voltmeter reads the voltage specified for this test by the manufacturer. This is usually 5.5 volts on 6-volt systems and 10.6 on 12-volt systems. Read the ammeter. With the motor running at its maximum speed place a speed indicator against the drive end of the armature shaft and read the speed. The motor current and speed under no load should be 5.5 volts and 60 amps at 2600 rpm for 6-volt systems. For 12-volt systems with the solenoid on the motor the readings should be 11 volts and 65-100 amps at 3600-5100 rpm.

Check the brush action while the motor is running. If the brushes do not ride the commutator smoothly, or if the current draw and speed are not within the specifications then check the motor for the following:

Low speed and low current. Look for high resistance in the starting motor. This may be caused by a dirty commutator, worn brushes, faulty brush leads, and low brush spring tension.

Low speed and high current. This indicates excessive friction due to tight, dirty, or worn bearings, loose pole shoes causing the armature to drag, bent armature shaft, shorted or grounded armature, or grounded field coils.

Failure to operate with high current. This is often a direct ground in the motor terminal, switch, field coils, or armature. Frozen bearings and mechanical defects may cause this too.

Failure to operate with no current draw. This means an open circuit. The field coils, armature coils (usually with burned commutator bars), worn brushes, broken or weak brush springs, or dirty commutator may be the cause.

Excessive arcing. This is caused by commutator troubles such as low brush spring tension, worn commutator bars, shorted commutator, or worn brushes. An open circuit in the armature will cause arcing and a burned spot on the commutator.

Excessive brush movement. A worn commutator or low spring tension may be the cause of this.

Stall Torque Test

The stall torque test measures the current draw and torque developed by the starting motor at a specified voltage while the starting motor is made to work against a spring scale. Fig. 3. The results of the test are compared to the manufacturer's specifications to determine the condition of the starting motor.

To make the test, securely mount the starting motor in a vise on a work bench. Connect an ammeter and a variable resistance (turned to maximum resistance) in series with the starting motor terminal and the battery. Fig. 3 shows the connections for a starting motor with a Bendix drive. For a starting motor with an attached solenoid, the connections are made as shown in Fig. 2. The connections for the stall torque test are identical to those for the no load test. The ammeter should have sufficient capacity to handle the stall current (which can become as high as 600 amperes). Connect

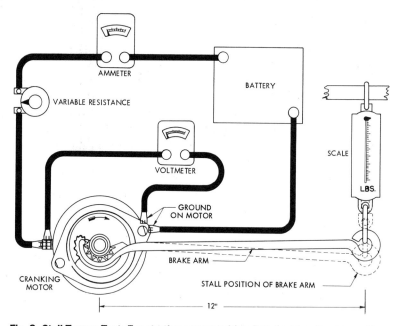

Fig. 3. Stall Torque Test. For starting motors with a Bendix drive the connections are made directly to the starting motor terminal as shown. With the variable resistance adjusted to provide a specified voltage, the ammeter reading and torque measured by the spring scale are compared to manufacturer's specifications. Delco-Remy Div.—General Motors Corp.

one voltmeter lead to the starting motor terminal and the other to a clean ground on the motor frame. Connect a torque arm and spring scale to the drive pinion as shown. Fig. 3.

Before the drive pinion can be attached to the torque arm it must be moved to its extended or drive position. If the starting motor being tested has a Bendix drive, the drive pinion must be threaded to the drive position by hand. If the starting motor being tested employs a solenoid shift lever to engage the pinion, the pinion must be moved to the drive position by manually shifting the solenoid shift lever. Engage the torque arm to the pinion as carefully as possible so that the torque arm will not slip when current passes through the starting motor.

Gradually turn out the variable resistance to obtain the voltage at which the test must be made as specified by the manufacturer. Note the ammeter and spring scale readings. The stall torque will be the product of the spring scale reading (in lbs) times the length of the torque arm (in ft). The result is expressed as lbs/ft (pounds-feet). As an example, a typical 12-volt starting motor develops a stall or lock torque of 15.5 pounds/feet at 580 amperes and 5 volts. The stall torque and ammeter readings should fall within the specifications of the manufacturer.

If the stall torque and current are both low, high resistance is indicated in the internal connections or between the brushes and commutator. A high current reading with low stall torque may be caused by a defective armature or field windings. If the stall torque and current are not within the manufacturer's specifications, the starting motor should be disassembled and the parts checked to determine their condition.

Locked Resistance Test

This test requires the same equipment and hook-up as the stall torque test. However, the pinion must be locked securely so that it cannot turn while the test is being conducted (Fig. 4). Adjust the voltage, by means of the variable resistance, to the voltage specified by the manufacturer (usually 3.5 to 4.3 volts on 12-volt systems). The motor current draw as read on the ammeter should be within the manufacturer's specifications (300-360 amperes are typical readings).

If the current draw is less than specified by the manufacturer, it indicates excessive resistance within the motor circuit. A current draw higher than the specified range indicates a short or ground.

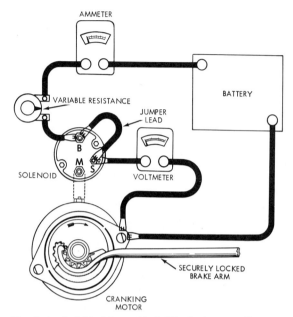

Fig. 4. Locked Resistance Test. The test connections are made to a starting motor with an attached solenoid as shown. The jumper activates the solenoid (to close the contact to the starting motor) when the variable resistance is turned out.

Starter Circuit Resistance Tests

The starter circuit resistance is measured by determining the voltage drop in the circuit. If the voltage drop is greater than what is considered normal for the circuit, the voltage available at the starter will be reduced. A lower than normal voltage drop indicates a lower than normal resistance. Both conditions are indicators of trouble in either the starting motor circuit, the starting motor, or both.

Check Voltage Drop in Starting Motor Circuit. Test the battery electrolyte specific gravity and if it reads 1.220 or less recharge the battery before proceeding with the test. Disconnect the ignition coil secondary cable from the center of the distributor cap and ground it against the engine. Use a low-reading voltmeter, connected into the circuit as shown in Fig. 5 to make the following tests.

Check the voltage drop between the insulated (positive) battery

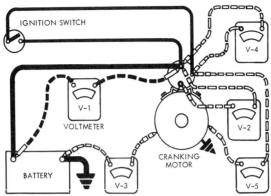

Fig. 5. Checking voltage drop in the cranking motor circuit. Oldsmobile Div.—General Motors Corp.

post and the battery terminal on the solenoid while the engine is being cranked. This is shown on V-1 in Fig. 5.

Note the voltage drop between the battery and motor terminals on the solenoid during cranking. Position V-2 of Fig. 5.

Determine the voltage drop between the grounded (negative) battery post and the starter housing during cranking. Position V-3, Fig. 5.

If the voltage drop in any of these three tests exceeds 0.2 volts it indicates excessive resistance in that part of the circuit.

If voltage drops greater than 0.2 volts (abnormal resistance) are found in tests V-1 and V-3 the trouble usually is a poor connection at the battery posts, solenoid terminal, or battery ground connection and can be corrected by cleaning and tightening the connections. To determine which connection is at fault test each one for voltage drop as shown in Fig. 6.

The test in V-2 of Fig. 5 checks the resistance across the switch terminals in the solenoid. If the resistance is high disassemble the switch and then clean the terminals or replace the switch.

If the solenoid fails to pull in when trying to start the engine look for excessive voltage drop in the solenoid control circuit. To check the resistance crank the engine and measure the voltage drop between the battery (Bat) and the switch (S) terminals on the solenoid. Position V-4, Fig. 5. This measures total resistance offered by the connecting wires and switches. The voltage drop should not

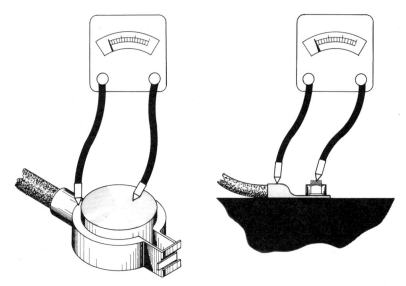

Fig. 6. Checking voltage drop (which indicates a poor connection) at the cable connections.

exceed 3.5 volts. If the resistance is high then test each connection in the circuit as shown in Fig. 6 to determine where the fault lies. Clean and tighten the connections.

If the voltage drop is within satisfactory limits measure the voltage available at the solenoid switch terminal, Fig. 5, position V-5. The solenoid should pull in when the voltage is 7.7 volts or more. If it fails to do so, replace it.

Check Current Draw of Solenoid. Check both the pull-in and the hold-in windings for current draw to determine if the solenoid is in a satisfactory condition. If the solenoid has not been removed from the starting motor it will be necessary to disconnect the connector strap from the terminal on the solenoid before making the tests.

To check the current draw of the hold-in winding connect a variable resistance and ammeter in series with a 12-volt battery and the switch (S) terminal on the solenoid. Fig. 7. Connect one terminal of a voltmeter to the switch terminal and ground the other on the solenoid case. Adjust the voltage with the variable resistance to 10.0 volts and note the reading on the ammeter. The reading should be

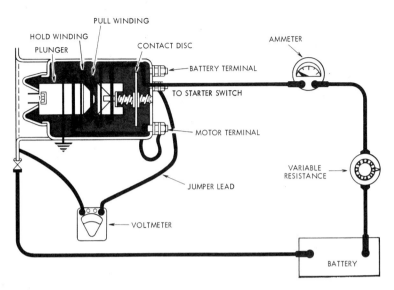

Fig. 7. Checking the current draw of the solenoid windings. Oldsmobile Div.— General Motors Corp.

within the manufacturer's printed specifications for the solenoid being tested (10.5-12.5 amps on some and 15.5-17.5 on others).

To check the current draw for both solenoid windings use the same hookup but ground the solenoid motor terminal to the case with a jumper lead as shown in Fig. 7. Adjust to 10.0 volts and note the ammeter reading. The reading should be within the specifications for the solenoid being tested (42-49 amps on some and 47-54 on others).

Test Neutral Switch. When testing the neutral switch on cars equipped with automatic transmissions remove the secondary ignition wire from the center of the distributor cap and ground it against the engine. Turn the starter (ignition) switch on and move the shift selector lever through all positions. The starter should engage only in the "park" and "neutral" positions. If the starter operates in other positions of the lever either adjust the neutral switch or replace it if it is defective.

To adjust the neutral switch loosen the screws that hold the switch in place on the steering column, Fig. 8. Place the transmission selector lever in the neutral detent position. Move the switch

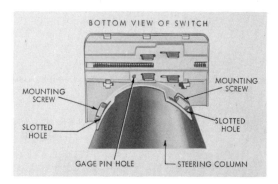

Fig. 8. The cranking circuit neutral switch, seen from bottom. The switch is correctly aligned when a small gage pin can be inserted in the hole shown. Ford Div. —Ford Motor Co.

operating lever (not seen from the underside of this particular switch) until a small diameter pin can be inserted in the gage pin hole on the bottom of the switch. Fig. 8. Tighten the screws and remove the gage pin. Finally check the operation of the selector lever to make certain that the starting motor operates only in the "park" and "neutral" positions.

DISASSEMBLY AND REPAIR OF STARTING MOTOR

Remove the starting motor from the engine and remove or disengage the solenoid switch. Remove the through bolts that hold the starter together. The commutator end plate, starter housing, and drive housing can now be separated. Fig. 9. On some motors the brushes will have to be disconnected from the field coils before the end plate can be removed. Remove the armature from the main housing. Remove the snap ring and retainer from the armature shaft and remove the overrunning clutch starter drive mechanism from the shaft.

Clean all parts of the starting motor by wiping them with a clean cloth. Clean Bendix drives with a petroleum safety solvent and a stiff brush. Do not clean the armature, field coils, screw shaft assembly on barrel type drives, or the overrunning clutch drive by any of the hot or cold degreasing methods. Degreasing may damage the insulation so a short or ground may develop. It will also remove lubricant originally packed in the overrunning clutch.

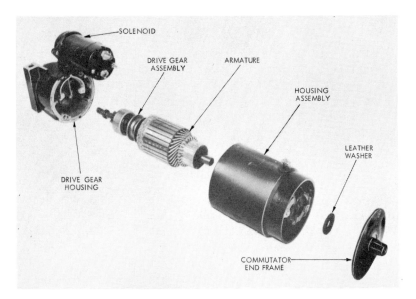

Fig. 9. Starting motor disassembled. Oldsmobile Div.—General Motors Corp.

After cleaning the various parts of the starting motor, visually inspect for mechanical defects and wear. Check with the proper equipment for electrical defects. The following inspections and tests will indicate the parts to be replaced and the repairs that must be made to restore the starting motor to a serviceable condition.

Armature Tests and Repairs

The armature should be checked for mechanical defects before checking it for grounds or short circuits in the coils or commutator.

Inspect the armature for a worn or bent shaft, worn commutator, or scored laminations. See that the windings are properly staked and soldered to the commutator. Replace the armature if the shaft bearing surfaces are worn. If the shaft is bent straighten it or replace the armature. Remove rust on the shaft. Turn down the commutator on a lathe if it is dirty or has worn spots or if the mica is high. Burned spots on the commutator are an indication of an open circuit in the armature coil which will prevent proper operation of the motor. If the commutator has burned spots the loose connections at

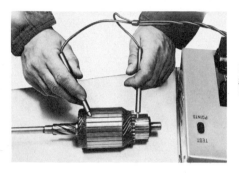

Fig. 10. Testing the armature for ground. Chevrolet Div.—General Motors Corp.

the burned bars should be restaked and soldered. Use a resin flux.

Check the iron core of the armature for scoring which would indicate it is rubbing against the pole shoes. Replace the bushings in the commutator end plate and pinion housing if the core is scored.

Test Armature for Ground. To test the armature for ground place one test prod of a 110 volt test lamp on the commutator and the other on the armature core or shaft. Fig. 10. Do not touch the test prods to the bearing surface on the shaft as the arc formed may burn the surface. If the test lamp lights the armature coils are grounded and must be replaced.

Test Armature for Short Circuit. Test the armature for a short circuit on a growler. Place the armature in the V slot of the growler and turn on the switch on the growler. Place a hacksaw blade on the core of the armature as shown in Fig. 11 and rotate the armature slowly by hand. If the armature coils are shorted the hacksaw blade will be attracted to the core and will vibrate.

If the growler test indicates a shorted coil take a hacksaw blade and clean between each commutator bar and at the top and back of the riser for each bar. Retest the armature. If the short circuit has not been eliminated replace the armature.

Repair Armature with an Open Circuit. Open circuits in a starter armature usually occur at the point where the armature coils are soldered to the commutator risers. An open circuit is usually indicated by the burned condition of the commutator bar to which the open circuited coil is attached.

To repair an open circuit coil scrape all dust and dirt away at the point where the armature coil is soldered to the riser. Resolder

Fig. 11. Testing the armature for short circuit with a growler. Plymouth Div.—
Chrysler Corp.

the joint using a high temperature solder and resin flux. While soldering be careful not to short circuit the adjacent coils or commutator bars. After soldering true up the commutator and riser bars on a lathe.

Resurface the Commutator. Mount the armature in a lathe so that it runs true. Take light cuts until the commutator is completely cleaned. Remove burrs with No. 00 sandpaper.

Some manufacturers recommend that the mica of starting motor armatures be undercut. Others advise against this practice. Those who do not recommend undercutting feel that the slot formed provides a place where copper dust worn from the brushes can collect between the segments, resulting ultimately, in a short. Molded commutators are not to be undercut and only lightly turned.

Where undercutting of the mica is specified the commutators are undercut on a machine designed for the purpose. If such machines are unavailable a hacksaw blade can be used for the job. The sides of the blade are ground thin to fit the space between the commutator segments. The undercutting tool should be about 0.002 in. wider than the mica. Undercutting should be clean and square and should remove all mica to a depth of 1/32 in. Remove all burrs with No. 00 sandpaper.

Field Coil Tests and Repairs

Check the starter terminal and replace if the threads are stripped. Examine the soldered connection at the starter terminal and resolder if necessary. Inspect the field coil insulation. If it is worn or damaged the coils should be rewrapped or replaced depending on the extent of the damage. Test the field coils with a 110 volt test lamp for open or grounded circuit.

Test for Open Circuit. To test the field coils for an open circuit place one test prod on each of the field coil leads as shown in Fig. 12. If the test lamp does not light there is an open circuit in the field coils. To determine if one or more field coils have an open circuit test each coil separately by placing the test prods on the leads of each coil. If the field coils have an open circuit replace them.

Note: The above test indicates only a continuous circuit in the field coils. It does not indicate whether the windings within the coils are short circuited. No test will detect short circuited field coils because the difference in current draw between normal and

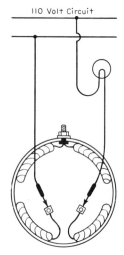

Fig. 12. Testing the field coils for an open circuit.

shorted field windings is very slight. If shorted coils are suspected install new field coils and check for improved performance.

Test for Ground. To test the field circuit for grounds place one test lamp prod on the starter terminal and the other on an unpainted surface of the motor frame. Fig. 13. If the test lamp lights the field coil circuit is grounded.

Some motors use a shunt field coil which is normally grounded. For this test be sure the shunt coil is disconnected. The shunt coil can be identified easily as it will have fine wire rather than copper ribbon as the motor coils have. The shunt coil serves to limit the top speed of the motor.

If a ground exists unsolder and separate the field coil leads from the terminal stud. Place one test lamp prod on the terminal stud and the other on the motor frame. If the lamp lights the stud is grounded. Remove the stud and replace the insulating washers.

If the terminal stud is not grounded then test each field coil for ground by placing one test lamp prod on a field coil terminal and the other on the motor frame. If a coil is grounded either replace or remove and retape the grounded coil.

Replace Field Coils. When removing the field coils from the starting motor housing mark the pole shoes for replacement in exactly the same position. To disassemble the field coils remove the nut and washers from the starter terminal. Remove the screws securing the pole shoes to the starter housing and take out the field coils and pole shoes from the housing.

110 Volt Circuit

Fig. 13. Using a test lamp to test the field coils for ground.

Grounded field coils may sometimes be repaired by reinsulating them. Remove the damaged portion of the taping and rewrap with new insulating tape. After taping apply insulating varnish to the field coil assembly. Avoid bulkiness as this may cause the pole shoes to cut through the new insulation and produce another ground when the coils are reinstalled. Field coils that cannot be repaired must be replaced. If only part of the field coil assembly is to be replaced unsolder it at the starter terminal.

Clean the starter housing before replacing the field coil assembly. Place the field coils in the housing with the terminal properly entered in the hole in the housing. Place the pole shoes in the field coils according to the marks before disassembly and install the pole shoes with a pole shoe spreader. While tightening the screws strike the housing with a soft face hammer to assist in seating the pole shoes. Install the insulating bushing and washers on the starter terminal and tighten. Test the field coil circuit for open and grounded circuits with a 110 volt test lamp to make certain the installation is satisfactory.

Test Brush Holders. Test the brush holders for ground by placing one test lamp prod on an insulated brush and the other prod on the starter housing or end plate, depending on the design. Fig. 14. If the test lamp lights the brush holder is grounded and the brush holder or end plate should be replaced. Check all insulated brush holders this way.

Disconnect the grounded brush leads from the end frame and clean the terminals. Reconnect if the brushes are satisfactory for re-use.

Inspect Brushes and Holders

Inspect the brushes and replace if they are oil soaked, if the leads are loose in the brushes, or if they are worn more than half their original length. Make sure the brush holders are clean and that the brushes are not binding in them.

When replacing brushes of the type where the leads are riveted to the end frame be sure to remove the rivet and to securely stake the new rivet to make certain of a good contact.

Brushes soldered to the field coils should be unsoldered and the loop in the field coil lead opened. Insert the new brush lead to its full depth in the loop and clinch before soldering. Make certain the

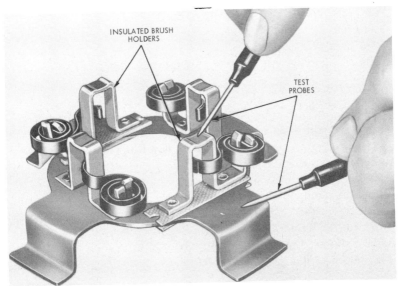

INSULATED BRUSH
HOLDERS

TEST
PROBES

Fig. 14. Testing insulated brush holder for ground. Plymouth Div., Chrysler Corp.

joint is well soldered. Use a high temperature solder and a resin flux.

Check Brush Spring Tension. Partially reassemble the starting motor so the brushes are resting on the commutator. The full brush surface should ride on the commutator with proper spring tension. Check the brushes to be sure they slide or swing freely in their holders and are in alignment with the commutator bars.

Hook a spring scale close to the brush and pull in a line away from the brush. Take the reading just as the spring leaves the brush. The spring tension varies on different makes of starting motors. Some require 24-28 oz while others may take more or less. Replace the spring if the tension is incorrect.

Inspect Drive Housing

Inspect the drive housing. If it is cracked or damaged it should be replaced. Install the drive housing on the armature shaft and check the fit of the bushing. If the bushing is worn so that side play exists, replace it.

Inspect Commutator End Plate

Examine the commutator end plate and replace if it is bent, cracked, or damaged. Check the fit of the bushing and the armature shaft. If side play exists replace the bushing.

Inspect Overrunning Clutch

Check the drive assembly for wear and make sure the clutch slides easily on the armature shaft. If the pinion teeth are chipped, cracked, or worn replace the drive assembly. Check the internal splines for wear or damage.

Place the drive assembly on the armature shaft and turn the pinion by hand. In one direction the clutch should release and the pinion turn smoothly and freely. Turning it in the opposite direction should lock the pinion. Replace the drive assembly if the pinion slips in the driving directions or rolls roughly in the overrunning direction.

Inspect Inertia (Bendix) Drives

Replace the drive spring if it is cracked, broken, twisted, or if the loops or tangs are bent. Examine all the parts of the assembly and replace any that are worn or damaged.

When working on the Folo-Thru type of drive be careful not to turn the pinion out to its fully extended position. The pinion becomes locked to the shaft by a pin that drops into a detent in the shaft. To return the pinion to its "at rest" position once it has locked requires the drive assembly to be driven at a speed fast enough to release the detent pin by centrifugal force. The starting motor usually can be installed with the drive in extended position. When the starting motor is operated the drive will release in the normal manner.

STARTING MOTOR REASSEMBLY

Assemble the starting motor by reversing the procedure used during disassembly. Make certain that all electrical connections are clean and tight. Soldered connections should be made with a resin flux and high temperature solder. Make *no load* and *lock torque* tests on the starting motor to determine if the voltage, current draw, and torque are within the specifications.

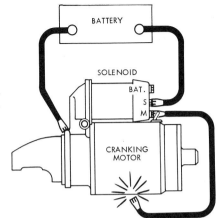

Fig. 15. Circuit connections for checking pinion clearance. Delco-Remy Div.—General Motors Corp.

Check Pinion Clearance

After the overrunning clutch type starting motor is assembled and before it is reinstalled check the assembly for pinion clearance. There must be sufficient clearance between the pinion in the engaged position and the retainer and snap ring on the armature shaft or between the pinion and drive housing to prevent jamming.

Fig. 16. Checking pinion clearance on a reassembled starting motor of the overrunning clutch type. Delco-Remy Div.—General Motors Corp.

When checking the pinion clearance use a voltage that will advance the pinion to the drive position but without operating the motor. A 6-volt battery can be connected to the solenoid switch terminal. This will operate the pinion but will not be sufficient to operate the starting motor. Ground the other battery post to the housing. Fig. 15. Use a heavy jumper cable to momentarily make connection between the solenoid motor terminal and the housing. This shifts the pinion into cranking position where it will remain until the battery is disconnected.

Press the pinion back toward the motor to remove loose play and check the clearance between the pinion and retainer. Fig. 16. The clearance should be 0.010-0.140 in. Excessive clearance indicates wear of the shift lever mechanism or improper assembly. Worn or defective parts must be replaced as there are no provisions for adjustment on late model starting motors.

TRADE COMPETENCY TEST

1. Describe how a starting motor can be tested under load while mounted on the vehicle.
2. What is the purpose of the no load test?
3. How is the lock torque test made?
4. How does the lock resistance test differ from the lock torque test? What trouble is indicated when the current draw is less than specifications?
5. How does a higher than normal voltage drop through a starter circuit affect the circuit?
6. What is the cause of excessive voltage drop in a circuit?
7. How would you test a neutral switch while it is mounted on the vehicle?
8. How would you test an armature for a ground circuit? For a short circuit?
9. How would you test the field coils for an open circuit? For grounded coils?
10. How would you test insulated brush holders for ground?
11. When should starting motor brushes be replaced?
12. How would you check the spring tension on starting motor brushes?
13. What tests should be made on starting motors that have been overhauled?
14. Why should the overrunning clutch never be washed in kerosene to clean it?

CHAPTER 6

DC CHARGING SYSTEMS

The charging system recharges the battery and maintains a supply of electrical current to meet the operating needs of an automobile.

The generating system includes the generator, generator regulator, charge indicator, storage battery, wires to connect the units, and the ground through the engine and battery ground cable to complete the circuit.

Although the battery was discussed in Chapter 2, it must be considered as a part of the charging system, since, in conjunction with the generator regulator, it controls the generator charging rate.

Due to its limited capacity the storage battery can supply the electrical requirements of the automobile only for a short period depending on the amount of energy consumed.

When the engine is running the generator restores to the battery the current used for starting and other electrical needs. When current demands exceed the generator output the battery supplies the additional current required. When the generator output exceeds the current consumption the excess current recharges the battery. The generator output must, in addition to meeting the demands of the electrical systems, keep the battery charged.

The generator is a dynamo or machine that converts mechanical energy produced by the engine into electrical energy. Fan belt driven, the generator supplies current to the storage battery and the connected electrical load at operating speeds. The current is produced in the generator by electromagnetic induction. For many years generators employed on automotive vehicles were the direct current (DC) type. The alternating current (AC) generator, or alternator, has replaced the direct current generator. However, the number of older cars still in use which employ the DC type genera-

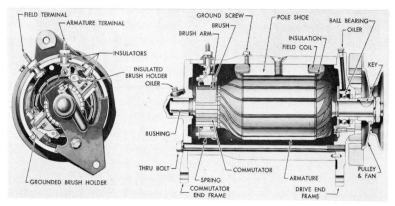

Fig. 1. Sectional view of an automotive generator. Chevrolet Div.—General Motors Corp.

tors is quite large. The mechanic will often be required to service these units; he must therefore be familiar with the construction and repair procedures for this generator. Some types of generators are used in other equipment which the mechanic might service.

COMPONENTS OF THE GENERATOR

Six- and 12-volt generators are similar in construction with the exception that 12-volt generators have their field coils and armature wound for 12-volt operation and have a higher wattage output (volts × amperes). Most 12-volt generators have copper-plated field terminals to distinguish them from 6-volt generators.

The generator, shown in Fig. 1, consists basically of a frame, or housing, pole shoes, field coils, an armature, brushes, a commutator end plate and a drive end plate. These components are described in detail.

Generator Frame

The generator frame is a cylindrical steel housing to which soft-iron pole shoes are attached by screws (Fig. 2). The pole shoes become north and south poles of electromagnets when current flows through the field windings, the frame acting as the return circuit for the magnetic field. Generators may have either two or four pole shoes. Fig. 2. Some generators have brush holders mounted on the inside at the commutator end of the frame.

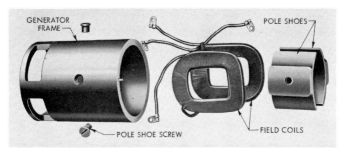

GENERATOR FRAME   POLE SHOES   POLE SHOE SCREW   FIELD COILS

Fig. 2. Generator frame, field coils, and pole shoes. Delco-Remy Div.—General Motors Corp.

Field Coils

The field coils (Fig. 2) of automotive generators are wound with an enameled, cotton-covered wire. Some field coils are wrapped with a cotton tape, impregnated with an insulating varnish and baked. Other field coils are wrapped with a plastic material. The coils are connected in series and are secured in the generator frame by the pole shoes. When current flows through the field coils, the pole shoes become magnetized, producing a magnetic field between the inner faces of the pole shoes. Two or four field coils are generally used in automotive generators, the individual field coils being wound so that the adjacent pole shoes have opposite magnetic polarity.

When the flow of current through the field coils is stopped, a small amount of magnetism remains in the iron pole shoes. New or newly rebuilt generators may have no residual magnetism, in which case they must be polarized by passing a current through the field coil before the generator will produce an electric current.

The field coils are connected in parallel (shunt connected) with the armature. As a result, only a portion of the current developed by the armature flows through the field coil circuit. Depending upon the design of the generator, one terminal of the field coil assembly is connected to the armature through an insulated brush, either directly to the brush or externally through a regulating device. The other terminal of the field coils is either grounded to the generator frame or grounded through a regulating device.

The field coil assembly offers resistance to the flow of current, the amount of resistance depending upon the size of the wire used and the number of turns of wire in each coil. The amount of current that flows through the field coil circuit is controlled by the resistance of the coil circuit and the voltage applied. The current draw on 6-volt generators varies from 3.5 to 6.0 amperes and from 1.9 to 3.0 amperes on 12-volt generators.

Armature

The generator armature consists of a shaft, a soft iron laminated armature core, commutator, insulation, and the coil windings (Fig. 3). The laminations are stamped from thin sheet iron and pressed on the shaft to form the core. The laminated core has a number of slots running lengthwise which contain the armature coils. The armature revolves between the pole shoes with a clearance of 1/64 in. (or less) between the core and the pole shoes. This reduces the amount of resistance to the flow of magnetic lines of force between the pole shoes. In addition, the iron core tends to collect the lines of force traveling between the pole shoes, concentrating them where they can be cut by the armature coils.

The commutator is pressed on the shaft and is composed of copper segments insulated from each other and from the shaft (Fig. 3). The armature contains a number of coils, each composed of five, six, or more turns of enameled, cotton-covered wire, the ends of which are soldered to the commutator riser bars. The armature coils fit into the slots in the core, and are insulated from the core by

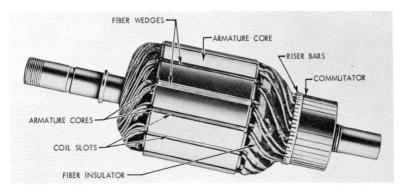

Fig. 3. Generator armature showing parts. Delco-Remy Div.—General Motors Corp.

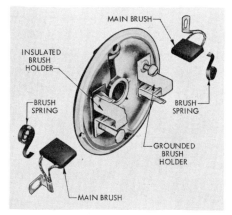

Fig. 4. Commutator end frame supporting the brushes. Ford Motor Co.

insulators at the ends of the core, and insulating material placed between the coils and the core slot. The coils are usually anchored in the slots by a fiber wedge driven the length of the slot.

Generator Brushes

The generator brushes, Fig. 4, ride on the surface of the commutator and transfer current generated in the armature conductors to the field circuit and to the external generating circuit. The brushes are mounted in brush holders and are held in contact with the commutator by spring pressure. The brushes used in generators are made of either carbon or graphite. The brushes fit into the brush holder with a sliding fit and are connected to their proper point by means of a "pigtail" anchored to the brush. To assure a good transfer of current from the armature to the brush, the brush should be in full contact with the commutator and the commutator should be clean and round.

Commutator End Frame

On some generators the commutator end frame provides a support for the brush holders and has either a bushing or ball bearing mounted in the frame which supports the commutator end of the armature (Fig. 4). On other generators the brushes are located within the housing. The end frame encloses the brush end of the generator and provides a support for the armature bushing. Fig. 5. One of the brush holders is grounded directly to the frame; the other brush holder is insulated from the frame.

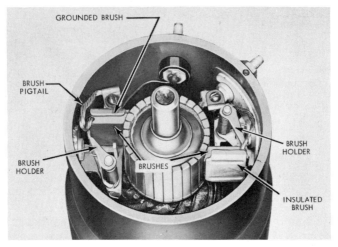

Fig. 5. Commutator end frame housing the brushes and supporting the armature bushing.

The commutator end frame is positioned on the generator housing by mating the small dowel and the hole provided for this purpose. This automatically places the main brushes at the "neutral point."

Drive End Plate

The drive end plate supports the front end of the armature in a ball bearing, and is usually provided with a bracket by means of which the generator is attached to the engine. The end plate has openings which permit the circulation of air through the generator. An oil cup may be mounted on the end plate for lubrication of the bearing. Most bearings are pre-lubricated type and require no further lubrication.

OPERATING PRINCIPLES OF A DC GENERATOR

All generators operate on the basic electrical principle that whenever a conductor cuts through magnetic lines of force an electric current is induced in the conductor. When the conductor moves parallel to the lines of force no current is induced in the conductor. The amount of current induced in a conductor depends upon the strength of the magnetic field (number of lines of force), the number

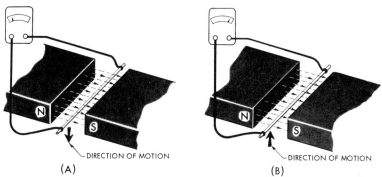

DIRECTION OF MOTION   DIRECTION OF MOTION
(A)   (B)

Fig. 6. Generating electricity by induction.

of wires cutting the field, and the speed with which they pass through the field.

Inducing Current

The generation of an electric current by the induction principle can be demonstrated by using two bar magnets and a length of wire. If the wire is moved downward between the two magnets so that the wire cuts through the magnetic lines of force as shown in Fig. 6, left, a voltage will be induced in the wire which will cause current to flow. This can be proved by connecting a sensitive ammeter to the two ends of the wire as shown to make a complete circuit. Movement of the wire through the field will cause the ammeter pointer to move to one side of the scale, indicating that current is flowing in the circuit. If the wire were to be moved *upward* through the magnetic field, as shown in Fig. 6, right, the ammeter pointer would move to the opposite side of the scale (to the right of zero) indicating that the current generated is flowing in the opposite direction. When the wire is moved parallel to the magnetic field, the ammeter pointer remains at zero, indicating that no current is being generated.

The direction of flow of the current generated by moving a conductor through a magnetic field can be determined by using the Left Hand Rule. By wrapping the fingers of the left hand in the direction that the lines of force wrap around the conductor, the thumb will point in the direction of current flow.

Automotive generators use electromagnets in place of bar magnets since they produce a stronger magnetic field resulting in a greater number of lines of force. Fig. 7 illustrates a simple shunt generator consisting of (1) field coils wrapped around facing pole shoes which create a magnetic field as current flows through the coils; (2) a single loop armature which, as it revolves, carries conductors through the magnetic field; and (3) a commutator and brushes to carry off the current induced in the armature conductors. When, as shown, the field coils are connected in parallel with the armature, the generator is said to be "shunt wound".

Note that the construction of the generator shown in Fig. 7 is basically the same as that for the starting motor discussed before. If this simple generator is connected to a battery instead of to the load shown it will run as a motor. The current flowing through the field coils magnetizes the pole shoes around which the field coils are wound, creating a magnetic field between the pole shoes. The lines of force thus created cause the armature to turn. When the battery is disconnected a small amount of magnetism remains in the iron pole shoes. This is called residual magnetism. Without residual magnetism (the presence of a magnetic field across the pole shoes) the generator could not function. Residual magnetism remains in a generator for a considerable period of time. This is why generators which have been stored for a long time begin charging immediately upon being installed in the vehicle.

The passing of current through a generator is called polarizing.

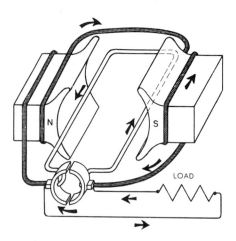

Fig. 7. Simple direct current generator. Compare to starting motor.

Generators that are properly polarized will, when driven in the proper direction, produce a current that flows in a direction that is in accordance with the polarity of the electrical system.

When the single loop armature coil (Fig. 7) is rotated in a clockwise direction through the residual magnetic field the two sides of the coil cut through the magnetic lines of force, resulting in a voltage being induced in the coil winding. This causes current to flow. Applying the Left Hand Rule, the current flows away from the viewer in the right hand side of the coil. In the left hand side, the current flows toward the viewer. The induced current flows from the left hand commutator segment and brush, through the external circuit, and returns to the armature coil through the opposite brush and commutator segment. As the field coils are connected in parallel with the armature, only a portion of the current generated in the armature coil flows through the field windings. The current flows through the field coils in the proper direction to strengthen the magnetic field between the two pole shoes. This further increases the amount of current induced in the armature coil.

Maintaining Current Flow in One Direction

As the armature rotates, an alternating current is induced in the armature coil as the sides of the coil change position with respect to the magnetic field. However, *since the segments of the commutator rotate with the coil,* they change brushes at the same time the current flow reverses in the coil. This results in a direct current that always flows in one direction in the external circuit. If the brushes are properly located at the "neutral point", the changeover occurs without arcing at the brushes.

Providing a Continuous Current Flow

The armature coil shown in Fig. 7 is made up of a single loop of wire. The amount of current induced in this coil depends in part on the number of magnetic lines of force which the coil cuts through per unit of time. Assume for the moment that the magnetic lines of force are perfectly straight as they extend from the north to the south pole shoe. When the armature is in a vertical position, the motion of the loop as it rotates is nearly parallel to the magnetic lines of force. Since the coil cuts through no lines of force, no current is generated in the coil. As the coil rotates clockwise from its vertical position, the movement of the coil becomes less parallel and increasingly more perpendicular to the lines of force. Finally, at the horizontal position shown in Fig. 7, the movement of the coil is almost entirely perpendicular to the magnetic lines of force. More lines of force are being cut per unit of time and maximum current is being generated.

Thus, as the coil rotates from a vertical position, the current induced in the coil goes from zero to maximum (coil in horizontal position), and back to zero as the coil rotates through the horizontal to the opposite vertical position. For this reason (since the armature is composed of only a single loop) the output of the generator is of a pulsating nature.

To produce a continuous flow of current, generators used in automotive vehicles have a number of coils equally spaced around the armature. Each coil in turn is made up of numerous turns of wire. The larger number of coils results in an overlapping of current impulses, providing a steady, continuous flow of current.

In order to have as many coils of wire in the armature cutting the magnetic lines of force as possible to increase output and reduce pulsations, a definite pattern for winding a two pole generator armature is followed. An armature wound in this manner is referred to as being lap wound, Fig. 8.

Only two coils are shown for clearness. Two pole generators must have the sides of the coils located at opposite or nearly opposite sides of the armature. As illustrated, the coil starts at No. 1 commutator bar, passes through slot No. 12 in the core to the back of the armature, from where it returns through slot No. 4. Several turns of wire are wrapped around slots Nos. 12 and 4, the number

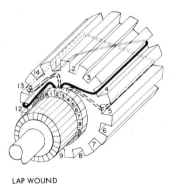

Fig. 8. Lap wound type of armature.

LAP WOUND

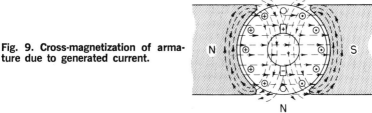

**Fig. 9. Cross-magnetization of arma-
ture due to generated current.**

depending upon the number of turns required in the armature coil. From slot No. 4, the coil wire is connected to commutator bar No. 2.

The next coil would start at commutator bar No. 2, pass through slots Nos. 13 and 5 in the core, and connect to commutator bar No. 3. The winding progresses around the armature in this manner until each slot in the core contains the sides of two coils and each commutator bar has the terminal ends of two coils soldered to it. When the armature is wound in this manner, the main brushes of the generator are located opposite each other, 180° apart.

Armature Reaction

As the armature rotates the side of each armature coil that passes by the pole shoe having north magnetic polarity has a voltage and current induced in one direction, while the opposite side of the same coil passing by the pole shoe having south magnetic polarity has a voltage and current induced in the opposite direction.

The effect of the current flowing through the armature coils is to magnetize the armature core in a cross direction (across the vertical diameter), giving one side of the core a north polarity and the other side a south polarity. In the generator, the cross-magnetizing lines of force pass through the armature core and pole shoes at right angles to the magnetic field produced by the field coils (Fig. 9).

Magnetic fields traveling in different directions cannot exist at the same place at the same time, and the reaction that takes place distorts the lines of force from the pole shoes.

Neutral Point Location of Brushes

If the magnetic lines of force produced by the field coils always traveled in a straight line between the pole shoes, the neutral point would be at right angles to the lines of force and the brushes would

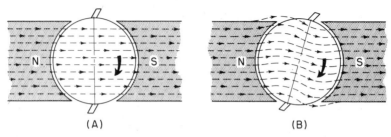

Fig. 10. Effect of armature reaction on brush position.

be located as shown in A, Fig. 10. However, when the generator is in operation, armature reaction causes the magnetic field between the pole shoes to shift in the direction of rotation. With the magnetic field shifted or twisted as shown in B, Fig. 10, it will be necessary to move the brushes forward, with respect to the rotation of the armature, to locate the brushes at the neutral point. With the brushes at the neutral point the armature coils are cutting the maximum number of lines of force and deliver the maximum voltage to the brushes. Since continued movement of the armature causes the armature coils to move past the brushes and in an opposite direction through the magnetic field, the neutral point is also the point at which current reversal take place in the armature coils. For several degrees at the neutral point, the armature coils are moving parallel to the lines of force, and no current is being generated in the armature coils. As a result, a minimum of arcing occurs at the brushes when the generator is operating with the brushes properly set at the neutral point. Since the brushes are permanently attached to either the generator frame or commutator end frame, the brush position is not considered adjustable.

Usually, the brushes are set slightly ahead of the neutral point. As a result of this, the armature will rotate in the direction the generator is normally driven when a battery is connected to the brushes of the generator.

DIRECT CURRENT GENERATOR

For a complete understanding of the two brush generator, a knowledge of how the generator is constructed is necessary.

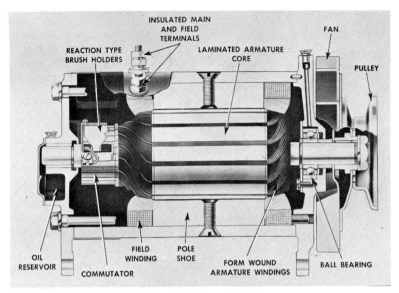

Fig. 11. Two pole, two brush generator. Delco-Remy Div., General Motors Corp.

Construction

The construction of a two pole, two brush generator is illustrated in Fig. 11.

Two pole, two brush generators have two brushes mounted in a fixed position on the commutator end plate and are spaced 180° apart. One of the brush holders is grounded directly to the frame, while the other brush holder is insulated from the frame. Two field coils are employed, both being wound in the same direction to produce magnetic poles of opposite polarity at the inner faces of the pole shoes. One terminal of the field coils is connected to the insulated brush. The other terminal is grounded either within the generator or externally through a regulator. With the field coils connected in this manner (in parallel with the armature) the total voltage generated in the armature is imposed upon the field coil circuit. Generators are classified according to whether the field coil circuit is internally or externally grounded, and according to the polarity of the generator.

Externally Grounded ("A" Circuit) Generator. In generators in which the field circuit is externally grounded, one terminal of the

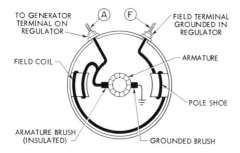

TO GENERATOR
TERMINAL ON
REGULATOR

FIELD TERMINAL
GROUNDED IN
REGULATOR

FIELD COIL

ARMATURE

POLE SHOE

ARMATURE BRUSH
(INSULATED)

GROUNDED BRUSH

Fig. 12. "A" circuit generator
with field circuit externally
grounded.

field coils is connected to the insulated brush and the other to the insulated F terminal in the generator frame (Fig. 12). The F terminal is connected to the generator regulator and grounds the field coil circuit through the regulator. The insulated brush is connected to the insulated A terminal in the generator frame.

Internally Grounded ("B" Circuit) Generator. On generators in which the field circuit is internally grounded, one of the field coil terminals is grounded within the generator, usually through the grounded main brush as shown in Fig. 13. The other field coil terminal is connected to the insulated (field) terminal, F, in the generator frame. The insulated main brush is connected to the insulated (armature) terminal, A, in the generator frame. When properly connected in the generating circuit, the F terminal connects the field coil circuit to the armature circuit (and insulated main brush) through the generator regulator.

It is important that you be able to distinguish between internally and externally grounded field generators, since the two types require two fundamentally different types of regulators and two different checking procedures.

Polarity. Generators are also classified according to their polar-

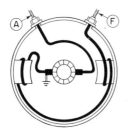

Fig. 13. "B" circuit generator with
field coils internally grounded.

ity. Generators may have either positive or negative polarity. The polarity of a generator must be the same as the polarity of the battery.

OPERATION OF A GENERATOR

When the armature in a generator begins to revolve, the armature coils cut the residual magnetic lines of force that exist between the pole shoes generating a voltage in the armature coils. Since the field coils are connected to the armature circuit the total voltage generated in the armature coils is imposed on the field coil circuit. The amount of current flowing through the field coil circuit is controlled by the resistance of the field circuit and the voltage applied.

The current flowing through the field coils causes an increase in the number of lines of force between the pole shoes. This in turn increases the amount of current generated in the armature coils. As the generator speed increases the continued increase in the amount of current flowing in the field coil circuit causes a greater and greater amount of current to be generated in the armature coils until, without some form of regulation, the generator would burn up and destroy itself.

Without such regulation, the output of the generator increases with speed. If resistance to the flow of the generated current is encountered, the voltage automatically increases until the resistance is overcome, or, at about sixty volts, the current starts to jump to ground at the commutator. At this time, the amperage through the field coils will be eight or ten times normal and the field coils will burn out. Alternately, if litte resistance to the flow of current is encountered the *amperage* will increase as the generator speed is increased. This high amperage can cause the generator armature to burn out.

All two brush generators have their charging rate externally controlled by means of a regulator. The regulator controls the amount of current flowing through the field coil circuit, thus limiting the output. Fig. 14 illustrates the charging characteristics of a regulated generator.

OTHER TYPES OF DIRECT CURRENT GENERATORS

Various designs of direct current generators have been used to

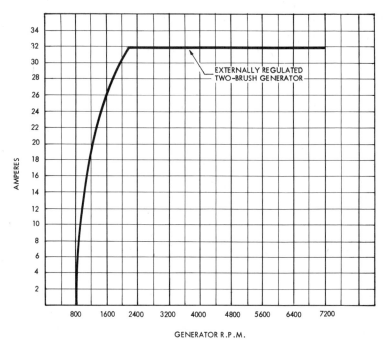

Fig. 14. Charging characteristics of a generator. The charging rate reaches its maximum at a speed of about 2000 rpm and remains constant even though the speed increases.

supply the current requirements of the automobile. Some of these are still being used in farm and road building equipment, stationary power engines, etc.

An early design that was widely used until replaced by the two brush generator was the three brush generator. On such generators the charging rate was self-regulated. The generator was designed to take advantage of armature reaction, which in conjunction with a third brush, permitted control of the current flowing through the field coils, thereby controlling the charging rate.

Other generators had extra field windings which changed the operating characteristics of the generator to give them a higher output.

Such generators were known as split-field and divided-field generators. Others, because of their heavier construction and higher output were known as heavy-duty generators.

DC GENERATOR CONTROL SYSTEM

This section is confined to the three unit vibrating type of regulator which has been in use almost exclusively from 1940 until the time that automobile manufacturers started changing over to the AC system beginning in 1960.

Operating principles and test procedures are the same regardless of the voltage of the particular charging system being serviced. When voltage and amperage readings are given they are general and apply to the 12-volt system. Always refer to the automobile manufacturer's test specifications for the particular make and model of regulator.

Many different makes of generator-regulator test equipment are on the market. While the general procedures for checking generator output and regulator limiting factors are correct, the manufacturer's directions for using any specific piece of test equipment always must be followed.

DC CHARGING CIRCUIT CONTROL

The output of a generator depends upon three factors: (1) the number of lines of magnetic force developed across the pole shoes by the field coils, (2) the number of turns of wire in the armature coils, and (3) the speed at which the lines of force are cut (rpm's of the generator armature). The number of turns of wire in the field coils are fixed by the design of the generator, and also the number of turns of wire in the armature coils. The speed at which the generator armature revolves is dependent upon the speed of the engine. However, the number of magnetic lines of force produced by the generator field coils can be changed by varying the amount of current flowing through the coils. This, then, is the method used to control the charging rate of a generator to meet the varying demands on the electrical system.

The electrical requirements of an automobile vary considerably depending upon the connected electrical load. To satisfactorily meet these varying electrical requirements, and to prevent the battery from becoming overcharged, a device known as a regulator is employed in the DC charging circuit, which automatically increases or decreases the generator output in accordance with the demands of the electrical system. Basically, the regulator controls generator output by varying the amount of current flowing through the generator field coils.

Two field coils are generally employed in a generator and are connected so that the field circuit is either internally or externally grounded, depending upon the design. As the armature begins to revolve the armature coils cut the residual lines of magnetic force between the field shoes. Since the field coils are connected into (parallel to) the armature circuit, the voltage induced into the armature is impressed upon the field coils. This increases the number of lines of magnetic force between the pole shoes and consequently a greater amount of voltage is generated in the armature coils. In addition, as the speed of the generator increases the lines of force are cut faster inducing still more voltage in the armature coils. The regulator prevents an excessive voltage and current build-up by inserting a resistance in the field coil circuit whenever the generator output reaches a predetermined value.

BASIC GENERATOR REGULATOR UNITS

The regulator is made up of three units, a cutout relay, a current regulator (limiter), and a voltage regulator (limiter). See Fig. 15. These units are interconnected, so that the operation of one unit is dependent upon the operation of the other two units.

Just as generators differ in their polarity and in the method of completing the field circuit, the generator regulators used with each type of generator are different and are not interchangeable with other types. Generator regulators are designed for use with (1) negative ground systems; (2) positive ground systems; (3) generators with externally grounded field circuits; and (4) generators with internally grounded field circuits. The actual construction of the regulator units may vary to some extent in regard to internal circuitry; e.g., the use of two contacts instead of one in the voltage regulator, or a different type of spring or adjustment. Some regulators are connected between the field and ground, while others are connected between the field and armature brush.

Regardless of the variations relative to polarity, construction, and circuit hook-ups all DC generator regulators operate on the same basic principles and contain the same units; namely, a cutout relay, a current regulator, and a voltage regulator. While the cutout relay has no regulating features other than opening and closing the charging circuit, it is always considered and serviced as a part of the generator regulator. Each of the units will be discussed separately;

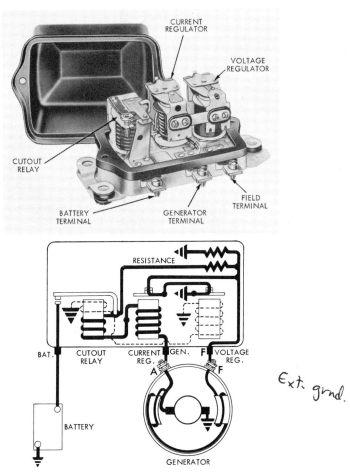

Fig. 15. A generator regulator in a charging circuit.

however, the relationship of each to the other units must constantly be kept in mind.

Cutout Relay

The cutout relay automatically connects the generator to the battery when the generator is charging, and automatically disconnects the battery from the generator when the generator is not charging. Battery voltage is higher than generator voltage when the generator is not charging. A device is therefore needed to open the circuit, otherwise the battery would discharge through the generator.

The cutout relay is brought into operation when the generator output reaches a predetermined voltage, generally between 11.8-13.5 volts when utilized with a 12-volt system (or at least 0.5 volts below the voltage limiter setting). At this point the cutout relay contacts close, completing the circuit between the generator and battery, so that electricity can flow from the generator to the battery. When the generator charging rate is reduced to the point where the flow of electricity is from the battery to the generator, generally between 0 and −6 amperes, the contacts open, disconnecting the circuit between the generator and the battery.

The cutout relay consists of a form of electromagnet, an armature (a metal strap hinged on one end with a contact point on the opposite end and held a predetermined distance away from the electromagnetic core by a spring), and a stationary contact point. See Fig. 16.

The electromagnet is composed of two coil windings on an iron core. One coil is a series winding (current coil) composed of a few turns of heavy wire. The other is a shunt winding (voltage coil) composed of many turns of fine wire. The two coils are wound so that electricity flows from the generator through both in the same direction. The voltage winding, connected in parallel with the charging circuit, has one end of the winding connected to the armature of the relay and the other grounded. The series winding (current coil) is connected in series with the generating circuit so that the generator output can flow to the battery when the contact points are closed. One end of the series winding is connected to the armature terminal of the generator and the other end terminates at the relay armature contact point (the movable contact on the generator cutout). The battery circuit is connected to the stationary contact point.

As the generator begins to charge electricity flows through the parallel winding to ground. The amount of electricity flowing through the voltage coil determines the number of lines of magnetic force being produced. As the charging rate increases the strength of the magnetic field increases to a point where the magnetic attraction is great enough to pull the armature down against spring tension, bringing the contact points together. The output of the gener-

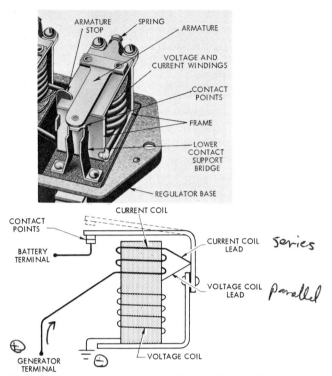

Fig. 16. Cutout relay. Delco-Remy Div.—General Motors Corp.

ator now will also flow through the current coil and contact points to the battery. Because the parallel (voltage) coil is made up of fine windings, its resistance is high; therefore the flow of electricity will be primarily through the heavier (low resistance) series winding. As current flows through both coils in the same direction, the pull on the armature is increased by the magnetism created by the current coil. Basically, the parallel winding acts as a pull down coil and the series winding as a holding coil.

When the generator speed decreases to the point where the generator output drops below the battery voltage, the current flows from the battery to the generator, reversing the flow of current in the current winding. The magnetism created by the current winding is now opposed to that created by the voltage winding, reducing the magnetic pull on the armature. The magnetic force acting on the armature becomes smaller than the force exerted on the armature by its return spring. This permits the spring to pull the contacts apart, disconnecting the generator from the battery.

Generator Regulation

We have just seen that for electricity to flow from the generator through the cutout relay to the battery, the voltage output from the generator must exceed that of the battery. A 12-volt battery in a charging circuit with a normal voltage drop of 0.5 volts would require a generator output of over 12.5 volts in order to force an appreciable amount of electricity into the battery. If the generator voltage was 14.5 volts, the generator voltage would be 2.0 volts greater than the combined battery-and-line drop voltage. This differential in voltage would cause electricity to flow from the generator to the battery.

With a constant circuit resistance, the greater the difference in voltage between the generator and battery, the more electricity the generator can force into the battery. The smaller the voltage difference, the smaller will be the amount of electricity that can be forced into the battery.

The battery, which has a voltage of its own, represents a means of moving electrons when the battery circuit is completed. The electrons move out through the negative terminal, returning by way of the positive terminal. This flow of electrons represents an opposing voltage to the movement of electrons from the generator. In the generator-battery circuit, the battery voltage is referred to as a counter electromotive force (counter EMF). The effective voltage in the generator-battery circuit therefore is the difference between battery voltage and generator voltage.

Since the voltage in any circuit cannot exceed the amount of voltage required to overcome the resistance to electron movement in the circuit the generator output will not exceed that required to overcome the resistance of the circuit.

Before electricity can flow into a battery the generator output voltage must be higher than that of the battery. As the battery becomes fully charged the counter EMF increases and the generator voltage output increases. By using a limiting device (regulator) to limit the generator output voltage to that of a fully charged battery plus the amount of voltage drop in the charging circuit, the generator output can be automatically stopped when the battery becomes fully charged. If more electricity is forced into a fully charged battery, the additional energy will be dissipated in the form of heat, causing the water in the battery to decompose into gases.

When a battery is fully charged and the regulator is limiting the generator voltage output, if an additional electrical load is turned on, an additional (parallel) path for electricity to flow is created. Since voltage cannot exceed that required to overcome resistance the voltage in the circuit drops (adding another circuit reduces total resistance). The regulator no longer limits the generator and its output increases to supply the additional electrical requirement.

Either voltage or current (amperage) can be limited by reducing the electricity flowing to the generator field coils. The present method of doing this is to use vibrating contact points to insert resistance into the field coil circuit. By using two vibrators it is possible to limit both the voltage and the amperage output. Basically, when the regulator contact points are closed generator field coil electricity goes through the contacts to complete the circuit to ground with minimum resistance. This results in the generator magnetic field strength being at maximum; if generator speed is great enough, either high voltage or current will then flow from the generator. When the contact points are open the field electricity must instead go through a resistor, which is in series with the field coils. The resistor reduces the electricity in the field coils, reducing the

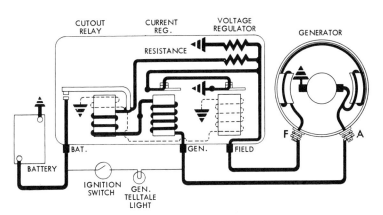

Fig. 17. Regulator for externally grounded generator, type A. Chevrolet Div.— General Motors Corp.

magnetic field strength in the generator. This will limit either the generator voltage or current.

In the case of the regulator used with the externally grounded (Type A) generator, Fig. 17, the regulator resistance is inserted between the field coils and ground when the regulator points are open. The regulator used with the internally grounded (Type B) generator, Fig. 18, has the resistance inserted between the insulated side of the circuit and the generator field coils when the regulator contact points are open. The type of generator can be determined by inspecting the connections at the brushes and the field coils. If the field coil lead is connected to the insulated commutator brush then the generator is of the externally grounded type. If the field coil lead is connected to the grounded commutator brush or to the frame of the generator the generator is of the internally grounded type.

Current Regulator

The purpose of the current regulator (limiter) unit is to protect the generator from overheating and burning out. A conductor of a given size can only carry so much current without overheating. Ex-

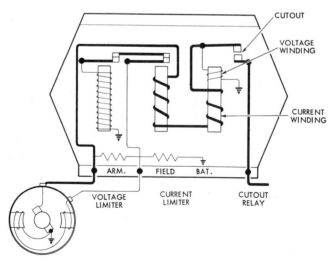

Fig. 18. Regulator for internally grounded generator, type B'.
Ford Div.—Ford Motor Co.

cessively high amperage (current) flow through the armature windings and commutator bars can cause both to overheat and can melt the solder holding the armature windings to the commutator bars. By limiting the generator circuit output excessive heating can be prevented.

The current regulator unit is a form of electromagnet. A few turns of heavy wire are wound on an iron core. This winding is in series with the armature circuit between the generator and battery. One end of the coil is connected to the armature terminal of the generator while the other end is connected to the battery through the cutout relay, Fig. 17. All electricity produced by the generator must flow through the current winding. Located above the iron core is an armature (a metal strap hinged on one end and having a contact point on the other end). A spring holds the armature point in contact with a stationary point. With the contact points closed in the cutout relay, voltage regulator, and current regulator units, the generator field circuit is connected to ground. In the case of the regulator used with the *externally* grounded generator, Fig. 3, the electricity is picked up at the main armature brush and flows through the field coils, both contact points and then to ground. With no resistance in the field coil circuit other than normal line drop, generator output is imposed upon the field coils and as generator speed increases, generator output increases.

In the case of the regulator used with the internally grounded generator, the electricity flows through the closed contact points of the current regulator and the voltage regulator, through the field coils and then to ground inside the generator.

As the current limiter coil is in series with the main (armature) charging circuit, all of the charging current goes through the coil. Because of this, the coil is said to be current sensitive. In any coil of wire the magnetic field produced by the coil will depend upon the current flowing in the circuit; therefore, the higher the generator output, the more current that will be flowing through the current limiter coil and the stronger will be the magnetic field surrounding the coil. In other words, the strength of the magnetic field is directly proportional to the generator output. The armature points are held closed by spring tension. When the magnetic strength created in the current limiter coil becomes great enough to overcome armature spring tension, the contact points open and a resistance is inserted in series with the field of the generator. The resistance between the field coils and ground reduces the electrical flow through the field coils, which in turn reduces the number of magnetic lines of force which can be cut by the armature coils, thereby reducing the generator output.

When the generator output is lowered the amount of electricity flowing through the current sensitive winding (current limiter coil) is reduced. With less electricity flowing the magnetic pull of the coil is no longer great enough to hold the contact points open against spring tension. When the contact points close the generator output rises again. As the magnetic field again builds up in the current limiter coil the points again are opened. The points open and close (vibrate) at speeds from 30 to 50 times per second. The points vibrate at the rate of speed necessary to prevent the generator current output from exceeding the value for which the spring tension is adjusted. Changing the spring tension, which holds the contact points closed, will therefore change current output.

Voltage Regulator

Generator voltage, if uncontrolled, could become extremely high, causing the battery to be overcharged, and accessories to burn out. On the other hand, the generator output voltage must be great enough to handle the electrical load and keep the battery charged. Generator voltage must exceed battery voltage or the battery cannot be charged. It is the difference between generator and battery voltage that causes current to flow.

If the state of charge of the battery is low the terminal voltage is low. When the generator is operating its voltage will rise above battery voltage and cause electricity to flow into the battery. If the speed of the generator is relatively high its voltage will be high, and the effective voltage, the difference between battery and generator voltage, will be high. This condition will cause a high initial charging rate and current output will be at or near the allowable maximum. As the battery state of charge rises the battery terminal voltage will also rise. If the generator output voltage is limited at a certain maximum as battery voltage becomes higher, due to being subjected to a charge, the effective voltage becomes less, and the charging rate therefore drops off. With proper voltage control, battery voltage will almost equal generator voltage, with only a small amount of current flowing to maintain maximum battery charge.

Limiting the generator voltage at too low a rate would prevent the battery from ever becoming fully charged. If the voltage limit is set too high, the battery will be over-charged before terminal voltage causes the charging rate to be reduced. Accurate limit setting is therefore essential if the proper charging rate is to be maintained. This is determined by the voltage regulator armature spring tension.

The voltage regulator, like the current regulator, is a form of electromagnet. Many turns of fine wire are wound on an iron core. This winding is connected between the armature circuit and ground. Due to the way the coil is connected into the circuit it is known as a shunt or parallel winding; it is parallel to the armature circuit. Located above the core is an armature (a metal strap hinged on one end and having a contact point on the other end). A spring holds the armature contact point tightly against a stationary point. When the contact points of the voltage regulator, current regulator, and cutout relay are all closed, maximum generator output will occur if generator rpm's are high enough as no limit is placed on the electrical flow into the generator field coils.

The voltage regulator (limiter) coil is a voltage sensitive coil because of the manner in which it is connected into the charging circuit. The magnetic field produced by the coil winding is directly proportional to the voltage produced by the generator. When the generator output voltage is low only a small amount of electricity will flow through the voltage limiter coil to ground, and the magnetic field will be comparatively weak. As the generator voltage rises, more and more electricity will flow through the limiter coil and the magnetic field will become strong enough to overcome contact point armature spring tension and open the contacts. Opening the contact points inserts a high resistance in series with the field coil circuit. This resistance causes the field current to be reduced, which in turn reduces the number of lines of magnetic force that can be cut by the armature. As the generator output is reduced, the voltage through the limiter is reduced, and spring tension closes the contact points. When the contact points close, the voltage rises and the magnetic field builds up to where the points are opened again. The points will open and close (vibrate) at the speed necessary to hold the voltage at the value for which the spring tension is set. In operation, the voltage limiter contact points will <u>vibrate</u> at speeds of 50 to 250 times per second, depending upon the state of charge of the battery.

The voltage and current limiters are never in operation at the same instant. The conditions which cause a current limiter to operate are opposite those which cause the voltage limiter to operate. As an example, when battery voltage is low, (immediately after operating the cranking motor for a few seconds) the current flow from the generator will be high and needs to be limited to prevent the generator from burning out. When the battery is near full charge, the voltage from the generator will be high, to overcome the counter EMF from the battery, but because the voltage differential is small, the current flow will be low. It is possible, under certain circumstances, that for a moment both units will operate until the voltage limiter comes into continuous operation.

Resistors

Two resistor units are normally used in the regulator circuit regardless of the type of generator employed on the vehicle. One function of the resistors is to prevent arcing at the contact points. When the contact points are closed, electricity builds up in the field windings of the generator, producing a strong magnetic field. When either one of the regulator contact points open, resistance is inserted into the field circuit suddenly, reducing current flow, and causing the magnetic field in the generator to collapse. As the magnetic field collapses across many turns of wire in the field coils, a high voltage is induced. Two resistors are needed to absorb this surge of induced voltage, which would otherwise badly arc and destroy the contact points.

One resistor installation, shown in Fig. 17, where the regulator is located between the field and ground, has a higher resistance value than the other. One terminal of each resistor is connected to the field circuit. The opposite terminal of one resistor is grounded directly to the regulator base, while the other is grounded to the base through the closed voltage limiter contact points.

When the voltage regulator is in operation only the resistor with the higher value is connected in series with the field coil circuit and in the instantaneous circuits which develop. When the current regulator operates to prevent the generator from exceeding its maximum output, the two resistors are connected in parallel with each other and in series with the field circuit. The total resistance offered by two resistance units in parallel is less than the resistance offered by the smaller resistor. The reason for variation in resistance is that when regulating voltage output, a higher value of resistance is required to control the voltage surge induced in the field circuit than is needed in order to control the excess flow of current.

One of the resistors, in the slightly different circuit shown in Fig. 15 whereby the regulator is located between the field coils and armature circuit, is connected between the field circuit and the armature circuit, while the other is connected between the field circuit and ground. The combined resistors are able to absorb the induced field current. While the resistors are always connected into the circuit they are not effective when the contact points are closed. Electricity always follows the path of least resistance, therefore, as long as the contact points are closed the electricity takes the easier path and completes its circuit to ground through the field coils without flowing through the resistance units. When either one of the contact points are opened the electricity must flow through the resistor in order to complete its circuit.

The regulator illustrated in Fig. 19 has three resistors. Two resistors (located below the single resistor unit) are in series with the field coils when either the current regulator contacts or voltage regulator contacts open. The single resistor located above the two resistors is so connected into the circuit as to absorb the surge of current which may be induced in the voltage windings of the cutout relay or voltage regulator.

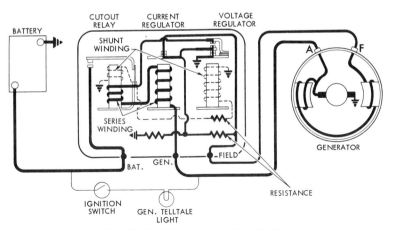

Fig. 19. Double contact voltage limiter.

Double Contact Point Voltage Regulator

Some vehicles with high electrical demands such as police vehicles, light delivery trucks used extensively in urban areas, or vehicles equipped with air conditioning may use a *high output* generator with a type of regulator that has double contact points on the voltage limiter armature, Fig. 19. The single type regulator points cannot adequately handle the greater field current needed for these higher output generators. The tendency of the generator is to produce an even greater voltage than can be controlled by a single point set. It also produces, at high speeds and light loads, an increasingly higher charging voltage. This is known as voltage creep.

The double contact type voltage limiter has the capacity to further reduce generator field current and thus can limit the charging voltage to its specified value.

The cutout relay and current limiter is the same type as that used in the standard regulator. (The voltage limiter has a contact point located on the armature strap which is in contact with the stationary point when the voltage regulator is not limiting, the same as in the standard regulator). Attached to and part of the armature is a second metal strap with a contact point located above the stationary point. The stationary contact has a corresponding point on top, as well as on the bottom, so that when the armature is pulled down beyond where the circuit is just broken, the upper contact point will touch the point located on top of the stationary contact. In normal position, the armature spring holds the armature lower point in contact with the lower point on the stationary contact unit. This set of contacts is in series with and grounds the generator field circuit. Fig. 20. In ordinary operation the lower set of contacts limits, by inserting a resistance into the field circuit, in exactly the same man-

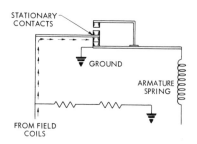

STATIONARY CONTACTS

GROUND

ARMATURE SPRING

FROM FIELD COILS

Fig. 20. Lower contact points in operation.

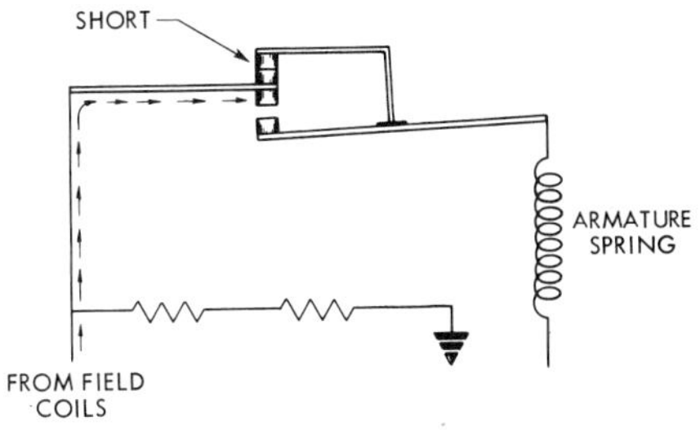

Fig. 21. Upper contact points in operation.

ner as the standard regulator, i.e., the lower set of contacts vibrates.

When the generator field requirements are low, such as under high speed operation and low electrical draw, the magnetic attraction in the voltage limiter coil, because of the high output of the heavy duty generator, is great enough to pull the upper set of contact points into operation. Fig. 21. This set of contacts will vibrate according to regulator setting and generator output. The upper strap of the voltage regulator armature strap is connected to the generator armature circuit. When the upper contacts of the voltage regulator close, the field coils are shorted out (no voltage difference across the field coils and therefore no current flow through the coils). The vibration of the upper contact points alternately shorts out the generator field coils and inserts a resistor in series with them. Shorting out the field coils reduces generator output more than merely inserting a resistance.

Temperature Compensation

Generator regulators operate under varying temperature conditions. All copper wire windings (coils) increase in resistance when they become hot. Owing to the effect of heat on the operating characteristics of the regulator windings, the regulator must be compensated for changes which occur in the coil resistance. Due to these changes in resistance, the regulator coil windings produce a weaker magnetic field when hot than when cold. This would mean that in order to obtain the same magnetic attraction to pull the armature contact points open, when the ambient temperature is high, there would have to be a greater flow of electricity. Rather than compensating, by increasing the electrical flow, a bimetal hinge is used.

With the voltage limiter, compensation beyond that required for changes in ambient temperature permits the limiter to operate at a higher voltage than when hot. This is a desirable feature, since a higher voltage is required to charge a battery when temperatures are low. Temperature compensation of the current limiter also permits the generator to deliver a higher output when the ambient temperature is low, and causes the output to taper off to some extent, when the regulator unit reaches normal operating temperature. Normal ambient temperature is considered to be 125°F.

Both the voltage and current limiters use a bimetal hinge to attach the armature to the support frame. With a bimetal hinge arrangement, the hinge adds its tension to that exerted by the armature spring, thereby requiring a higher than normal electrical output to be generated to produce a magnetic field strong enough to open the contact points. When the regulator unit has reached operating temperature, the bimetal hinge loses some of its tension, resulting in a return to normal output. Because the regulator is compensated for temperature variations the voltage and current limiters must be adjusted after they have reached normal operating temperature. If adjusted while cold the contact points will open at a correspondingly lower voltage when the regulator reaches its operating temperature.

Normal ambient temperature is considered to be 125°F and published specifications are given for this temperature reading, however, it is not always possible to obtain a normal temperature reading. Some manufacturers give the voltage range for the different temperatures readings. Table 1 is a typical ambient temperature voltage chart. Ambient temperature is the temperature of the air surround-

**TABLE 1. VOLTAGE REGULATOR SETTING
AND AMBIENT AIR TEMPERATURE**

REGULATOR AMBIENT TEMPERATURE DEGREES FAHRENHEIT	12 VOLT REGULATOR NORMAL VOLTAGE RANGE
165	13.2 – 14.2
155	13.35 – 14.35
145	13.5 – 14.5
135	13.65 – 14.65
125	13.8 – 14.8
115	13.95 – 14.95
105	14.1 – 15.1
95	14.25 – 15.25
85	14.3 – 15.3
75	14.45 – 15.45
65	14.6 – 15.6
55	14.75 – 15.75
45	14.9 – 15.9
35	15.05 – 16.05
25	15.2 – 16.2

ing the regulator and is generally measured by a special thermometer that is clipped onto the regulator cover with approximately ¼ inch clearance between the thermometer and regulator cover.

Regulator Polarity

Regulators are not interchangeable for use on either negative or positive ground systems. In addition, the charging system maximum output will vary between makes and models of vehicles. Different regulators are used with the different generator ground systems. It is essential that the regulator be specifically designed for the particular electrical system it is to be used with.

When the regulator contact points are vibrating (operating), there will be a slight arcing, regardless of the use of absorbing resistors. The arcing, although slight, will create enough heat so that there will be a small spot of molten metal between the contact points each time they separate. The usual tendency is for the molten metal to stick to the positive contact point so that a build-up of metal will occur on the positive contact point and a crater will result in the negative contact point. To help overcome this condition to some extent, the negative contact point is made of a different material than the positive point. When electricity flows through the contact points, in the proper direction, the transfer of metal between contacts is thereby kept to a minimum. If a regulator for one polarity is installed in a charging circuit designed for the opposite polarity, the electricity will pass through the contact points in the wrong direction and shorten the life of the contact points considerably. This points up the importance of polarizing the generator before starting the engine, if there is any chance that the generator polarity may have been reversed during the process of servicing. Polarizing the generator is the passing of electricity through the generator field coils. In the case of the generator with an externally grounded field, ground the field terminal. Momentarily connect a jumper wire between the battery and generator armature terminal. This permits a momentary surge of current to flow through the generator which correctly polarizes it. With an internally grounded field generator, disconnect the wire attached to the generator field terminal, and momentarily connect a jumper wire between the generator field terminal and the battery.

TRADE COMPETENCY TESTS

1. What is the purpose of the generator?
2. What is the function of the field coils?
3. What is residual magnetism?
4. What controls the amount of current that flows through the field coils?
5. What is the purpose of the armature coils?
6. What is the purpose of the generator brushes? Of what materials are they made?
7. Can you explain how a current can be induced in a conductor?
8. What factors control the amount of current induced in a conductor?
9. How is the alternating current induced in a loop type armature converted into direct current?
10. How is the output of all generators controlled?
11. What is armature reaction?
12. Why do the generator main brushes have to be at the neutral point?
13. What variations are to be found in the field coil circuits of two-brush generators?
14. Can you describe how a two-brush generator operates? How is the output controlled?
15. What is the purpose of polarizing a generator? How is this done?
16. What is the purpose of the generator cutout relay?
17. What is the function of the generator regulator?
18. What is required before the generator can force current into a battery?
19. What is the function of the resistors in a generator regulator?
20. Can you trace the flow of current from the generator to the battery?
21. Why are two or more resistors used in most regulators?
22. Why must regulators be compensated for temperature? What effect does compensation have on the output?
23. If the external load becomes greater than the current output of the generator, where is the excess current obtained?
24. What effect would a high setting of the current limiter have on the generator?
25. Is the lowering of cutout closing voltage accomplished by increasing or decreasing armature spring tension?
26. Can you explain how the voltage regulator operates to limit generator output?
27. How does the current limiter function to regulate the current output?

CHAPTER *7*

DC CHARGING
SYSTEMS SERVICE

The generating system consists of three principal units, the storage battery, a generator, and a generator regulator, functioning together to supply the electrical needs of the vehicle. In the generating and battery system, most problems start with an indication of trouble with the battery. Either the battery has failed, is low in charge, or the charging rate is too high.

GENERATOR CIRCUIT TROUBLE SHOOTING

The trouble shooting procedure usually starts with tests to determine whether or not the battery is capable of accepting a charge. If the tests indicate that the battery is still good, then the other units in the charging system are tested one by one until the trouble is located. Most of the tests are made without removing the individual units from the vehicle. The most commonly encountered problems with direct current generators, along with possible causes and corrective procedures, are outlined in the trouble shooting chart which follows (Table 1).

If the battery remains satisfactorily charged, if it does not use an excessive amount of water, and if there is no evidence of damage to the generator, lights, or other voltage sensitive equipment, there should be no need for checking or adjusting the regulator. When there is an indication of trouble in the charging system, it must be remembered that the entire system is inter-related, so that each unit which makes up the system must be checked. Malfunctioning of one part may affect the operation of other units. A faulty battery may affect regulator operation. A generator incapable of meeting output requirements will affect the battery charge and so will an improperly adjusted regulator. Abnormal resistance anywhere in the charging system may also affect regulator operation.

TABLE 1. GENERATOR TROUBLE SHOOTING.

Trouble	Cause	Remedy
(1) Generator has no output	(a) Defective generator	(a) Test and repair or replace generator
	(b) Defective regulator	(b) Test regulator and adjust or replace
	(c) Grounded or open lead from armature terminal of generator to regulator	(c) Repair or replace
	(d) Grounded or open field lead	(d) Repair or replace
	(e) Broken or loose drive belt	(e) Replace or tighten belt
(2) Generator has low output	(a) Slipping drive belt	(a) Adjust belt
	(b) Low current or voltage limiter setting	(b) Test and adjust generator regulator
	(c) High resistance in charging circuit	(c) Test circuit resistance and repair
	(d) Defective generator	(d) Test generator output and repair or replace
(3) Generator has excessively high output	(a) Defective regulator	(a) Test generator regulator and adjust or replace
	(b) Low resistance	(b) Short in battery; replace battery
(4) Generator noisy	(a) Defective bearing	(a) Replace bearing
	(b) High mica	(b) Undercut mica
	(c) Commutator out-of-round	(c) True up commutator
	(d) Defective worn brushes	(d) Replace brushes
(5) Generator output normal but battery low in charge	(a) Low current or voltage limiter setting	(a) Adjust or replace regulator
	(b) Excessive resistance	(b) Check voltage drop in charging circuit
	(c) Driving habits: short trips, excessive electrical load Slow speed driving	(c) Charge battery

Battery

While this section is concerned with servicing of the regulator, the other charging system units must still be given consideration. Generator-regulator circuit trouble is usually indicated by a battery which is low in charge due to a low generator output or complete absence of charge. A battery which needs charging is indicated by a slow cranking speed. Test the battery with a hydrometer to see if it is discharged. A complete test of the battery should be made if there is any question about its condition, as it could be that it will not properly take or hold a charge.

Battery Connections

Battery terminals, because of the heavy current flow which takes place when the cranking motor is operated, must be kept clean and tight or excessive resistance may occur. If there is any question relative to the condition of the battery terminals and cables make a test for high resistance. To make a resistance check (voltage drop test) an expanded scale voltmeter is used. Connect one lead (prod) to the battery post and the other lead (prod) to the battery terminal (cable connection). Operate the cranking motor. If the voltmeter reads more than 0.2 volts, the terminal should be removed, cleaned, the battery post cleaned, the terminal reinstalled and tightened. Check the other battery post and terminal in like manner. The other ends of battery cables should also be checked by placing one prod on the the terminal bolt and the other prod on the terminal while operating the cranking motor. The same voltage drop limit applies to this end of the cable, as to the battery terminal.

After the battery and battery connections have been eliminated as a possible source of trouble the next logical unit to check is the generator since it supplies the electricity for charging the battery. When it is necessary to check the generator output or regulation always follow manufacturer's specifications for the particular make and model of charging system units.

INSPECT GENERATOR

To obtain maximum service from a generator with a minimum of trouble, it should be inspected at regular intervals to determine its condition. The frequency with which generator inspections should be made is determined by the conditions under which the generator operates. Dust, dirt, water, high-speed operation, and high temperatures are all factors which cause the bearings, the commutator, and the brushes to wear.

Essential steps in a periodic inspection procedure are lubrication (where required) and inspection of the generator mounting and fan belt. In addition, examine the wiring, since defective wiring or loose or corroded connections will prevent normal generator or regulator operation.

Generators with hinge cap oil cups should be given three to five drops of medium engine oil at regular lubrication periods. Some generators have sealed ball bearings that do not require lubrication. Do not over lubricate, as excessive lubricant may find its way onto the commutator where it reduces the generator output and increases commutator and brush wear.

If there are indications of oil or grease on the commutator it usually can be dissolved by squirting carbon tetrachloride on the commutator while the generator is running. Examine the commutator through the slot in the housing and if the commutator is badly grooved, worn or dirty, the generator should be disassembled and the commutator turned and the mica undercut.

Check the generator mounting for looseness and tighten it if necessary. Check the belt to make sure that it is in good condition and has the correct tension. Slackness in the belt tension permits the belt to slip, resulting in rapid belt wear and a low or erratic generator output. Too much tension on the belt causes rapid belt and bearing wear. Instructions for the proper adjustment of the generator drive belt is in the section, "Install Generator."

GENERATOR OUTPUT TEST

Before removing a generator, it is advisable to check the generator output to make sure the trouble is in the generator rather than in the battery, regulator, or wiring system. To check a direct current generator for electrical output, connect a 0-50 amp ammeter in series between the battery and generator output terminal or, more conveniently, between the battery (BAT) terminal on the generator regulator and the battery as shown in Fig. 1. Connect an electric

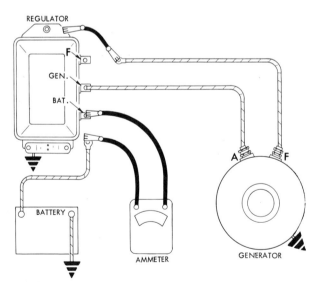

Fig. 1. Testing generator output in an "A" circuit system.

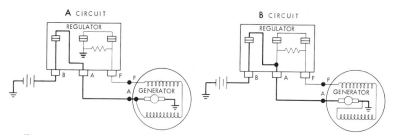

Fig. 2. A and B circuits. A is externally grounded. B is internally grounded.

tachometer (if available) between the distributor terminal on the ignition coil and ground.

Determine if the generator is of the "A" type circuit (field externally grounded) or the "B" type (field internally grounded). Fig. 2.

If a field winding is connected to an insulated brush, it is type "A". If there is no connection to the field coils at the insulated brush, it is type "B". (Note: All Ford Motor Co. cars use the type "B" circuit. Other domestic cars use type "A" circuit.) Disconnect the field "F" wire at the regulator and if it is the "A" type, ground it to the regulator base. If the circuit is the "B" type, connect the disconnected field wire to the regulator armature terminal. By always disconnecting the field wire, possible damage to the regulator will be avoided, especially if it is the double-contact type.

Start the engine and run at the specified speed for the generator being tested (usually 1200 or 1500 rpm). If a tachometer is not available to determine engine speed, open the throttle about one-fourth of the way. Read the generator output on the ammeter, which should reach or exceed the specified current output, for which the generator is rated. (30 ampere generator, 35 ampere generator, etc.).

If the generator output does not meet specifications, it must be removed, disassembled, tested and repaired. This procedure is covered later. If the generator output meets specifications, the charging system trouble is in the regulator or wiring system.

CHARGING CIRCUIT RESISTANCE TESTS

An excessive voltage drop in the charging circuit (caused by poor connections or other high resistance) tends to keep the generator charging rate low and the battery in a discharged condition.

Connect a 0-50 amp ammeter in the charging circuit between the battery and the battery terminal on the regulator Fig. 2. On the "A" circuit generator disconnect the field lead at the regulator field terminal, and with a jumper wire, ground the field lead to the regulator base. On the "B" circuit generator, connect a jumper wire between the "field" and "armature" terminals. Operate the engine at a speed that will give about a 20 ampere normal charging rate.

To check for abnormal generator circuit resistance, measure the voltage drop in each lead of the circuit as indicated in Fig. 3. The V-1 reading measures the voltage drop (resistance) in the lead from the battery to the battery (BAT) terminal of the regulator. The V-3 reading measures the voltage drop in the lead from the armature terminal of the generator to the generator (GEN) terminal of the regulator. Neither reading should exceed 0.3 volts. The V-2 reading measures the resistance of the battery ground strap. The voltage drop should not exceed 0.1 volts.

If at any point, the voltage drop indicated exceeds the limits, it indicates high resistance in that part of the circuit. To correct, clean and tighten all connections. If this fails to correct the exces-

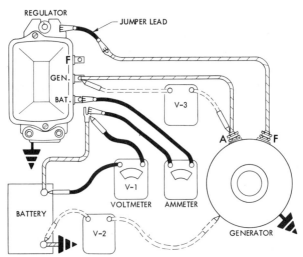

Fig. 3. Testing voltage drop in an "A" circuit generator system.

sive resistance, replace the faulty wire. Remove the jumper wire and re-connect the field lead to the regulator field terminal.

In many cases the above corrective procedures will eliminate the excessive resistance in the generator circuit; the generator output should now be normal. If, however, the output to the battery still does not meet requirements, check and adjust the voltage setting of the regulator according to the directions.

DISASSEMBLY AND REPAIR OF GENERATOR

If the preceding tests indicate that the generator is at fault it should be removed from the vehicle for disassembly and repair. Although direct current generators are quite similar in construction, there are some variations in their design. Due to their design characteristics the disassembly procedures given in this section must necessarily be general. However, an examination of the generator to be disassembled will indicate which parts must be removed for complete disassembly.

To disassemble the generator remove the through-bolts that hold the generator together. Remove the commutator end frame from the generator. Remove the brush lead screws from the brushes (when employed), and remove the brushes. Fig. 4.

Cleaning

With the generator completely disassembled wash all parts in a petroleum safety solvent. Gasoline should not be used because of hazards involved. Do not clean the armature and fields in a degreasing tank as the compounds used in these tanks may cause damage to the mica or enamel insulation. Ball bearings should be thoroughly cleaned, blown off with compressed air and oiled. Do not spin the bearing with compressed air while drying, since this may damage the bearing. Sealed ball bearings should not be cleaned as cleaning will destroy the lubricant.

After disassembling and cleaning, the various parts of the generator can be more thoroughly inspected and tested to pin point the trouble within the generator and to determine which parts are in a serviceable condition, which parts can be made serviceable with minor repairs, and which parts require replacement.

Field Coil Tests

Check the field coils and if the tape is burned or brittle, the

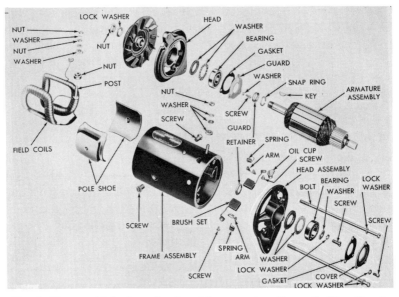

Fig. 4. Disassembled view of automobile generator. Plymouth Div.—Chrysler Corp.

field coils should be replaced. Field coils with worn spots in the taping can be retaped provided they are otherwise satisfactory.

Open Circuit. Place one test prod on the field terminal in the generator frame and the other on the opposite terminal of the field coils (Fig. 5).

If the test lamp does not light, the field coils have an open circuit. Check the soldered connection between the field coils and at the field terminal and resolder if necessary. Check the ground connection (if field is grounded) or the terminal at the insulated brush. If necessary, remove the connection, clean, and replace. If an open circuit still exists, replace the field coil assembly. Defective field coils are replaced with the aid of a pole shoe screwdriver and spreader as illustrated in Fig. 6.

NOTE: *Before making the following test, disconnect the grounded field connection on generators having one end of the field circuit grounded in the generator housing.*

Grounded Circuit. Place one of the test prods on the field coil terminal in the generator frame and the other on the frame (Fig. 7).

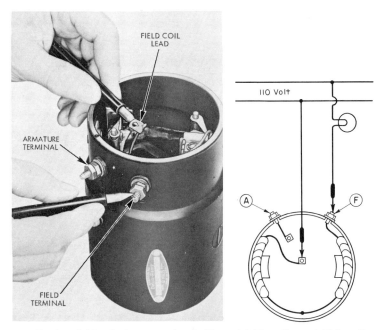

Fig. 5. Testing field coils for open circuit. Chevrolet Div.—General Motors Corp.

Fig. 6. Replacing pole shoes with a pole shoe screwdriver.

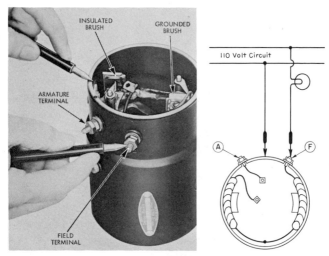

Fig. 7. A, Testing field coil circuit for ground. B, diagram of the circuit and test. Chevrolet Motor Div.—General Motors Corp.

If the test lamp lights, the field circuit is grounded. The point of ground is sometimes indicated by smoke. Check the wire connecting the field coils to make sure that it is not grounded to the frame. If the field coil circuit is grounded, disconnect the field coil wire from the field terminal in the housing and test the field terminal for ground by placing one test prod on the field terminal and the other test prod on the frame. If the test lamp lights the field terminal is grounded. Replace the insulating washers and bushing if the field terminal is grounded. Replace the field coils if the ground cannot be readily repaired.

Short Circuit. To determine if the windings of the field coils are short-circuited, connect a battery and ammeter in series with the field coils to determine the amount of current they draw. Fig. 8.

NOTE: *Some manufacturers recommend checking field current draw at five volts on six-volt systems and ten volts on twelve-volt systems, while others recommend checking at six and twelve volts respectively. When checking at five or ten volts a variable resistance should be connected in series with the ammeter and battery. A voltmeter should be connected to the coil leads and the voltage reduced by means of the resistance to the specified value. For proper battery*

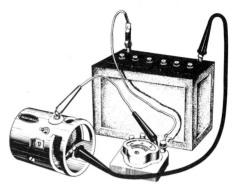

Fig. 8. Testing the field coil for short circuit.

voltage and ammeter readings check the manufacturer's specifications.

Connect the test leads to the field coil terminals and note the reading on the ammeter (Fig. 9). Depending upon the generator, the field current draw may vary from 1.4 to 4.5 amperes or more. If the current draw is more than is specified by the manufacturer for that particular generator, there is a short in the field coils. To determine if one or more coils are shorted, connect the test leads to the terminal wires leading from each coil, and note the current draw on the ammeter. In generators with two field coils, the current draw for each coil should be twice the total amount specified by the manu-

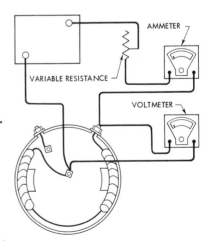

Fig. 9. Testing the field current draw.

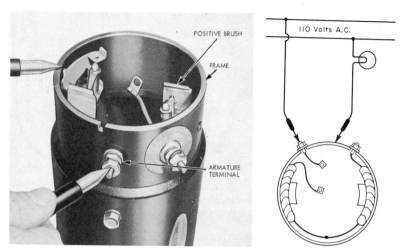

Fig. 10. Testing terminal for ground. Chevrolet Motor Div., General Motors Corp.

facturer. In generators with four field coils, each coil should draw approximately four times the total specified amount. Replace the field coils if they are shorted.

If the current draw is less than that specified, there is a high

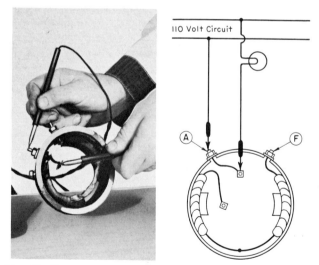

Fig. 11. Testing generator brush lead for continuous circuit. Chevrolet Motor Div.—General Motors Corp.

resistance in the field circuit. To remove the high resistance, re-solder all soldered terminals. Clean the terminals and their attachment points and reconnect the terminals. Recheck the current draw.

Armature Terminal for Ground. Place one test lamp prod on the armature terminal and the other on the frame as shown in Fig. 10. If the test lamp lights, the terminal is grounded. Replace the terminal insulating washers and bushing to remove the ground.

Brush Lead to Armature Terminal. Place one test lamp prod on the armature terminal and the other on the end of the brush lead as shown in Fig. 11. If the test lamp does not light, the brush lead has an open circuit, and the terminals should be resoldered or the wire replaced.

ARMATURE TESTS

Replace the armature if the insulation is burned or brittle, if the core is damaged, or if the bearing surfaces are scored or worn.

Examine the commutator. If it is dirty, rough, scored, has burned spots, is worn out of round, or has high mica, it should be turned down on a lathe and undercut. Check to see that the armature coils are securely soldered to the risers. If, due to extreme heat, solder has been thrown from the riser at the point where the armature wires are soldered, resolder the wires to the bars. A loose connection at this point could result in an open circuit in the armature windings. Test the armature for grounded coils with a 110-volt test lamp, and for short and open-circuited coils with a growler.

NOTE: *Before testing the armature for ground, blow off with compressed air the copper and brush dust that collects on both ends of the commutator. An accumulation of dust can form an electrical path between the commutator bars and shaft, causing the armature to be grounded.*

Grounded Circuit. Place one test lamp prod on the armature core or shaft and the other on the commutator as shown in Fig. 12. If the test lamp lights, the armature is grounded.

Short Circuit. To test the armature for short-circuited coils, connect a growler to a 110-volt alternating current outlet and place the armature on the growler. Hold a thin strip of steel, such as a discarded hacksaw blade, over the armature core, as shown in Fig. 13,

Fig. 12. Testing the armature for ground. Chevrolet Motor Div.—General Motors Corp.

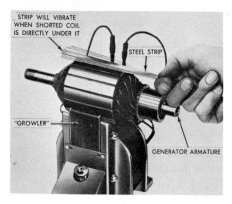

Fig. 13. Testing the armature for short in coils. Ford Motor Co.

and revolve the armature. If the hacksaw is attracted to the armature core and vibrates, the armature is short-circuited. To determine whether the armature or commutator is shorted, clean out the slots between the commutator bars and recheck the armature. If the saw blade still vibrates, the armature should be replaced.

Most automotive armatures can be tested for short-circuited coils by the foregoing method. However, the armatures employed in some high-output generators have extremely low resistance and are wound in such a manner that they will test shorted by the method just described. A growler equipped with an AC voltmeter with a total scale reading of two to three volts (Fig. 14) is required to test this type.

These armatures are checked for shorts by measuring the voltage induced across adjacent commutator bars by the growler. If one or more armature coils are short circuited the reading will be nearly zero when testing the shorted coil.

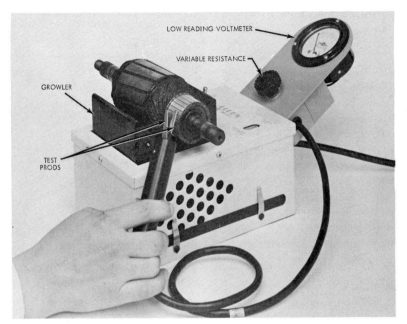

LOW READING VOLTMETER

VARIABLE RESISTANCE

GROWLER

TEST PRODS

Fig. 14. Testing the armature for short and open circuited coils. Allen Electric & Equip. Co.

Armatures can also be checked for an open circuit on a growler equipped with the low reading AC voltmeter. If an open circuit exists, the meter reading will be extremely high when testing the coil in which the open circuit is located.

Armatures that are grounded, shorted, or that have an open circuit that cannot be readily repaired must be replaced. Replacement is usually on an exchange basis where the faulty armature is exchanged for a rebuilt armature. It will be necessary to remove the pulley and drive end plate if the armature is to be replaced or if the commutator is to be turned. Place the armature in a vise equipped with soft jaws and remove the nut holding the pulley in place. Use a puller to remove the pulley, remove the woodruff key which keeps the pulley from turning on the shaft, and then remove the end plate.

Commutator. If the commutator is worn, rough, out of round, or scored, the armature should be centered on a lathe or an armature lathe fixture and a light cut taken from the commutator (Fig. 15).

Fig. 15. Cutting down a commutator in an armature lathe fixture. Plymouth Div., Chrysler Corp.

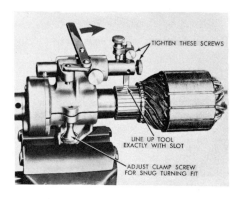

TIGHTEN THESE SCREWS

LINE UP TOOL
EXACTLY WITH SLOT

ADJUST CLAMP SCREW
FOR SNUG TURNING FIT

Fig. 16. Undercutting a commutator. Polish with sandpaper to remove burrs caused by undercutting. Ford Motor Co.

Only enough metal should be removed to clean up the commutator. After turning, the commutator should run true within 0.003 in.

After turning down the commutator, the mica between the commutator bars may need to be undercut. This can be done with an undercutting tool, Fig. 16, or with a hacksaw blade, the teeth of which have been ground off flat with the sides of the blade, Fig. 17. The cutting tool or hacksaw blade should be about 0.002 in. wider than the mica and the mica should be cut away clean between the

Fig. 17. A hacksaw blade can be used to undercut the mica on a commutator.

COMMUTATOR

Fig. 18. Proper and improper undercutting. Ford Motor Co.

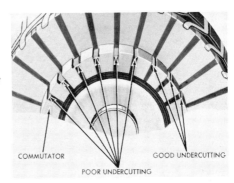

COMMUTATOR   GOOD UNDERCUTTING
POOR UNDERCUTTING

commutator bars to a depth of 1/32 in. Fig. 18. After undercutting, the commutator should be polished with No. 00 sandpaper and blown off with compressed air to remove all particles of abrasive from between the commutator bars.

NOTE: *Never use emery cloth to polish the commutator.*

Inspect Insulated Brush Holder

To test the insulated brush holders for ground, place one test lamp prod on the metal parts of the brush holder and the other on the commutator end frame on which the brush holder is mounted. (Fig. 19). If the test lamp lights the brush holder is grounded and should be repaired or replaced.

Inspect Brushes. Replace the brushes if they are oil soaked, if the pigtail is loose at the point where it is connected to the brush, or if the brushes are worn more than one-half their original length. Check the brushes to be installed in the generator to be sure that they fit freely in the brush holders.

Brush Spring Tension. The brush spring tension should be checked with a spring tension scale, graduated in ounces, while the

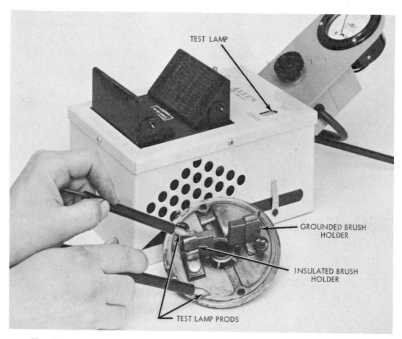

TEST LAMP

GROUNDED BRUSH HOLDER

INSULATED BRUSH HOLDER

TEST LAMP PRODS

Fig. 19. Testing the insulated brush for ground. Allen Electric & Equip. Co.

brushes are resting on the armature. Place the hook of the scale as close to the brush as possible and exert an outward pull in a line parallel with the brush, Fig. 20. Notice the tension scale reading just as the brush leaves the commutator. Brush spring tension varies on different makes of generators from fifteen to sixty ounces.

Excessive brush spring tension causes the commutator and brushes to wear rapidly. Low spring tension is often responsible for a reduced generator output and for arcing at the brushes, resulting in a burned commutator.

The tension exerted by the brush springs must be within the limits specified by the manufacturer if the generator is to charge satisfactorily. Tension specifications given by the manufacturers are for new brushes.

Inspect Commutator End Plate

Inspect the commutator end plate assembly, and replace it if it is damaged. Check the bushing in the end plate, and if it is worn so

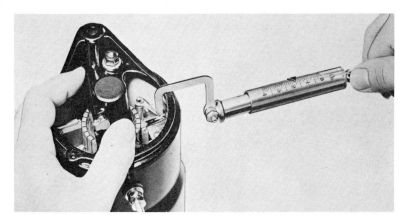

Fig. 20. Testing the spring tension of the brushes. Chevrolet Div.—General Motors Corp.

that the clearance between the shaft and bushing is 0.004 in. or more, replace the bushing. NOTE: *On some makes of generators, the bushing and end plate are not serviced separately and must be replaced as a unit.* Replace the felts or oil seals.

Inspect Drive End Plate

Replace the drive end plate if it is cracked, distorted, or otherwise damaged. Replace the end plate if the ball bearing fits loosely in the recess in the plate. Replace the bearing if it is discolored due to heat, if it is worn, or if it feels rough when turned. Replace the felts or oil seals regardless of their condition.

Fit Generator Brushes

When generator brushes are replaced, the new brushes must seat perfectly on the commutator. Although the edges of the new brushes come preshaped to conform to armature curvature, the brushes must still be shaped to the precise curvature of the armature to assure proper current transfer.

There are two methods of obtaining correct brush-to-armature fit. Brush-seating compound can be applied to the armature while the armature is turned by hand. Turn the armature only long enough to obtain the correct brush curvature. Use compressed air to remove the residue from the armature and brushes.

The other method is to sand the brushes to the correct shape with

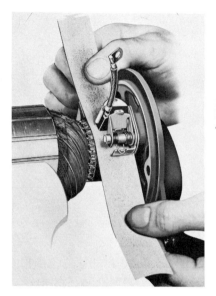

Fig. 21. Sanding the generator brushes for correct fit. Electric Auto-Lite Co.

No. 00 sandpaper. To sand the brushes on a disassembled generator, place the commutator end frame on the armature, install the new brushes in the holders, and position the brush springs. Place a strip of No. 00 sandpaper between the brush and commutator with the abrasive side toward the brush, Fig. 21. Form the sandpaper around the commutator so that the brush is forced toward the brush holder. Several strokes are usually sufficient to seat the brush. Brushes are seated properly when they show 100 percent contact with the commutator. Do not sand the brush more than necessary, as this merely shortens the life of the brush. After sanding, blow the sand and carbon dust from the armature and brush holder. Never use emery cloth to seat the brushes because particles of emery may become permanently embedded in the commutator or brushes.

ASSEMBLE GENERATOR

To assemble the generator reverse the procedure followed during disassembly. Make certain that all connections are properly made and are clean and tight. After completion of assembly test the generator, either on the vehicle or on a test bench, Fig. 22, to see if the repairs have corrected the difficulty and the generator is capable of delivering its rated output.

Polarizing

Whenever a generator has been overhauled or for any reason has lost its residual magnetism, it will not start to charge, and its magnetism must be re-established with the correct polarity for the electrical system in which it is to be used. This must be done before the engine is started.

Field Externally Grounded. Ground the field terminal. Momentarily connect a jumper wire between the battery and the generator armature terminal. This permits a momentary surge of current to flow through the generator which correctly polarizes it.

Field Internally Grounded. Disconnect the wire attached to the generator field terminal, and momentarily connect a jumper wire between the generator field terminal and the battery terminal. This allows a momentary surge of current through the field windings which correctly polarizes the generator.

Motorizing Test

After the generator is assembled, it may be given a motorizing test to determine if the amount of current required for running as a motor is within the limits specified by the manufacturer. The motorizing test can be made on a generator test bench or with a battery and ammeter.

NOTE: *Some manufacturers recommend that their generators be tested for motorizing at six volts on six-volt systems, and at twelve volts on twelve-volt systems. Others require that generators manufactured by them be tested at five and ten volts respectively. When testing generators at five and ten volts, an ammeter and variable resistance should be connected in series with the battery and generator. Also, a voltmeter should be connected to the generator terminals to indicate the voltage at which the test is being performed.*

Based on the generator type and design, certain connections have to be made on the field circuit for the motorizing test. If the generator is of the "A" type circuit (field externally grounded) connect a jumper wire between the generator field terminal and ground. If the generator is of the "B" type circuit (field internally grounded) connect a jumper wire between the field and armature terminal of the generator.

NOTE: *When motorizing a generator, connect the battery according to the polarity of the generator being tested. On positive ground generators, ground the positive battery post. On negative ground generators, ground the negative battery post.*

To motorize a generator which should be checked at twelve volts, connect a battery and ammeter in series between the armature terminal on the generator and the proper battery post. Ground the generator frame to the other battery post. With the connections made, the generator should operate as a motor, and the current draw read on the ammeter should be within the manufacturer's specifications (from four to six amperes on most generators).

When checking the current draw on generators that should be tested at five or ten volts, connect an ammeter and a variable resistance in series between the armature terminal on the generator and the proper battery terminal. Ground the generator to the other battery terminal. Adjust the voltage to the specified value by means of the variable resistance, and read the current draw on the ammeter.

If the current draw during the motorizing test is not within the desired limits it indicates a faulty armature or field coils, poor connections, or excessive drag on the armature. Special attention should be given to the fit of the brushes on the commutator. If necessary, the generator can be operated as a motor for a short period to produce the desired brush fit. After the run-in period, the generator should be permitted to cool to room temperature before repeating the motorizing test. During the motorizing test, the generator is polarized correctly so that when the generator is charging, the current produced will flow in the proper direction.

Bench Output Test

Generator output may be tested on the engine or it may be tested on a generator test stand. When testing a generator on the vehicle, the engine speed can be varied to suit the generator. On generator test stands, the speed is varied by means of a variable speed motor or by means of a mechanically variable drive. Generator test stands generally consist of an ammeter, a voltmeter, a load rheostat, some means of driving the generator, and a battery, plus suitable leads and the necessary switches.

A typical, variable-speed generator test stand is shown in Fig. 22. Since generator test benches vary considerably in their construction, the manufacturer's instructions for each particular test bench

Fig. 22. Testing a generator on a test bench. Allen Electric and Equip. Co.

should be carefully followed when mounting, connecting, and testing the generator.

NOTE: *Generators are rated at a higher voltage than the normal battery voltage. The carbon pile rheostat is employed to increase the resistance of the charging circuit so that the desired voltage can be obtained.*

Connect the generator to the instruments on the test bench and to the driving motor. Make certain that the generator is connected to the battery according to the polarity of the generator. Start the driving motor and operate the generator in the direction it is supposed to run. Increase the generator speed slowly, and as the output increases, hold the voltage at the specified value by adjusting the carbon pile rheostat. Manufacturer's specifications generally give the maximum voltage and current output, and the generator speed at which they should be attained.

If the repairs have been properly made the generator should test within the manufacturer's specifications as given in the service manuals.

INSTALL GENERATOR

Attach the generator to the engine with the front and rear mounting bolts and connect the wires to the generator terminals. Inspect the drive belt. Replace the belt if it is worn, frayed, glazed, or if any of the plies have separated. Install the belt and fasten the clamp bolt.

The belt is generally adjusted by loosening a clamp bolt and moving the generator outward. (Fig. 23). Adjust the belt to the manufacturer's specifications and tighten the adjusting strap (clamp) bolt. The tightness of the belt is checked by applying a five pound pressure at a point midway between the pulleys. When pressure is applied by pressing down with the thumb and measured with a ruler the belt should be depressed from $\frac{1}{4}''$ to $\frac{1}{2}''$ depending upon the manufacturer's specifications.

Belt tension can also be checked with a tension gage, (Fig. 24).

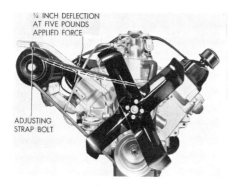

Fig. 23. Fan belt adjustment on a V-type engine. Plymouth Div., Chrysler Motor Corp.

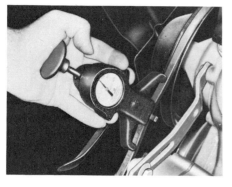

Fig. 24. Fan belt tension being checked with gage. Tension should be between 70-140 lbs. Chevrolet Div., General Motors Corp.

Depending upon the manufacturer's specifications the belt should be adjusted to a tension of 70 to 140 pounds.

REGULATOR INSPECTION

Before testing the regulator itself, make sure all wires in the circuit are in good condition and that all connections are clean and tight. Poor wires and bad connections will affect regulator operation. Resistance in the generator-regulator circuit can be checked by a voltage drop test. Use the same hook-up as for the generator output test, and with the generator output at approximately 20 amperes, check the voltage at the battery terminals and at the A (armature) terminal of the generator, Fig. 25. If the difference is greater than 0.6 volts, a high resistance is present. Clean and tighten all connections and re-check. After the generator and the generator-regulator circuit have been eliminated as the source of trouble, check the regulator itself.

REGULATOR TESTING AND ADJUSTMENT

It is possible to disassemble some regulator units and replace the resistors, coils, and contact points. However, it is generally considered impractical to do so because of the time involved as opposed to the availability and relative low cost of new replacement regulators and commercially rebuilt units obtainable on an exchange basis. Service work, except for testing and adjusting, is usually confined to cleaning the contact points.

Adjusting the Regulator

Battery polarity varies with different makes and models of vehicles. Therefore, always make sure the correct polarity is followed according to the battery and the circuit.

Make sure the connections are correct between the leads and terminals to prevent damage to the test equipment, wiring or regulator. After any regulator or generator tests have been made or either unit has been removed and reinstalled, the generator should be polarized to make sure the polarity throughout the system corresponds to the battery polarity. This prevents arcing and burning of contact points. When the field is externally grounded, polarize the generator by momentarily connecting a jumper wire between the A (armature) and B (battery) terminals of the regulator. When internally grounded, disconnect the F lead from the regulator and momentarily

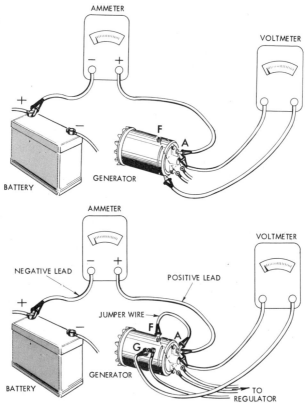

Fig. 25. Testing generator output. Top, For externally grounded generators attach ground jumper to the field terminal. Bottom, For internally grounded generators connect the jumper between the armature terminal and the field terminal. Circuit resistance is checked by connecting a voltmeter between the armature terminal and ground, and between the battery terminal and the ground, while the generator is charging at about 30 amps. The voltage drop between the two tests indicates the resistance in the circuit. Ford Motor Div., Ford Motor Co.

connect it to the regulator B terminal. Never operate the generator with an open circuit (leads disconnected) as this may damage the generator.

The information which follows is general in nature. Follow manufacturer's instructions and specifications carefully to get correct settings and to prevent serious damage to equipment. The accompanying illustrations are typical of those test set-ups used when separate resistance units and meters are used. Again, a few simple rules for using electrical test equipment must be carefully followed: an ammeter must be used in *series* in the circuit—one wire is unhooked and the ammeter inserted in the circuit; a voltmeter must be hooked up *parallel*—across the circuit—so that the circuit need not be broken. The resistance units are placed in series in the circuit. The fixed resistors impose a fixed load on the circuit. The variable resistance serves to lower the battery voltage, thus simulating a discharged battery. Operating the cranking motor for a period of time, then turning on the headlights and other accessories while making the voltage regulator test can be used in place of a variable carbon-pile resistance unit if one is not available.

Always set the voltage regulator before setting the current regulator.

Current and voltage regulator limiting settings are adjusted by changing the armature spring tension, which is directly proportional to the charging rate. Spring tension may be changed, depending upon the construction of the regulator, by bending a spring hanger, Fig. 26, by bending an adjusting arm, Fig. 27, or by turning an adjusting screw, Fig. 28.

Cutout Relay Test

The cutout relay is normally checked and adjusted for closing voltage without removing it from the car. Connect a voltmeter between the A (armature) terminal and ground. Remove the B (battery) lead from the regulator and insert an ammeter between the B terminal of the regulator and the battery, Fig. 29. Start the engine and observe the voltmeter while gradually increasing engine speed. When the cutout relay contact points close, the voltage will drop back slightly and a current flow will be indicated by the ammeter. The highest reading observed just before the voltage drops back is the cutout relay closing voltage. This should be about 11.8 to 13.75 volts for a 12-volt system. Slowly decrease engine speed and observe the discharge rate just before the contact points open. The discharge rate should be between 0 and −10 amperes when the contact points open.

The cutout relay closing voltage is adjusted by increasing or decreasing the spring tension which holds the contact points open. This is done by bending the spring hanger, as shown in Fig. 26, or by turning an adjusting screw, as shown in Fig. 28. Increasing the

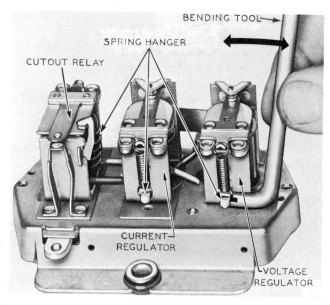

Fig. 26. Adjusting the spring tension on a voltage regulator by bending a spring hanger. Plymouth Div.—Chrysler Corp.

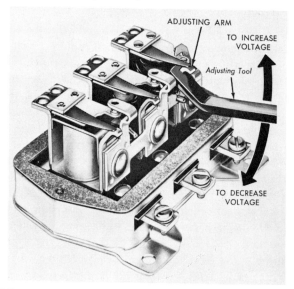

Fig. 27. Adjusting a cut-out relay closing voltage by bending an adjusting arm. Ford Motor Div.—Ford Motor Co.

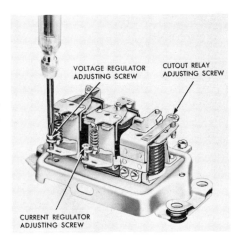

Fig. 28. Location of regulator adjusting screws. Chevrolet Div. —General Motors Corp.

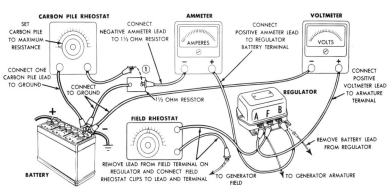

Fig. 29. Regulator test connection diagram. Note connections on voltage regulator at A, F, and B. Ford Motor Co.

spring tension raises the closing voltage; decreasing spring tension reduces closing voltage.

Another method of checking cutout relay closing voltage is to connect an adjustable resistance unit between the F (field) terminal of the regulator and the generator field lead. See Fig. 29. The positions of the test meters remain unchanged. Operate the engine at about 1500 rpm (or approximately ¼ full throttle) with the resistance (field rheostat) turned to maximum resistance, slowly decreasing resistance until the cutout relay contact points close. Note the closing voltage. It should fall within the range indicated above.

The directions given above for adjusting the cutout relay are valid for every make of generator regulator.

Voltage Regulator Tests

Connect one voltmeter lead to the B (battery) terminal of the regulator and ground the other lead. Insert a ¼ ohm resistance between the B terminal of the regulator and the battery lead. The addition of this resistor simulates the condition of a fully charged battery. Generator voltage will quickly rise to the value at which the voltage limiter is set. Insert a variable resistance between the F (field) regulator terminal and the field lead, Fig. 30.

Operate the engine at about 1500 rpm. Cycle the generator by turning the variable resistance, inserted in the field circuit, toward the open position (increase the resistance) until the cutout relay contact points open. Then, turn the field control in the opposite direction and note the voltmeter reading as the voltage regulator points re-close. This should be between 13.8 and 14.8 volts, depending upon temperature and manufacturer's specifications. Adjust the voltage output by changing the armature spring tension through bending the spring hanger, Fig. 26, or by turning the adjusting screw, as shown in Fig. 28. Increasing the tension on the spring increases voltage output; decreasing tension lowers the voltage output.

Current Regulator Tests

Remove the ¼ ohm fixed resistor that was used to simulate a

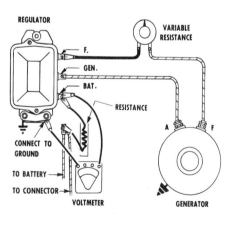

Fig. 30. Checking a Delco-Remy voltage regulator. Chevrolet Div., General Motors Corp.

fully charged battery in the test of the voltage regulator. In the test of the current regulator we want to set up a condition where (1) the generator current will quickly rise to a value at which the current regulator contacts open, and (2) the voltage is kept low so that the voltage regulator contacts will not open and restrict the current output of the generator.

Start the engine and increase the speed to about 2000 rpm. At the same time add a load to the circuit by increasing the resistance until the ammeter reads 28 to 32 amperes. Increase or decrease the armature spring tension to obtain the correct amperage reading if the amperage does not meet manufacturer's specifications.

Manufacturer's specifications for testing and adjustment must be followed in every case. A slight error in the setting of a unit may cause improper functioning, such as a run-down or an overcharged battery, or damage to the generator or regulator. Manufacturers of electrical test equipment make an automotive regulator test kit consisting of an ammeter, voltmeter, a variable resistance, fixed resistors, and the necessary test leads. This is the combination of equipment most commonly used in the service field for testing and adjusting regulators.

Cleaning Regulator Contact Points

Inspect the contact points for any oxidation or pitting before making any regulator tests or adjustments. If air gap specifications are given, also check the air gap setting and correct as required. Many of the reported charging rate troubles arise from dirty and oxidized contact points which may cause a reduction in generator output. Oxidized contact points may also cause an abnormal fluctuation in the voltmeter and/or ammeter readings when testing the charging circuit.

Clean the contact points with a thin, fine-cut, flat spoon or riffler file. Whatever file is used it should not be allowed to become greasy and should not be used to file other metals. *Never use emery cloth or sandpaper to clean contact points;* particles of sand, emery, or metal may become embedded in the points causing them to burn rapidly. Clean flat contact points with a spoon or riffler file. A flat file is less likely to touch the center of the point where the most wear is apt to occur. Clean rounded contact points with a flat file. File the points just enough so that they present a smooth surface to each other. It is not necessary to remove every trace of pitting or burning. After filing, the points may be further cleaned by placing some carbon tetrachloride on a piece of linen tape or lintless bond paper and drawing it between the points.

The armature air gap may require an adjustment to compensate for the metal removed by filing. Specifications for the particular regulator will indicate whether or not the air gap is adjustable.

The armature air gap is the space between the armature and core of the winding. The operation of the cutout relay and voltage and current regulator is affected by the amount of air gap between the armature and the iron core. The greater the air gap, the stronger the magnetic pull exerted by the electromagnet must be to attract the armature. Consequently, on many cutout relays and regulators the armature air gap can be adjusted to the clearance specified by the manufacturer. If no adjustment is provided, a change in the air gap can be compensated for by changing the armature spring tension. Fig. 31 shows how the air gap on one type of regulator is checked and adjusted.

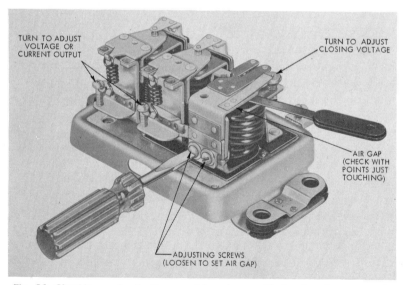

Fig. 31. Checking and adjusting regulator air gap. By turning the screws the armature may be moved up or down to obtain the correct air gap. Delco-Remy Div.—General Motors Corp.

Battery Water Consumption

The amount of water that a battery consumes can be considered an indication of the charging rate. The ideal regulator setting is one that will keep the battery charged without excessive use of water. Normal water usage should not be over one ounce of water per cell per 1,000 miles. If the water consumption is greater than that indicated, or if the battery is consistently low in charge, the voltage regulator may need to be "tailored" to take care of these undesirable features. If the amount of water used is excessive with the regulator correctly adjusted, reduce the voltage setting by 0.1 or 0.2 volts and check for reduced level of water consumption over a period of time. Repeat this procedure until the battery remains charged and the water usage is at the specified minimum. It rarely will be necessary to set the voltage regulator below 13.8 volts. In the case of a battery which is consistently undercharged at the normal regulator setting, increase the voltage setting 0.1 volt and check for an improved battery condition over a period of time. Repeat this process if necessary until the battery remains charged with a minimum amount of water consumption. It rarely will be necessary to set the voltage rating above 14.8 volts.

Ordinarily there should be no need to set a regulator at anything other than the specified ratings. In the case of a vehicle that is consistently operated in heavy traffic at low speeds, it is possible that the normal voltage setting is not high enough to permit the battery to become fully charged. This may require the installation of a generator and regulator of a greater capacity. Finally, some batteries may have abnormal charging characteristics. If this is suspected, carefully check out the battery and replace it if necessary.

TRADE COMPETENCY TESTS

1. Can you describe several methods for undercutting a commutator? How deep should the mica be undercut?

2. How would you test the insulated brush holder to determine if it is grounded?

3. What effect could low brush spring pressures have on generator operation?

4. How are the brushes sanded on a disassembled generator?

5. What does the motorizing test indicate?

6. What is the purpose of polarizing a generator? How is this done?

7. How would you check generator brush spring tension?

8. How do you make a generator output test?

9. What will cause a noisy generator?

10. What cautions must be taken in cleaning a generator?

11. How do you adjust belt tension?

12. How do you check for circuit resistance?

13. How often should a generator be inspected? What maintenance procedures should be performed?

14. What precautions would be taken when cleaning the armature and field coil assemblies?

15. How would you test the field coils for an open circuit? For a ground circuit? A short circuit?

16. How would you test the armature to determine if the armature coils are grounded? How would you test them for a short circuit?

17. What sort of trouble in the armature windings does a burned spot on the commutator indicate?

18. What are the results of an incorrectly adjusted belt?

19. What is the purpose of undercutting the mica in the commutator?

CHAPTER 8

AC CHARGING SYSTEMS

AC ALTERNATOR CHARGING SYSTEM

The purpose of a charging system is to supply electricity to take care of all electrical requirements and to maintain the battery in a fully charged condition.

Today's vehicles have more electrically operated accessories than ever before. Also, more time is being spent in slow speed driving because of greater traffic congestion. Both of these factors have contributed to the need for a generator that is capable of developing a higher charging rate, not only at slow vehicle speeds but also at engine idle. In order to meet these increased demands, a continuous output diode-rectified AC (alternating current) generator, commonly called an *alternator,* has been developed and is installed as regular equipment on all vehicles.

Basically, the standard production alternator is designed to replace the standard DC generator, and provide improved low-speed output. It is not designed to replace the heavy-duty DC generators that are needed to fulfill unusual demands in certain commercial operations and on police vehicles. Heavy duty alternators are available, and should be used where heavy duty service is recommended for special operating conditions.

Other advantages of an alternator are that it is more compact than a DC generator, weighs considerably less, and rarely requires service. A cutout relay is not needed and a current regulator (limiter) is not used in the alternator charging system. Fig. 1.

An alternator will deliver from 6 to 10 amperes at normal idle speed, while a DC generator, at the same speed, may not develop enough electrical flow to cause the cutout relay contact points to close.

The construction of the alternator also provides a distinct mechanical advantage. A DC generator is usually driven, through a

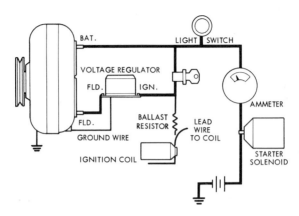

Fig. 1. An alternator or AC charging circuit.

belt and pulley arrangement, at about twice crankshaft speed. With high speed engines a DC generator could easily be subjected to armature speeds in excess of 10,000 rpm. Such speeds would cause the armature to be overspeeded and it would throw its windings. A pulley resizing could resolve the problem at high speeds but low speed output would be adversely affected by too slow an armature speed.

The alternator, however, because of rotor construction, is capable of rotational speeds of 15,000 rpm with no danger of physical damage. Thus, the alternator can use a smaller pulley than a DC generator and produce high output at low speeds with no high speed problems either.

The basic principle of producing electricity through the use of magnetism applies to the alternator in the same manner as it does to the DC generator.

ALTERNATOR PRINCIPLES

All generators and alternators produce electricity by means of the induction principle. When this principle is applied to a generator, it means that whenever a conductor cuts through magnetic lines of force an electrical current is induced in the conductor. The amount of electricity induced will depend upon the strength of the magnetic field (number of lines of force), the numbers of wires (conductors) cutting the field, and the speed with which they pass through the field.

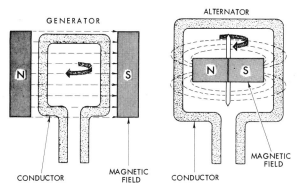

Fig. 2. In a generator the conductor rotates. In an alternator the field magnet rotates.

The alternator operates on exactly the same basic principle as the DC generator. However, because of construction differences, the principle is applied in a different manner. In the alternator the magnets, which create the magnetic lines of force, revolve; the conductors remain stationary. The induction principle still applies, in that if electricity can be induced in a conductor, formed into a loop, as it cuts through a magnetic field, it also holds that a magnetic field revolving inside a loop (conductor) also induces electricity in the conductor. Fig. 2 indicates how magnetic lines of force are cut to induce electricity in the generator and in the alternator.

Both the generator and the alternator produce alternating current which must be changed into direct current before it flows into the external circuit. In the generator, the field coils (which produce the magnetic lines of force) are stationary; the conductor coils, mounted in the armature, rotate between the magnetic poles. The armature also consists of a commutator, which converts the alternating current to direct current before it leaves the generator.

In the alternator, the conductor coils are stationary in the frame and are called the stator. The field magnet, called the rotor, turns inside the stator. The stator contains more and larger loops of conductors (wires) than the generator armature, thus permitting more electricity to be induced.

There are six pairs of north and south poles in the rotor which produce the magnetic field, compared to the two poles of a standard

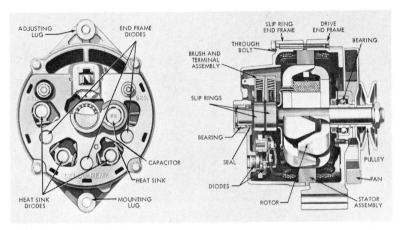

Fig. 3. **Cutaway view of an alternator.** Cadillac Motor Div. General Motors Corp.

generator. A coil located inside the rotor increases the number of lines of force when an electrical current is applied to the coil. Two slip rings and brushes connected to the battery are used to excite the magnetic field when the ignition switch is turned on. The output current is picked up from stationary terminals on the stator. The alternating current is changed to direct current (rectified) by the use of six diodes.

Because there are six magnetic fields instead of only one, the frequency of the current is also higher. Fig. 3 is a cutaway view of a typical alternator, while Fig. 4 shows a disassembled view.

ALTERNATOR CONSTRUCTION

The alternator in common use today, is made up of four major units: a stator assembly, a rotor assembly, and two end frame assemblies. The stator assembly consists of coils of wire wound into slots in a laminated iron frame, Fig. 5. The conductors are in the form of three continuous coils of wire. One end of each coil is attached to a common connection, while the other end of each coil is connected to a separate pair of diodes. The stator assembly is positioned between the two stationary end frames.

The rotor assembly contains a coil of wire (field coil) mounted between two interlocking iron pole pieces. Each of the pole pieces has six poles (fingers) which intermesh as shown in Fig. 6 to provide

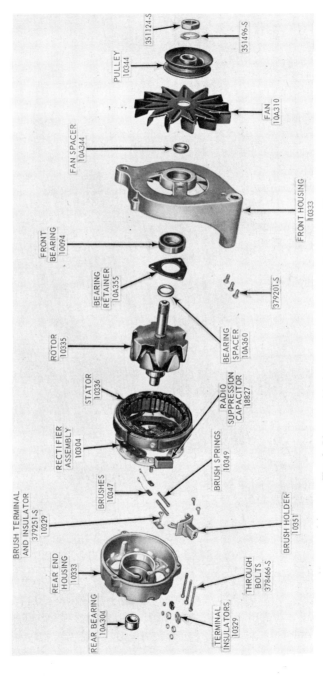

Fig. 4. Disassembled view of an alternator. Ford Motor Co.

351124-S

351496-S

PULLEY
10344

FAN
10A310

FAN SPACER
10A344

FRONT HOUSING
10333

FRONT
BEARING
10094

BEARING
RETAINER
10A355

372201-S

ROTOR
10335

BEARING
SPACER
10A360

STATOR
10336

RADIO
SUPPRESSION
CAPACITOR
18827

RECTIFIER
ASSEMBLY
10304

BRUSH SPRINGS
10349

BRUSH TERMINAL
AND INSULATOR
379251-S
10329

BRUSHES
10347

BRUSH HOLDER
10351

REAR END
HOUSING
10333

THROUGH
BOLTS
378466-S

REAR BEARING
10A304

TERMINAL
INSULATORS
10329

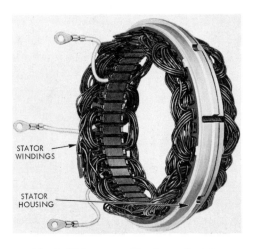

STATOR
WINDINGS

STATOR
HOUSING

Fig. 5. Stator assembly of an alternator.

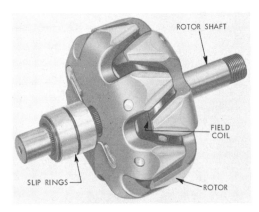

ROTOR SHAFT

FIELD
COIL

SLIP RINGS

ROTOR

Fig. 6. Rotor assembly of an alternator.

a total of twelve poles for the complete rotor assembly. The rotor
shaft is supported by prelubricated bearings in each end frame, and
turns inside the stator assembly.

Two slip rings, one insulated from the rotor assembly and frame
and the other grounded to the assembly, are mounted on one end
of the rotor shaft. One lead of the field (rotor) coil is grounded to
the rotor shaft while the other wire lead is attached to the insulated
slip ring. An insulated brush riding on the insulated slip ring is

connected to the battery through the ignition switch. When the ignition switch is turned on, electrical energy from the battery flows through the insulated brush and slip ring to the field coil, completing the circuit through the ground brush and slip ring. Thus this alternator is type B with an internally grounded field circuit.

The end frames contain the bearings which mount the rotor. Attached to the rear end frame is a heat sink containing three diodes. These diodes are insulated from the frame, yet mounted in such a manner that heat can be more readily dissipated from the diodes than from the rest of the unit. Three ground diodes are pressed into the same end frame. See Fig. 3. The rear end frame also contains the two slip ring brushes. One brush is insulated from the frame while the other is grounded. Springs in the brush holders result in the brushes being held in constant contact with the slip rings.

ALTERNATOR OPERATION

When a magnet is rotated inside a loop of wire (conductor) so that the magnetic lines of force are cutting across the conductor, a voltage is induced, which causes current (electrons) to flow through a completed circuit. With the magnet (rotor) turning, as illustrated in Fig. 7, and the south pole (S) under the top loop of the conductor, while the north pole (N) is directly above the bottom of the loop, the induced voltage will cause current (electrons) to flow from A to B as shown by the arrows in the upper illustration. The student can verify this by applying the Left Hand Rule: With the fingers placed on the side of the conductor which first contacts the magnetic field, and with the fingers pointing in the direction of the field, the thumb points in the direction of electron flow. After the magnet has turned one-half revolution, the N pole will be under the top loop and the S pole will be above the bottom loop. The induced voltage will now cause the current to flow in the opposite direction, from B to A as illustrated by the arrows in the lower illustration. As the magnet is turned another one-half revolution, the direction of current flow will change back to the original direction of flow from A to B. The result is that the current will flow through the external circuit first in one direction and then in the other. The direction of current flow reverses every one-half revolution. This is the characteristic of alternating current (AC) as developed by an alternator.

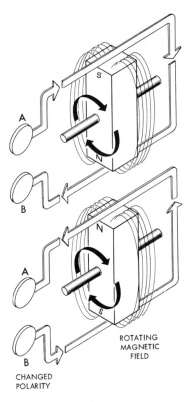

Fig. 7. Current flow in an alternator showing changing polarity.

For purposes of illustration the rotor has been considered to be a bar magnet or a two pole electromagnet. In actual practice the rotor will normally have twelve poles. In addition to multiplying the number of lines of force by means of the number of poles, a coil containing many turns of wire is located between the two interlocking rotor pole pieces. This coil supplies additional lines of force to the pole pieces. Electricity, supplied by the battery, is carried to the rotor coils by means of slip rings and brushes at one end of the rotor assembly.

Magnetic lines of force always concentrate at the N and S poles and diminish on either side of the poles. Because the amount of voltage induced is proportional to the number of lines of force cutting across a conductor in a given length of time, more voltage will be induced when the rotor poles are passing close to the con-

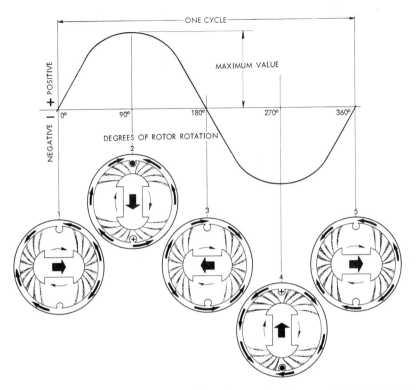

Fig. 8. Rotor cycle (current cycle). The voltage varies in amount as the rotor cuts the various numbers of lines of force. The voltage curve is not due to rotor speed.

ductor. It is obvious, for this reason, that the amount of voltage being induced will be constantly increasing and decreasing, even though the speed of the rotor may be constant. Fig. 8 illustrates how the induced voltage varies in relation to the pole position.

In the location numbered 1, the rotor is at right angles to the conductor, therefore no lines of force are being cut and no voltage is induced. As the rotor turns, lines of force are being cut so that when position 2 has been reached the rotor has moved 90°, and the greatest number of lines of force has been cut, resulting in the maximum amount of voltage being induced. Moving from position 2 to 3, fewer number of lines of force are cut, reducing the flow of current to 0 when 180° is reached. When the rotor is moved from position 3 to position 4, when the rotor reaches position 4 or 270° the maximum number of lines of force has been cut and maximum voltage induced. During this quarter revolution however, the lines of force leaving the N pole are being cut by the upper portion of the conductor loop and the S pole's magnetic lines of force are being cut by the lower portion of the conductor loop. The induced voltage is now flowing in the opposite direction and is at maximum value. Finally to complete the full cycle, the rotor moves from position 4 to 5 and the induced voltage tapers off to 0 at 360°. The complete cycle results in the voltage curve as illustrated, and is commonly referred to as a Sine Wave. The Sine Wave represents the induced voltage output of a single phase, two pole alternator (AC generator).

If the rotor were to make 60 complete turns every second, it would result in 60 cycles of electricity being produced per second. The number of cycles per second is called the frequency. Frequency continually varies, according to the speed of the alternator, and therefore is of little significance in the overall operation.

Thus far we have considered only a single loop, or phase, of wire in the stator, which results in a low voltage output. Three factors are involved in increasing alternator output: (1) voltage increases as the speed of the rotor increases; (2) voltage will also be increased as the strength of the rotor's magnetic field is increased; and (3) voltage will increase as the number of turns of wire in the stator coils are increased.

To bring about increased alternator output in actual practice, the stator is made up of three separate windings (coils), each containing many turns of wire. Each separate winding is called a phase, hence the term "3-phase" is attached to the alternator. The three stator coils may be interconnected in two different ways: one arrangement is called the 3-phase *Y connection* stator; the other arrangement is called the 3-phase *Delta connection* stator. See Fig. 9. The 3-phase Y connected stator is the arrangement most commonly found in today's alternators. In both cases the stator coils will be connected to diodes.

The battery and all other electrical components used on the automobile require direct current (DC) for their operation. In the case of the DC generator, which was previously used as standard equipment on all automobiles, the alternating current produced

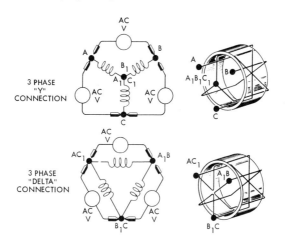

Fig. 9. Stator coil connections.

within the armature was changed into direct current by means of a commutator and brushes, a form of mechanical rectification. The alternating current (AC) produced within the stator of the alternator can be changed into direct current by a process of electrical rectification. Some of the early alternators used an externally mounted, dry plate, selenium rectifier. All alternators now have the stator windings connected directly to rectifying diodes mounted within the alternator housing. This permits the alternator to deliver direct current at the output terminal, the same as a DC generator.

The diode, a small "semi-conductor" (half conductor and half insulator) is an electrical one-way switch which allows electricity to flow in one direction only. The actual rectifying material consists of a very small metallic disk or wafer of pure silicon treated with a controlled impurity. A "getter" material is sometimes used to surround the silicon wafer so as to absorb unwanted impurities and prevent contamination of the silicon surfaces. Fig. 10 is a sketch of a diode. The nature of the silicon wafer is such that there will be a transfer of electrons through the diode in one direction only and not in the opposite direction when the diode is properly connected into a circuit with a given polarity.

The AC output of the alternator's 3-phase stator could be connected through an electronic device that would let the electricity, flowing in one direction only, go out into the circuit and prevent

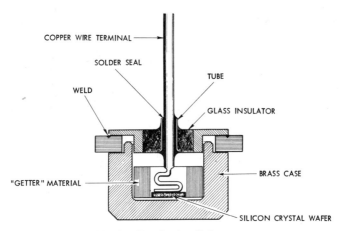

COPPER WIRE TERMINAL

SOLDER SEAL

TUBE

WELD

GLASS INSULATOR

"GETTER" MATERIAL

BRASS CASE

SILICON CRYSTAL WAFER

Fig. 10. Sketch of a diode

all electricity of opposite polarity, from flowing into the circuit. This would be half-wave rectification, since only half of the potential output of the alternator is being utilized.

Through the use of six diodes connected into the stator circuit, Fig. 11, it is possible because of the "Y" connection to obtain full-wave rectification. This full-wave rectification of the alternating current is accomplished in six stages. Due to the location of the stator coils in the housing, and their relationship to the moving rotor, each of the six stages occurs in sequence for a brief instant. In every case, the rotor position is such that induced electricity will flow out through one circuit and return through the second circuit, while opposing voltage will balance the third circuit causing it to be neutral. To understand the electrical flow in the 3-phase full wave diode rectified alternator, the six steps or stages are illustrated and explained in the following figures. The order in which the various stages occur has been arranged in this particular sequence to simplify the manner in which rectification takes place.

In Fig. 11 the rotor is in such a position that the electrical flow is from the junction of the phase one stator coil to the positive diode located in the heat sink. Arrows show the direction of the electrical flow with the black arrowhead (symbol for diode) indicating the diode that is conducting electricity. From the alternator terminal the charging electricity flows to the battery or external load and

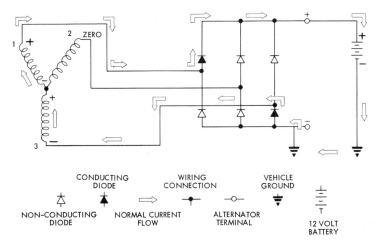

Fig. 11. Rectification of alternating current—Stage 1. Ford Div.—Ford Motor Co.

from there to ground which includes the alternator housing. The electricity then flows from ground to the diode connected to the phase three stator coil junction which has a negative voltage with respect to the phase one voltage. While a voltage difference exists across the other diodes, the voltage in each case is reversed in

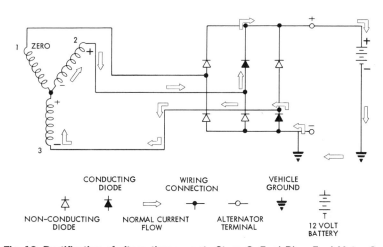

Fig. 12. Rectification of alternating current—Stage 2. Ford Div.—Ford Motor Co.

polarity relative to the diode, causing each remaining diode to act as a check valve, blocking the flow of electricity.

In the second stage of rectification, the phase one stator coil is neutral, phase two is positive and phase three is negative, Fig. 12. The electrical flow, therefore, must be through the positive phase two stator coil junction, into the heat sink, and through the number two positive diode. From the alternator terminal the electrical flow is through the battery or external load to ground. The flow from ground is through the third stage negative diode to the phase three stage junction, which is still negative.

During the third stage of rectification, the phase three coil is at zero potential (neutral), phase two is positive, and phase one has become negative. The electrical flow, illustrated in Fig. 13 is through the positive stage two stator coil junction, into the heat sink and the stage two positive diode. The diode is an excellent conductor in this direction and permits the electricity to flow to the alternator terminal. For the electricity to complete its circuit, the flow is from the terminal through the external load or battery to ground. The electrical flow is now from ground through the stage one negative diode and through the phase one stator junction.

When the rotor is lined up so that the fourth stage of rectification can take place, the phase two stator coil is at zero voltage (neu-

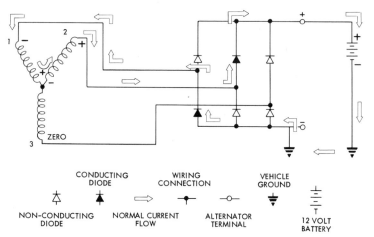

Fig. 13. **Rectification of alternating current—Stage 3.** Ford Div.—Ford Motor Co.

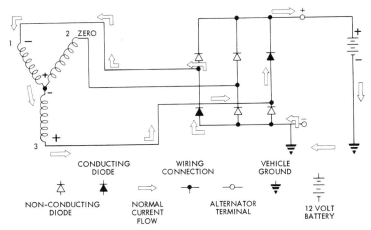

Fig. 14. Rectification of alternating current—Stage 4. Ford Div.—Ford Motor Co.

tral), phase three stator coil is positive, and phase one stator coil is negative. The flow of electricity shown in Fig. 14 is through the phase three stator coil junction, into the heat sink, through the third phase positive diode and to the alternator terminal. The electrical flow continues from the terminal through the battery or external

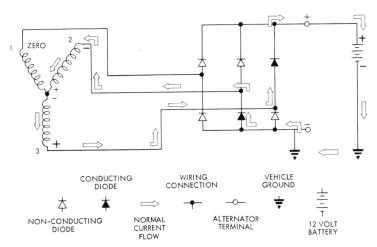

Fig. 15. Rectification of alternating current—Stage 5. Ford Div.—Ford Motor Co.

load to ground. From ground the flow is by way of the phase one diode, which is negative, and into the phase one stator coil junction.

The fifth stage of rectification has the rotor positioned so that the phase one coil is at zero potential (neutral), phase three coil is positive, and phase two coil has become negative. The electrical flow, Fig. 15, is through the phase three stator coil junction, to the heat sink, through the third phase positive diode and to the output terminal. In completing the circuit, the flow is continued to the battery or external load and to ground. The phase two negative diode carries the electricity through to the phase two stator coil junction thereby making a complete circuit.

The sixth stage of rectification occurs with the rotor positioned so that the phase three stator coil is neutral (zero flow of electricity), phase one coil is positive and phase two coil has become negative. The induced electrical flow, Fig. 16, is through the phase one stator coil junction, heat sink and phase one positive diode to the alternator terminal. From the alternator output terminal the flow is through the battery or external load to ground. The circuit is completed by the electrical flow through the negative phase two stator coil diode and through the phase two stator junction.

These six electrical flow changes are necessary to accomplish the full-wave rectification of a three phase alternator (AC generator).

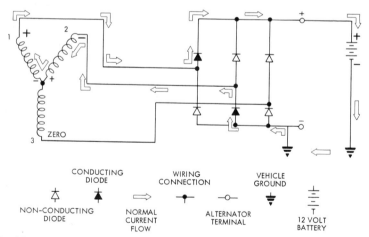

Fig. 16. Rectification of alternating current—Stage 6. Ford Div.—Ford Motor Co.

Factors Affecting Alternator Output

Several factors affect the output of the alternator. Electrical output will increase as the speed of the rotor increases. The voltage will be greater as the strength of the magnetic field of the rotor increases. The strength of this field depends upon the number of turns of wire in the rotor windings, the amount of electricity applied to the rotor coil through the brushes and slip rings, and the air gap between the rotor poles and stator. The smaller the air gap the more effective will be the strength of the field. Output will also increase as the number or turns of wire in the stator coils is increased, as more conductors will be cut by the magnetic lines of force from the rotor coil.

Another important factor having considerable bearing on the alternator output is referred to as "inductive reactance." Inductive reactance is a "built-in" current limiting factor and completely eliminates the need for a current limiter in the regulating system. When electricity moves through a coil of wire, a magnetic field is produced. When this electricity is alternating in nature the magnetic field produced will build up in one direction as the electrical flow increases and falls off as the flow decreases. When the direction of electrical flow is reversed, the magnetic field will again build up, but in the opposite direction. The field also decreases as the electrical flow decreases. Fig. 17 illustrates graphically how this change in direction of electrical flow causes a magnetic polarity reversal, as well as the build up and collapse of the magnetic field.

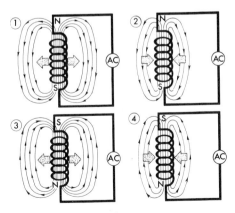

Fig. 17. Inductive reactance.

When the current flow through a stator coil increases, the magnetic lines of force extend outward and cut across adjacent coil windings. The direction that these magnetic lines of force cut the adjacent stator coil windings is such that the voltage induced in the coil windings is opposite to that applied to the coil. This opposing voltage limits (counteracts) the voltage being induced in the coil. This opposition to current flow is termed "inductive reactance." Since, with an alternating current source, the current is constantly changing, inductive reactance is always present.

The amount of "inductive reactance" is affected by the speed at which the lines of force build up and collapse (frequency). The speed of the rotor has a direct bearing on the charging rate. As the charging rate increases, due to an increase in rotor speed, the "inductive reactance" becomes more effective and further curtails the amount of current output. Because of this the need for a separate current limiting device in the regulator is eliminated.

Some alternators use an isolation diode in addition to the six-phase rectification diodes just discussed.

The entire DC output of the system passes through the "isolation diode." The isolation diode is not essential for rectification and is used to: provide an automatic solid state switch for illuminating the alternator charge-discharge light; automatically connect the volt-

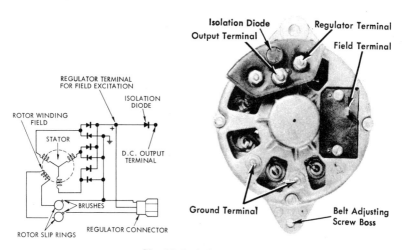

Fig. 18. Isolation diode.

age regulator to the alternator and battery when the alternator is operating; and eliminate electrical leakage through the alternator so that maximum leakage is less than one milliampere when the car is not in use, Fig. 18.

ALTERNATOR REGULATOR

While the regulator assembly may contain as many as three functioning units, the voltage limiter is the only external unit that actually performs a controlling function—it limits the DC output voltage according to external load and state of charge of the battery. This is brought about by controlling the electrical flow through the field coil in the rotor.

A current limiter is not required because the alternator is capable of self-regulating the current at a given speed and voltage by "inductive reactance." A cut-out relay is not required, because the action of the diodes prevents battery voltage from discharging through the alternator.

The regulator assembly most commonly used today consists of a field relay and a voltage limiter. One manufacturer has an ammeter in the charging circuit and therefore uses only a voltage limiter in the regulator assembly. The type of field relay in use today has eliminated the need for an indicator light relay.

Voltage Limiter

Regardless of the number of units in a regulator assembly, the voltage limiter functions in the same basic manner in all alternator regulators. The limiter is connected into the field circuit between the field terminal of the alternator and the battery and limits the voltage output by controlling the electrical flow to the field coil located in the rotor.

Fig. 19 is a wiring diagram of the voltage limiter used in conjunction with a charging circuit that includes an ammeter.

Line voltage (battery voltage less voltage drop to the connection) is imposed on the ignition terminal of the regulator through the ignition switch.

Field current, controlled by the regulator, is delivered to the F or "Fld" (field) terminal of the regulator and flows into the rotor field coil through the insulated brush and slip ring. The field circuit is completed through the ground slip ring and ground brush.

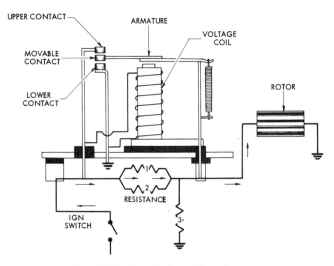

Fig. 19. Voltage limiter wiring diagram.

The two terminals, ignition and field, are insulated from the regulator base and connected by two parallel resistors, numbered 1 and 2 in Fig. 19. Number 3 resistor is grounded. Two parallel resistors dissipate heat better than a single unit.

Voltage control is accomplished by an electro-mechanical limiter consisting of a voltage coil with many turns of fine wire wound around an iron core. The core and winding are assembled on a metal frame. A flat steel armature supporting upper and lower contact points is attached to the frame by a flexible hinge and is centered above the core. A matching upper contact point is held by a contact support insulated from the frame. A matching lower contact point is fastened to a contact support grounded through the frame. The construction is basically that of the voltage limiter used with a conventional generator charging system.

The voltage coil is connected between the ignition switch terminal and ground. Battery voltage is therefore imposed on the regulator voltage coil as soon as the ignition switch is closed. The upper contact point is also connected to the ignition terminal of the regulator. The lower contact point, as previously mentioned, is grounded through the regulator base. The movable contact point is connected to the rotor (field) coil. A coil spring attached to the hinged end of the armature holds the upper contacts together, so that full battery voltage is also imposed on the field coil when the ignition switch is closed.

In actual operation the movable contact point (armature) seldom stays in one position. It may rest against the upper contact, vibrate between the upper contact and open position, or vibrate between open position and the lower contact point. When battery voltage is relatively low, the flow through the voltage coil will also be low and the magnetic pull of the voltage coil will not be enough to overcome the armature air gap and spring tension holding the movable contact against the stationary upper contact. With the two points together, the circuit is completed from the battery to the rotor (field) coil. As resistance is low, the maximum amount of electricity will flow through the field. With rotor field strength high, the alternator output will be at its maximum, according to rotor speed. Because electricity follows the path of least resistance, there will be no electrical flow through the resistance unit when the upper contact points are closed.

As the rotor continues to rotate the state of charge of the battery rises; more voltage will be applied to the regulator voltage coil. With increased voltage, the magnetic field surrounding the voltage coil will be increased in strength to where it will be able to pull the movable contact armature assembly away from the upper stationary contact point. When this happens the direct circuit between the battery and field coil is disrupted. The flow from the battery to the field coil is now through the two resistance units. This reduces the voltage across the rotor coil which, in turn, reduces the number of lines of magnetic force in the field coil and results in a reduction of alternator output.

One of the factors affecting the charging rate of an alternator is the number of magnetic lines of force that are being cut. Reducing the number of lines of magnetic forces reduces the charging rate when other factors remain the same. A lower charging rate also results in a reduced electrical flow through the voltage coil. The upper contact points will be pulled together by spring tension when the electrical flow is reduced in the voltage coil to the point where spring tension overcomes the magnetic pull.

When further reduction of the charging rate is required, the increased electrical flow through the regulator voltage coil will cause the armature to be pulled down into contact with the *lower* set of points. Since the lower stationary contact is connected to ground, the electrical flow from the battery will flow directly to ground, rather than to the (short circuited) field and voltage coils. Reduced output will cause the contact points to separate. The field current flow now alternates between that supplied by the battery through the resistor units (lower contact points open) and zero current flow (lower contact points closed).

The rate at which the regulator armature fluctuates (vibrates) between the lower contacts and mid-position (float), and the upper contacts and mid-position is determined by the electrical load, state of charge of the battery, and the specific alternator rotor speed. Upper stage regulation takes place generally at low speeds and when electrical loads are fairly high (or battery low in charge). The lower stage or shorting contacts will operate at higher speeds with light electrical loads (charged battery).

The third resistor, Number 3 in Fig. 19, absorbs the electrical surges developed in the field circuit, which build up with the rapid opening and closing of the contact points, protecting the contact points from excessive arcing.

The amount of spring tension holding the upper contacts to-

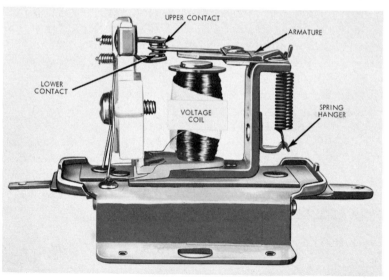

Fig. 20. **Voltage limiter construction.** Plymouth Div.—Chrysler Corp.

gether controls the voltage at which the regulator limits the alternator output. Increasing the spring tension results in the need for higher electrical flow through the voltage coil before the contact points are opened. In other words, the battery voltage must build up more before the regulator acts to reduce the charging rate by inserting resistance into the field circuit.

In the particular voltage limiter just discussed, the ground stationary contact point is located beneath the armature and the upper contact point is connected to line voltage. In another make of voltage limiter, the lower stationary contact point is connected to line voltage, while the upper stationary contact is grounded. The operating principles are exactly the same, the difference being in the armature hinge and spring arrangement. A typical voltage limiter is shown in Fig. 20.

Voltage Limiter With Field Relay

A few of the early regulators used, in addition to the voltage limiter, a field relay and an indicator light relay. Today's regulators do not use an indicator light relay. Instead, control of the indicator light is incorporated in the field relay. When the indicator light relay was used, turning the ignition switch on would energize the indicator light relay, causing the light to glow. When an electrical flow from the alternator was impressed on the indicator light relay coil winding, the contact points were pulled open and the light would no longer light.

The most common alternator regulator in use today consists of a double contact voltage limiter unit and a field relay. The voltage limiter operates to limit the alternator output to a pre-set voltage. The field relay is used to connect the alternator rotor field winding and the voltage coil of the limiter directly to the battery as soon as the alternator begins to produce electricity. When the ignition switch is closed (and before the engine is started), the indicator light glows to indicate the alternator is not charging. As soon as the alternator begins to charge the indicator light goes out.

In operation, when the ignition switch is closed, battery current will flow from the switch through the indicator light, causing it to glow, and through the resistor which is connected in parallel to the light. From there, the current flow is to the regulator ignition terminal. This terminal may be marked "I" or, in some cases, merely

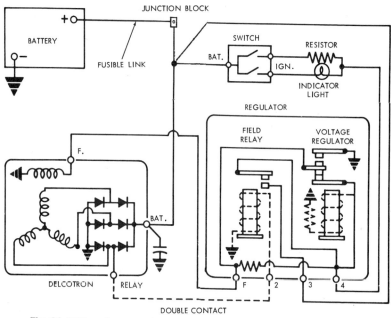

Fig. 21. Wiring diagram of regulator with voltage limiter and field relay.

numbered for identification purposes. In Fig. 21 the regulator indicator light terminal is identified as "Terminal No. 4." From the regulator ignition terminal the electricity flows through the (closed) stationary and movable contact points to the rotor field coil by way of the slip ring and ground brush.

The flow of electricity to the rotor coil is small because of the resistor in the circuit. However, the current still produces enough magnetic flux to permit the stator, after the engine is started, to develop sufficient electrical energy to close the field relay contact. The wiring diagram, Fig. 21, indicates the electrical circuit. In this particular diagram, the regulator field terminal is designated as "Terminal No. 2." Alternately, the terminal may be labeled "S" indicating stator. As soon as the alternator begins to charge, electricity flows from the stator to the field relay coil. When the magnetic field surrounding the field relay coil becomes strong enough, the contact point, located above the coil, will be pulled into contact with the stationary contact. When this happens, full line voltage is

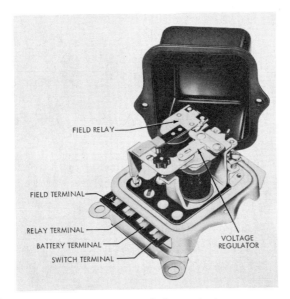

Fig. 22. Voltage limiter and relay.

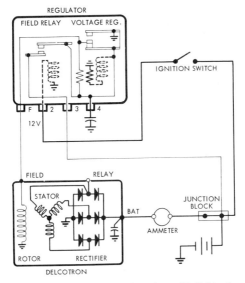

Fig. 23. Ammeter in conjunction with field relay.

impressed on the rotor field coil. The electrical path is now from the battery through the closed field relay contact points, through the closed voltage limiter stationary and movable contact points, to the rotor field coil through the regulator F (field) terminal. This produces maximum rotor field coil voltage and full alternator output. The light no longer glows, because there is a direct path to the rotor field coil, without passing through the resistance unit. Fig. 22 illustrates a typical regulator unit, consisting of a field relay and a voltage limiter.

When an ammeter is used in conjunction with a field relay, as soon as the ignition switch is turned on, the field relay contact points close and full line voltage is applied to the rotor field coil. Figs. 23 and 24.

The voltage limiter operates in exactly the same manner as the previously described regulator unit, consisting of only a voltage limiter. When the engine is first started, armature spring tension holds the armature contact point against the stationary contact, which is connected to the battery through the ignition switch and resistance. Voltage is impressed upon the rotor field coil and the voltage coil of the voltage limiter unit. As the state of charge of the battery becomes higher, the voltage impressed upon the voltage limiter coil becomes greater, until the magnetic attraction is great enough to pull the armature contact point away from the stationary contact. The flow of electricity to the rotor field coil is now reduced, because the only path the field current can now take is through the resistor units. This reduces the charging rate. When the voltage drops off, spring tension will close the contact points, and the charging rate will again rise.

With a fully charged battery, a light electrical load and high alternator rotor speed, the magnetic flux developed in the voltage limiter coil, due to the high current flow, will be great enough to pull the armature contact point into contact with the stationary point that is grounded. As the armature vibrates between mid-position (float) and ground, the charging rate is reduced a greater amount than when the armature vibrates between the mid-position and the contact connected to the battery.

The rate at which the armature opens and closes (vibrates) determines the amount of limiting which takes place. The voltage at which limiting takes place is determined by the amount of tension placed on the armature spring. The tension can be changed by

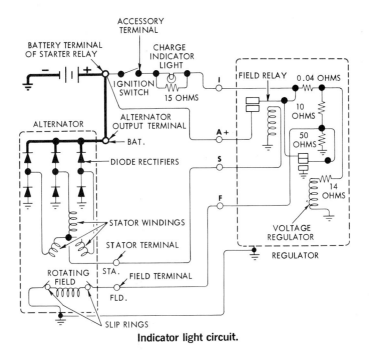

Indicator light circuit.

Fig. 24. An ammeter in conjunction with a field relay compared to indicator light circuit.

bending the spring hanger, or by changing an adjusting screw. The distance (gap) between the armature and the voltage coil core, as well as the contact point gap, has an effect on limiting the voltage output. Contact point gap, as well as the armature-to-core gap, can be adjusted to obtain proper limiter operation.

Temperature is always a factor in charging rate regulation as battery requirements vary with different temperatures. A higher voltage is needed to produce specified charging current at low temperatures, compared to normal temperature (approximately 75°-80°F). The reverse is true for extreme high temperature operation. This means that when adjusting the limiter setting, ambient temperature should be measured and compensated for in order to obtain a properly functioning voltage limiter.

On some installations a bimetal strip is used for an armature hinge. When this is the case, and if ambient temperature is low, more voltage is needed to create additional magnetic strength before the contact points can be opened. The bimetal hinge creates less resistance to bending when the temperature is high, therefore less voltage is required to open the contact points; thus limiter voltage is reduced.

A resistor is often connected in series with the voltage limiter coil. When the voltage limiter coil is cold, there is less wire resistance and more current would flow, thereby limiting at a lower voltage. The resistance unit reduces current flow permitting voltage to build up in the circuit to allow a higher voltage when cold. As the coil warms up a reduced voltage then occurs because less current can flow through the warmed coil. This arrangement effectively helps compensate for temperature variations and also acts as an absorber of induced high voltages caused by the operation of the voltage coil.

TRANSISTORIZED REGULATORS

Many vehicles are being equipped with a variety of transistor controlled voltage regulators. These regulators all operate with the same basic circuitry.

The transistorized regulator will be found as a separately mounted voltage regulator assembly or it may be built into or attached directly to the alternator.

Externally Mounted Transistor Regulators

The regulator is made up of transistors, diodes, resistors, ca-

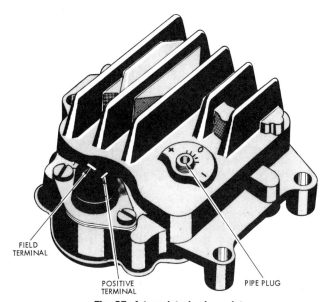

Fig. 25. A transistorized regulator.

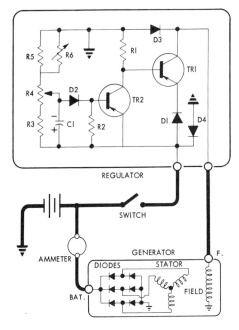

Fig. 26. Diagram of a transistorized regulator.

pacitors, and a thermistor. It operates to limit alternator voltage to a preset value by controlling or limiting generator field current. The thermistor functions to compensate for temperature variations. This type of regulator usually has a plug which can be removed to gain access to an adjustment screw for changing voltage settings by increments of .3 volt to a maximum of .6 volt. This unit has no moving parts and requires no periodic service. Fig. 25. Any malfunction requires replacement of the unit.

A closer look at the circuitry in Fig. 26 will provide an insight to the operation of this type of regulator. TR1 and TR2 are the two transistors used. D2 is the zener diode. The other resistors and capacitors operate as protective devices to prevent transistor damage. R6 is the adjustable resistance. The other diodes are also used to protect the transistors from damage electrically.

Notice that when the ignition switch is closed, current will flow into the emitter of TR1 where current can complete the base circuit through R1. With the TR1 emitter to base circuit complete, the emitter to collector circuit is also turned on providing the alternator with full field strength. Notice also at this time that TR2 does not have a completed base circuit because the zener diode D2 is

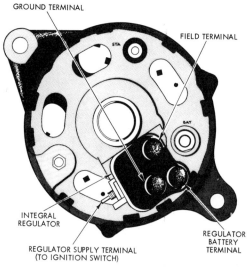

Fig. 27. An alternator with an integral regulator.

blocking it. This is because the charging voltage is not high enough for this diode to zener. TR2 is off.

As the generator increases the charging voltage to approximately 14.5 volts, this voltage will be impressed on the zener diode causing it to drop its resistance and allow TR2 to have a complete emitter to base circuit. Now TR2 is turned on and TR2 emitter to collector current will apply reverse bias to TR1 causing it to be turned off. When TR1 is turned off, the alternator field circuit is opened. With field current turned off the generator voltage will also drop. This will cause the zener diode D2 to once again block current. This will turn off TR2 and allow forward bias to TR1 which will turn the alternator field on again. As TR1 is on, TR2 is off; when TR2 is on, TR1 is off. This cycle will be repeated rapidly to control charging voltage. The transistor arrangement can cycle on and off at speeds of 2000 times per second with ease.

Internally Mounted Transistor Regulators

These units are usually of the integrated circuit type. The internal operation of the transistors is basically the same as the externally mounted transistor regulators. The illustration shows two

Fig. 28. Another alternator with built-in integral regulator.

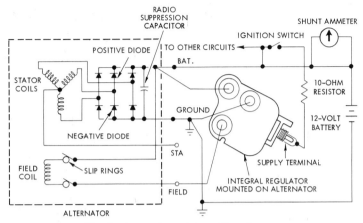

Fig. 29. Integral regulator wiring diagram.

typical regulator arrangements. Figs. 27, 28. In particular, it is very important to note that the alternator field circuit has been altered slightly. In other types of alternators, the field circuits are grounded within the alternators. When the transistor regulator is integral, however, the alternator field brushes are both insulated. This means that it is the type which has the field circuit grounded at the regulator (type A). Fig. 29.

Alternators which do not have integral regulators are Type B, internally grounded field.

General service to this type of transistorized regulator is not possible. No adjustments are possible. If the regulator malfunctions, it is to be replaced.

TRADE COMPETENCY TESTS

1. What has brought about the adoption of alternating current generating systems?

2. Can you describe the construction of an alternator?

3. How is the alternating current produced by the alternator converted into direct current?

4. What is the function of the regulator in alternating current systems?

5. What are the advantages of an alternator over a DC generator?

6. What are the major units which make up an alternator?

7. How is the field coil in the rotor energized?

8. How is increased output brought about in an alternator?

9. What is a diode and what is its purpose?

10. Can you explain the stages or steps in alternator rectification?

11. What is inductive reactance, and how is it brought about in an alternator?

12. Why isn't a cut-out relay needed in an alternator charging system?

13. How is voltage control obtained?

14. What is the function of the field relay and how does it work?

15. What are the two types of transistorized regulators?

16. Explain the basic transistor operation in the transistor regulator.

CHAPTER 9

AC CHARGING
SYSTEMS SERVICE

An alternator that is not producing electricity will result in the indicator light remaining on when the engine starts. In most cases when this happens the alternator is not revolving because of a defective drive belt or the alternator unit is faulty. A malfunctioning regulator can also cause a no charge situation.

When the different components which make up the battery charging system appear to be functioning but the battery is consistently undercharged or is overcharging (indicated by the excessive use of water) or light bulbs are continually burning out, a series of tests should be performed in order to isolate the trouble so correction can be made. The most common problem encountered is a consistently undercharged battery. For this reason one of the first tests to make is an alternator output test. The regulator cannot limit effectively if the alternator is not producing at its rated output nor can the battery be kept fully charged. When any abnormal condition exists it is always advisable to make a complete series of inspections and tests.

In thoroughly diagnosing the charging system the following tests and inspections should be performed. The battery condition is checked to find out if it can accept and hold a charge. The alternator output is measured to see if the alternator is capable of producing the specified voltage and amperage. A field relay check is made to be sure the unit is permitting full voltage to flow to the rotor field coil when the engine is operating. The voltage limiter must be operating properly to hold the output within specifications. Circuit resistance must be held to a minimum. A regulator limits voltage according to resistance created by the battery as it becomes charged. Any abnormal resistance in the circuit will therefore affect limiting.

A visual inspection is also important. Before making any tests, check for corroded battery cable connections, road dirt, salt, or electrolyte on the battery top. Check the alternator drive belt for tension and glaze. All connections must be clean and tight.

Alternator testing basically requires the same equipment needed for generator-regulator testing. This includes a jumper wire, ammeter, voltmeter, $\frac{1}{4}$ ohm fixed resistor, a battery post adapter, and a carbon pile variable resistor. A tachometer can be used to make sure the engine is operating fast enough when testing. The individual units can be used independently, however, many manufacturers make available an ammeter, voltmeter, and resistor unit (AVR) which is the most commonly used type of tester for regulator and alternator work.

Certain precautions must always be exercised when servicing an alternator because of the method of inserting the alternator into the battery circuit. Always disconnect the battery ground cable before removing the wire from the alternator output (Battery) terminal. There is no cutout relay in the circuit, therefore the output terminal is always hot whether the ignition is on or off. Grounding the output terminal or lead wire can result in a burned wiring harness or damaged alternator. Do not short across or ground any of the terminals on the regulator or alternator. Never operate the alternator with an open circuit, as might occur if a battery cable is disconnected while the engine is running. Always make certain the ground polarity of the battery and the ground polarity of the alternator is the same when installing a battery.

CHARGING SYSTEM DIAGNOSIS

The most common problem is a low or undercharged battery which results in a slow cranking engine plus hard starting. Headlights that are dim at engine idle also are an indication of a partially discharged battery.

One of the things that can be readily checked is the alternator drive belt. A belt that is glazed, worn, or loose may slip, and the alternator will not be able to operate at maximum charging speed. Check the belt for fraying, cracks, glaze, wear, and tension. If the belt is damaged, replace it with a new belt and adjust to the correct tension. If the belt is merely loose, adjust to the correct tension.

To replace or adjust the belt loosen the alternator mounting

Fig. 1. Checking belt tension with a gage.

bolts and adjusting arm bolt. Move the alternator toward or away from the engine until the correct tension is obtained. Two methods of checking and adjusting belt tension can be used. The best method is to use a belt tension gage. Install the gage on the drive belt, Fig. 1, and check the tension according to the manufacturer's instructions. A second method is the deflection method. When this method is used, press down with the thumb on the belt, in the center of the greatest span from the pulleys. The belt should not deflect in excess of 1/4" when pressure is applied with the thumb.

When there is any question about the condition of the battery, make a light load test. An expanded voltmeter having a range from 0-3 volts, Fig. 2, is needed for this type of test. To make the test

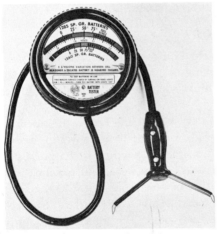

Fig. 2. Expanded voltmeter used for light load test of battery, ranges in reading from 0 to 3 volts.

operate the cranking motor for approximately 3 seconds, if the engine starts, shut it off immediately. Turn the headlights on and wait one minute before beginning the test. Leave the headlights on while testing each cell. A sufficiently charged good battery will have a reading of 1.95 volts a cell and the difference between cells of less than .05 volts. Any time there is more than .05 volt difference between the cells, the battery should be replaced.

Two methods of checking alternator output and voltage setting are given. One method of testing involves the use of a separate ammeter and a voltmeter. The preferred method, where it is possible to have a controlled load on the battery as well as simulating a fully charged battery, involves the use of an ammeter, voltmeter, and resistance units.

Checking Alternator Output—1st Method

To check alternator output when using only an ammeter and voltmeter, disconnect the ground cable from the battery. Remove the battery lead from the alternator terminal. Connect one lead of the ammeter to the battery lead which was just removed. Connect the other ammeter lead to the battery terminal of the alternator. Connect a voltmeter across the battery terminals. Remove the regulator leads (battery and field) or connector if leads terminate as a push-in connector and connect a jumper wire between the battery lead and alternator field terminal. (A+ to F, #3 to F, Battery to field). This energizes the rotor field coil directly from the battery bypassing the regulator. Install the battery ground cable. Start the engine and operate at 2,000 rpm's or more.

Checking Alternator Output—2nd Method

When a regulator test (AVR) unit is to be used, disconnect the ground terminal from the battery ground post. It will be assumed that the charging system has a negative ground. A battery post adapter should be installed as it makes the insertion of an ammeter into the circuit convenient and safe. The instructions which follow are for connecting a commonly used type of generator-alternator regulator test unit. Always consult the manufacturer's instruction for the particular test unit being used.

Remove the insulated battery terminal from the battery post (this is the positive post in most cases on today's automobiles). In-

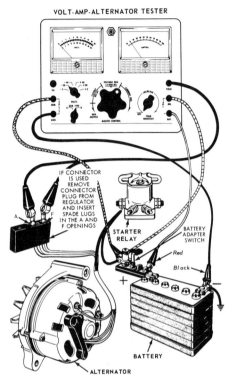

VOLT-AMP-ALTERNATOR TESTER

IF CONNECTOR
IS USED
REMOVE
CONNECTOR
PLUG FROM
REGULATOR
AND INSERT
SPADE LUGS
IN THE A AND
F OPENINGS

A   F

STARTER
RELAY

BATTERY
ADAPTER
SWITCH

Red

Black

+

BATTERY

ALTERNATOR

OUTPUT TEST

Fig. 3. Hook-up for alternator output test.

stall the battery post adapter onto the battery post, and the battery cable on the cable connector of the adapter. See Fig. 3. Connect the voltmeter leads across the battery terminals, negative lead to the battery negative post and the positive voltmeter lead to the positive battery terminal. Connect the ammeter regulator lead to the insulated (positive) battery cable. Connect the battery lead of the ammeter to the positive battery post. Install a jumper wire between the battery positive and the alternator field terminal. This can also be easily done at the regulator connector. Place the jumper in A+ to F or #3 to F, according to type of regulator designations. Fig. 3 illustrates the hook-up for making an alternator output test. Make sure the field resistance regulator (field rheostat) is in open position (maximum counterclockwise position). Reconnect the battery ground cable. Close the battery adapter switch and start the engine.

Open the battery adapter switch. Make sure all electrical accessories are turned off. Run the engine at approximately 2,000 rpm's. Adjust the field resistance control until the voltmeter reads output voltage.

Test Results and Conclusions

Observe the ammeter reading. Add 5 amperes to the reading to compensate for ignition and alternator field draw and compare the reading to the manufacturer's output specification. Do not allow the output to exceed 16 volts. If the alternator output does not meet specifications it must be removed from the vehicle for service.

If the output was high and then dropped back to a lower value, recheck to be sure the belt tension is properly adjusted.

An output amperage reading from 2 to 5 amperes below specifications usually indicates an open diode. A reading of 10 amperes below specifications usually indicates a shorted diode. There will usually be a noticeable whine in the alternator, particularly at low speeds, when there is a shorted diode.

With a fully charged battery it may not always be possible to get the specified amperage reading. Before condemning the alternator, turn the field resistance control to the maximum counterclockwise position. Rotate the front center control knob to the current regulator load position. Turn both the field resistance control and the center resistance control clockwise, maintaining a voltmeter reading of 12 volts, until the field resistance control is at its maximum clockwise position. With Method 1, to place a load on the battery, turn on all accessories and lights. Observe the ammeter reading. Stop the engine and turn the tester controls off and disconnect all test leads if the alternator needs to be repaired. If the output meets specifications, it indicates the regulator is faulty.

CIRCUIT RESISTANCE TESTS

Excessive resistance in the charging system can cause high voltage to develop. A voltage drop test should be performed to check for a high resistance in the insulated circuit (positive) and the ground circuit (negative). Loose or corroded connections are the common reason for such a problem. To check the insulated circuit, connect an expanded scale 0-3 range voltmeter lead to the alternator output terminal, and the negative lead to the positive battery post. It may be necessary to jab a sharp prod into the battery post and clip the voltmeter lead to the prod. Operate the engine at a fast idle speed. If the voltmeter reads over 0.3 volt, there is excessive resistance in the circuit. Remove, clean, install and retighten each connection between the alternator output terminal and the positive battery post. To check the ground circuit, connect the negative voltmeter lead to the alternator frame and the positive lead to the negative battery post. Operate the engine at a fast idle and observe the voltmeter scale. A reading of over .1 volt indicates a high resistance in the ground circuit. Remove, clean, install and retighten all ground connections between the alternator and battery negative post.

Checking Voltage Limiter

A fully charged battery should always be used when testing and adjusting the voltage limiter. Before making any limiter tests, operate the engine for approximately 20 minutes to normalize the regulator (bring it up to operating temperature). Use a regulator thermometer to measure the ambient temperature. In every case manufacturer's specifications should be followed relative to alternator output and ambient temperature.

Table 1, showing the relationship between ambient temperature and voltage setting, is an example of the effect temperature has on voltage setting.

To check the voltage limiter setting the same basic hook-up is used as for the output test except that the field control unit is not involved. The voltmeter is connected across the battery terminals, positive lead to positive battery terminal on the adapter, and negative (or ground) voltmeter lead to the negative battery terminal. The battery lead of the ammeter is attached to the positive battery post and the ammeter regulator lead is attached to the battery ter-

TABLE 1. VOLTAGE REGULATOR SETTING
AND AMBIENT AIR TEMPERATURE

Ambient Air Temperature °F	Voltage Regulator Setting (Volts)
25	14.4 – 15.0
50	14.3 – 14.9
7.5	14.1 – 14.7
100	13.9 – 14.5
125	13.8 – 14.4
150	13.6 – 14.2
175	13.5 – 14.1

minal lead of the battery adapter, Fig. 4. The voltage limiter test is made with the regulator at normal operating temperature, and the regulator cover in place. Make sure all accessories are turned off. Close the battery adapter switch and start the engine. Open the adapter switch. Run the engine at approximately 2,000 rpm's while making the test. Turn the center control knob to the cutout relay position. If the ammeter reads more than 10 amperes, the battery must be charged before continuing the test. Always remove the battery cables from the battery while it is undergoing a charge. With a fully charged battery, rotate the center control knob from the cutout relay to the ¼ ohm (Voltage Regulator) position. The ammeter should read less than 2 amperes. Cycle the regulator by rotating the tester control knob from the direct position to ¼ ohm position a couple of times. This tends to remove residual magnetism from the

VOLT-AMP-ALTERNATOR TESTER

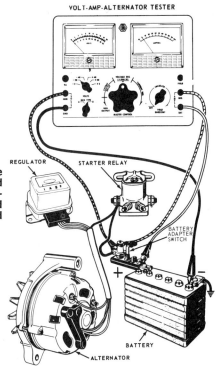

Fig. 4. Hook-up for checking voltage limiter setting, eliminating field control unit shown in Fig. 3. Regulator operating temperature should be normal, its cover in place, and all accessories turned off.

VOLTAGE LIMITER TEST

limiter unit eliminating a possible improper voltage limiter reading. Allow the battery to normalize for a short time and then read the voltmeter and thermometer.

The voltage should be within specifications, according to the ambient temperature, if not, make a voltage limiter adjustment. After each adjustment, the regulator must be cycled. Always make all checks with the regulator cover in place.

The regulator should be operating on the ground (shorting) contact points since the $\frac{1}{4}$ ohm resistor unit simulates a fully charged battery and the engine speed is high enough so that alternator output should be at its maximum. If the limiter is operating at the specified voltage, or if adjusting the armature spring tension brings the output to its specified reading, no further testing is needed.

If the battery does not remain charged, is overcharging, or it is impossible to obtain the proper reading through adjustment, it might be well to check the regulator further and make sure it is operating correctly on the set of contact points which are connected to the battery. To check the voltage difference, at which the regulator cuts back and begins to limit on the armature and battery connected set of contact points, slowly increase the resistance of the variable resistor, while operating the engine at approximately 1500 rpm's, until the regulator begins to limit on the other set of contacts. It is possible to determine when the transition takes place by watching the voltmeter; there will be a flicker in the meter reading and a change in the reading of from 0.2 to 0.7 volts. If the voltage change is not within limits, the core-to-armature air gap of the limiter must be adjusted. If increasing the resistance to the capacity of the variable resistor does not bring about the change, turn on the headlights for an additional load. A better method of determining when the transition takes place, is to use a set of earphones connected from the regulator field terminal to ground. As the resistance is increased, the vibrating sound will fade away, and then be heard after the change takes place. Removing the regulator cover and observing the change is another method, but the voltage readings will not be accurate while operating with the cover removed. Most manufacturers now specify that the regulator be replaced if the voltage settings do not fall into specified limits. If adjustment is to be attempted be sure to use a shop manual for the particular regulator involved. Each regulator has a slightly different procedure which is extremely sensitive and time consuming. Consequently it is more economical to replace the regulator if it does not meet specifications.

Field Relay Test

The field relay permits electricity to flow to the rotor field coil as soon as the ignition switch is turned on. The contact points in the field relay should close permitting full line voltage from the battery to flow into the rotor field coil. Correct adjustment is essential so that the relay coil may be fully energized when the output voltage reaches a predetermined amount.

If the vehicle uses an ammeter, the field relay will close when the ignition switch is turned on. Operation of the relay can be checked by removing the cover of the regulator and observing the point action at the relay as the ignition switch is turned on and off. If the relay points open and close it is not necessary to go any further. If it does not operate, use a voltmeter to determine if the battery voltage is reaching the relay terminal. If voltage is at the terminal and the relay doesn't operate, the regulator should be replaced. If no voltage is at the field relay terminal, a careful check of the wiring will be necessary to locate the source of trouble. Normally, the field relay gives no trouble at all. When the vehicle uses an indicator lamp, the field relay does not close when the ignition switch is closed. Instead only a small amount of current is supplied to the field (rotor) to allow the indicator light to operate. Fig. 5.

When the alternator begins to operate it will produce a voltage at the stator or relay terminal of the alternator. This voltage is applied to the field relay and causes it to close. This fully energizes the alternator field circuit and also causes the indicator to go out.

To test the field relay, disconnect the leads from the regulator. Remove the regulator cover. Use the same test unit that was used for the other tests and connect the positive voltmeter lead to the field relay terminal of the regulator. Ground the negative voltmeter lead to the regulator base. Connect a lead between the regulator base and the negative battery terminal. Connect one lead of the test unit field resistance control to the regulator field relay terminal. Attach the other field resistance control lead to the positive terminal of the battery. Fig. 5. Slowly turn the field resistance control knob clockwise from the off position and note the voltage at which the contact points close. If the closing voltage is not within manufacturer's specifications, adjust the relay.

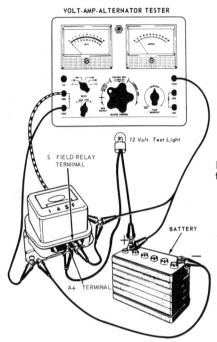

VOLT-AMP-ALTERNATOR TESTER

12 Volt Test Light

S FIELD RELAY
TERMINAL

BATTERY

A+ TERMINAL

FIELD RELAY TEST

Fig. 5. Field relay test using indicator light.

Voltage Limiter Adjustments

When alternator output meets specifications and the charging system is in a functional condition but the battery is consistently undercharged, or in a few cases overcharged, the voltage regulator (limiter) is generally at fault. As previously stated, the purpose of the regulator is to limit the charging rate according to the demands of the electrical load and the state of charge of the battery.

The only service that can ordinarily be done to the regulator is to clean the contact points. This should be done only when there is a constant fluctuation or erratic voltage reading which will be indicated when checking the voltage setting. As the contact point material of the voltage limiter is soft, a file should not be used to clean the points. A strip of #400 silicon paper or its equivalent, folded with the abrasive side out and pulled back and forth between the contact should provide the necessary cleaning. After cleaning, wash the contact surfaces with alcohol or carbon tetrachloride. In the case of the field relay contact points, a clean fine cut file may be used to remove a small amount of point material, if the surface is oxidized or rough. Never use emery cloth or sandpaper to clean any contact points. The contact point surfaces must be kept clean.

Three adjustments can be made to most voltage limiters, namely: armature spring tension, air gap (distance between the armature and voltage winding core) with the lower contacts touching, and point opening (distance between the upper contact and armature) when the lower contact points are touching. In most cases, the only adjustment the voltage limiter will require, in order to perform in a satisfactory manner, is to change the armature spring tension setting.

Voltage Setting. Always refer to the manufacturer's specifications whenever any adjustments are to be made. As removing the regulator cover usually changes the voltage reading, calculate how much of a change is necessary to bring the setting within the specified limits before removing the cover, and use this figure when changing spring tension, rather than the total final reading.

Increasing armature spring tension increases the voltage limiter rating. Decreasing armature spring tension lowers the voltage rating. The spring tension is changed on some regulators by bending the spring hanger, Fig. 6. Bending the hanger up, lowers the voltage setting, down increases voltage setting. It is advisable to use a bending tool as shown in Fig. 6. Wrapping tape around the tool eliminates the danger of creating a short circuit should the tool come in contact with metal parts. It is only necessary to move the hanger a small amount in most cases. The regulator unit illustrated in Fig. 7, has an adjusting screw located on the spring holder. With this arrangement, turning the screw clockwise increases voltage, counterclockwise decreases voltage. Always make the final setting by turning the screw clockwise, so that the spring holder is against the screw head. If the screw must be turned counterclockwise, turn it beyond the required amount, pry the holder up against the screw head and then turn the adjusting screw clockwise until the correct setting is reached. After making the correction, reinstall the regulator cover and check the voltage.

Point Opening. If the unit cannot be adjusted to the correct specifications or the voltage difference between operating on the

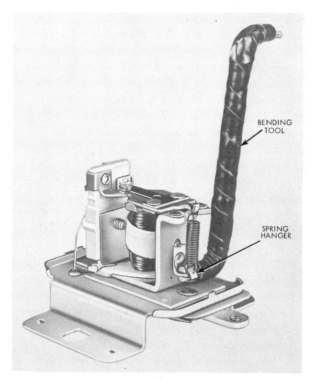

Fig. 6. Altering spring tension by bending spring hanger with tape-wrapped bending tool.

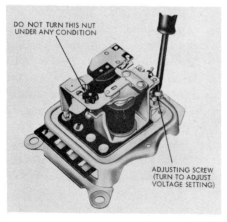

Fig. 7. Regulator unit with adjusting screw on spring holder. Turning this screw alters voltage.

upper contact points and lower contact points is not within specifications, it will be necessary to check the contact point gap and the core to armature gap. Specifications will indicate whether the point gap measurement is made at the upper or the lower contact points.

On one model of a regulator, in order to measure the contact point opening, it is necessary to lightly press the bottom armature contact against the bottom stationary contact point. Measure the air gap between the upper stationary contact point and the top armature contact with a feeler gage, Fig. 8. Bend the upper contact point arm up or down to obtain the correct gap. Make sure the contact points are properly aligned.

On some regulators, the point gap specification is given for the bottom point gap. With the upper contacts touching, measure

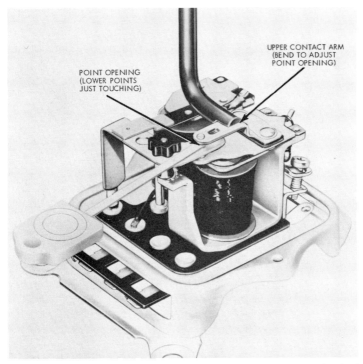

Fig. 8. Measuring contact point opening with feeler gage. Point opening is then adjusted by bending upper contact arm.

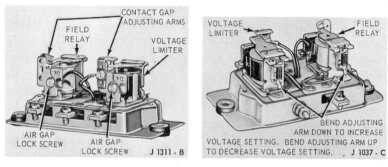

Fig. 9. Adjusting slot in lower contact point bracket on some regulators. By loosening the lock screw the entire bracket may be moved to obtain the correct core gap.

the distance between the bottom armature point and the bottom stationary contact with a feeler gage. Some regulators will have an adjusting slot in the lower contact point bracket, Fig. 9. If this is the case, loosen the lock screw ¼ turn and move the stationary contact arm up or down by inserting a screw driver in the slot, until

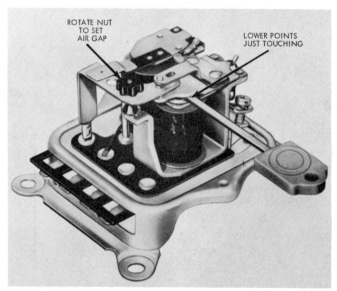

Fig. 10. Regulator with nylon adjusting nut on contact support.

the correct gap is obtained. Tighten the lock screw. If no slot is present in the stationary contact mounting, it will be necessary to bend the stationary contact bracket to obtain the correct gap.

Air Gap. One model regulator uses a nylon adjusting nut located on the contact support, Fig. 10 to control the air gap between the armature and voltage limiter core. Measure the gap with the lower contact just touching. Turn the nylon nut to obtain the correct gap setting. On another type of regulator, measure the gap between the armature and core with the upper contact points touching. If adjustment is necessary and there is an adjustment slot in the stationary contact mounting bracket, loosen the lock screw and move the entire bracket up or down to obtain the correct core gap. (Fig. 9)

With the regulator unit containing only a voltage limiter, con-

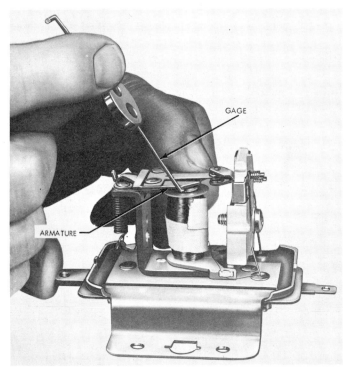

Fig. 11. Regulator unit containing only voltage limiter may be adjusted after testing with feeler gage and test lamp.

nect a small dry cell test lamp in series with the regulator FLD. and IGN. terminals. Insert a feeler gage of the correct thickness between the armature and core, Fig. 11. Press down on the armature, not the contact spring (reed). The upper contacts should just open, and the light should glow dimly. Insert a .004″ larger feeler gage and press down on the armature until it contacts the feeler gage. The light should remain bright. If adjustment is necessary, loosen the stationary contact point bracket and move it up or down.

FIELD RELAY ADJUSTMENTS

If it is necessary to change the field relay voltage setting, there are three adjustments which can be made, namely: the air gap, the contact point opening and the armature tension. Changing armature tension on the contact points, in most cases, will result in obtaining the correct closing voltage.

To change armature tension, use a bending tool and move the armature frame up or down to obtain the specified voltage reading, Fig. 12. If adjusting the armature tension does not bring about the correct closing voltage reading, check the air gap. Insert a feeler gage of the specified thickness between the field relay coil core and the armature, with the contact points just touching, Fig. 13. The air gap is changed in this particular regulator by bending the flat contact support spring. In the case of the regulator illustrated in Fig. 12, the air gap is changed by bending the contact post arm.

After adjusting the air gap, measure the contact point opening by inserting a feeler gage of the specified thickness between the contacts, Fig. 14. Adjust the contact point opening by bending the

Fig. 12. Changing air gap by bending contact post arm.

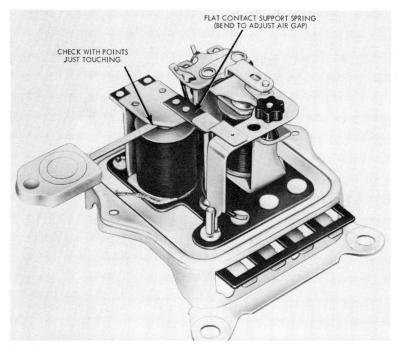

Fig. 13. Checking air gap by inserting feeler gage between field relay coil core and armature.

armature stop. The field relay illustrated in Fig. 14, does not have a separate adjustment for the contact point gap. Adjusting the air gap controls the point opening.

Tailoring Voltage Limiter Setting

Sometimes, with the limiter operating as specified, the battery remains undercharged or overcharged. An indication of overcharging is excessive use of battery water. A normal battery should not use over 1 ounce of water per cell per 1,000 miles. These conditions may be the result of underhood temperatures, the type of driving, excessive nighttime service or many other variables.

If no abnormal circuit conditions exist, and the battery is consistently undercharged, raise the voltage setting by 0.3 volt and check for an improved battery condition over a reasonable length of time. If the battery is overcharging, lower the setting by 0.3 volt and check

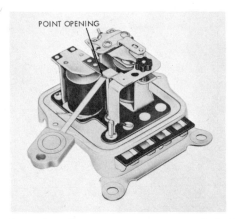

POINT OPENING

Fig. 14. Field relay having contact point gap and air gap adjusted by the same screw.

for reduced water usage over a period of time. Do not go beyond the recommended limits for the particular temperature range.

Indicator Light

The charge indicator light should come on when the ignition switch is turned on and go off as soon as the alternator begins to charge. Trouble in the charging system will usually show up by faulty indicator light operation.

If the light fails to come on when the ignition switch is turned on, check for a burned out bulb or fuse; then check the field relay unit. If the light stays on with the ignition switch turned off, check for a shorted positive alternator diode.

If the indicator light fails to go out when the engine is running, the trouble is either in the field relay or the alternator. Connect a voltmeter between the lead and alternator relay terminal. Operate the engine at a fast idle. Observe the voltmeter reading. If the voltage reading is 5 volts or more, either the relay is defective or the lead from the terminal to the relay is open. Check the lead with a test lamp. If the voltmeter reading is less than 5 volts, the trouble is in the alternator.

Sometimes feedback from the charge indicator light circuit to the accessory terminal of the ignition switch can cause an alternate flashing of the oil pressure warning light and the charge indicator light with ignition switch off. A shorted positive diode also can cause the battery to discharge through the field circuit because this will cause the field relay to be closed with the ignition switch off.

ALTERNATOR SERVICE

If the alternator output does not meet specifications, it should be removed from the vehicle for testing and servicing. Disconnect the battery ground cable at the battery post to prevent the leads from shorting and burning the wiring harness while being removed. Remove the leads from the alternator terminals. Remove the adjusting arm bolt and loosen the mounting bolts. Move the alternator toward the engine, until the belt can be removed from the pulley. Remove the mounting bolts and lift out the alternator.

Check the Field Coil Amperage Draw

The field coil amperage draw tests can be made with the alternator on or removed from the vehicle. Connect a test ammeter positive lead to the positive post of a fully charged battery. Connect one end of a jumper wire to the negative battery post and the other end to the alternator field terminal. Connect the negative ammeter lead to the alternator case, Fig. 15. Slowly rotate the rotor and check the amperage reading. A current flow, considerably above specifications,

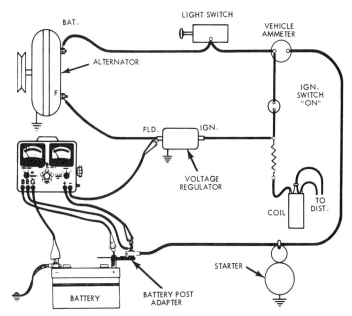

Fig. 15. Checking field coil amperage draw.

CONTACT
HEAT SINK

CONTACT EACH
TERMINAL

Fig. 16. Checking diode by means of alternator diode tester. Reading should be the same for all diodes.

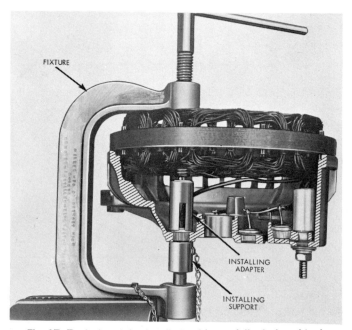

Fig. 17. Replacing defective diode with specially designed tool.

indicates a ground in the coil or the brush leads are touching ground or each other. Little or no current flow indicates the field or brushes have a high resistance or are open. If the test shows there is an open or short circuit and the brushes or brush holders are not at fault, the rotor assembly must be replaced.

Test the Diodes

Diodes may be checked electrically for an open or shorted condition, by using a 12 volt test lamp or an alternator diode tester. The alternator diode tester is more accurate and generally easier to use.

When using a test lamp disconnect the stator coils from the diodes. In some alternators, it may be necessary to cut the stator leads, if this is done make sure they are cut in such a manner that they can readily be soldered together again after all tests are completed.

Connect the test lamp leads across each diode, first in one direction and then in the other (ground and center lead). If the lamp lights in both directions the diode is faulty. The lamp should light when connected one way and not light when the leads are switched around the other way, if the diode is in satisfactory operating condition.

When using an alternator diode tester be sure to make the hook-up according to manufacturer's instructions. Fig. 16 illustrates an alternator tester used in checking a diode. As with the test lamp, there should be a meter reading, with the electrical flow in one direction and no reading with the electrical flow in the opposite direction. The meter reading should be the same for all diodes. The alternator must be disassembled if the diodes need replacement. A special tool is available for removing the defective diode and pressing in a new one, Fig. 17.

Disassemble the Alternator

One make of alternator has the insulated brush positioned vertically against one of the slip rings. To permit disassembly of the alternator without damaging the brush and holder assembly, remove the brush holder retaining screw, insulated washer, and field terminal. Lift out the holder and brush assembly, Fig. 18. Remove the ground brush by removing the retaining screw, and lift the clip, spring, and brush assembly from the end shield. Mark the end and

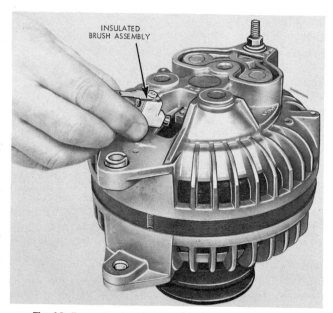

Fig. 18. Removing brush assembly from the end shield.

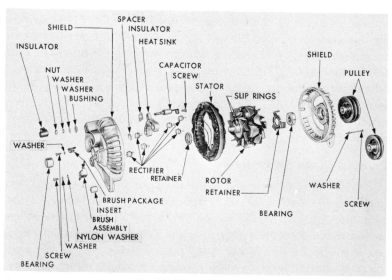

Fig. 19. Alternator parts.

center housing for alignment purposes when reassembling. Remove the through bolts and pry the assembly apart into three sections. Fig. 19 illustrates a disassembled alternator. In the case of most alternators, it will be possible to make all the necessary tests without further disassembly.

Test the Rotor

If a field coil test was made prior to disassembly and the test showed no abnormal conditions, further rotor testing would be unnecessary. If no tests were made, or upon checking an abnormal condition was indicated, further tests should be made. The rotor field coil is checked electrically for ground, short circuit, or open field coil. The tests may be made with a test lamp, preferably a 110 volt lamp or an ohmmeter.

To check for ground, connect one lead to a slip ring and the other lead to ground; if the lamp lights, or if the ohmmeter reading is low, the coil is grounded.

To check for an open circuit, connect one lead to each slip ring. If the lamp fails to light or the ohmmeter reading is high, the circuit is open.

To check for a shorted circuit, connect a 12-volt battery with an ammeter in series to each slip ring. Check specifications for the field amperage draw. The rotor assembly must be replaced if any abnormal condition exists. The pulley and end frame must be removed, if the rotor is to be replaced. A special puller is used to remove the pulley and end housing from the rotor shaft. If the slip rings are rough, grooved or worn, a light cut may be taken with a lathe to smooth and "true up" the surface. Do not remove any more material than is necessary to get a smooth surface. On one make of alternator the slip rings can be cut off and new ones pressed on if they cannot be remachined; however, it is generally advisable to replace the entire rotor assembly. Fig. 20 illustrates testing the rotor with an ohmmeter.

Test the Stator

Disconnect the stator leads from the diodes. It may be necessary to cut the wires. Be sure to cut the leads so they can readily be soldered back together after testing.

Check the stator for ground, by placing one test lead of a 110

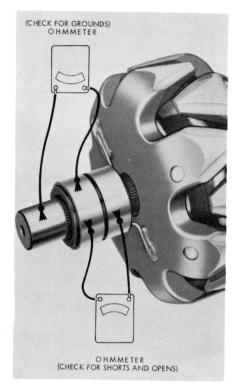

(CHECK FOR GROUNDS)
OHMMETER

OHMMETER
(CHECK FOR SHORTS AND OPENS)

Fig. 20. Rotor test using ohm-meter.

volt lamp or ohmmeter on one of the stator leads, and the other lead on the frame. If the lamp lights or the ohmmeter reading is low, the stator is grounded. Test the remaining two coils similarly.

To check for a continuous circuit, successively connect the test lamp leads or ohmmeter leads between all the stator leads. If the lamp fails to light or the ohmmeter reading is high, there is an open circuit in the stator winding and the stator must be replaced.

A short circuit in the stator windings is difficult to locate without special laboratory equipment. If all other electrical tests are normal and the alternator still fails to produce the rated output, a short circuit in the stator coils is indicated. Fig. 21 illustrates the testing of a stator.

Check the Brushes and Brush Holders

Use a test lamp to make sure one brush and holder is insulated

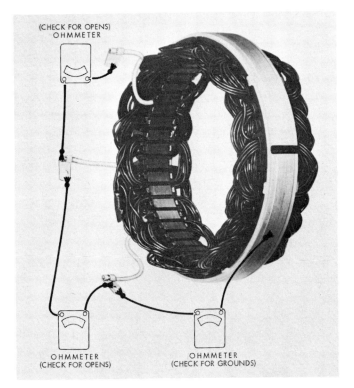

Fig. 21. Testing the stator coils for possible short circuit.

and the other brush holder is grounded. The brushes must be clean and move freely in the holder. Check the length of the brushes against specifications or compare with new brushes. Replace the brushes if they are worn. If there is any question about the brush springs having the necessary tension to hold the brushes solidly against the slip rings, install new springs.

If the brush holders have a small hole in the arm and matching holes in the end frame, when ready to assemble the unit, place a wire of the same size as the hole through the hole in the end frame and the hole in the brush holder arm. This will hold the brushes out of the way of the rotor during assembly. Remove the wire guides after the unit has been assembled.

Check the rotor support bearings for wear, roughness, or play.

Remove the bearing and replace with a new one if any wear, roughness or excessive play exists. These bearings are prelubricated and no attempt should be made to lubricate them. Replace the bearing if it is no longer lubricated.

The heat sink or diode plate containing the positive diodes is insulated from the frame, and normally should not be removed. If it must be removed, make sure all insulators are reinstalled correctly. Always check the plate with a test lamp to make sure it is insulated from the frame after reinstalling.

If a capacitor is used in the alternator circuit, always check against specifications for capacity, insulation, and ground, whenever the unit is disassembled for service.

Assemble the Alternator

After all the necessary tests have been conducted and corrections made, assemble the alternator. Install the brush assemblies if they were removed before disassembly. Install the alternator on the vehicle and adjust the drive belt to the correct tension, as given earlier in the chapter.

TRANSISTORIZED REGULATOR SERVICE

Externally Mounted Regulator

If this unit is defective it is recommended that it be replaced. Before condemning this type of regulator, a careful check of the other charging system components should be made.

The battery, connections, drive belt, and alternator should be

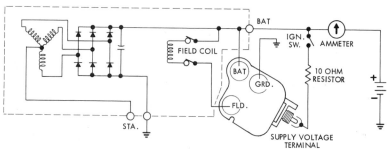

Fig. 22. Typical wiring diagram IC regulator circuit showing 10 ohm current limiting resistor. Autolite Div., Ford Motor Co.

in proper operating condition. These units can be tested as outlined earlier in this chapter.

A voltage regulator adjustment should only be made to keep the battery fully charged. No particular voltage is usually specified. Tailoring the voltage setting to keep the battery fully charged is a longer process. To do this, determine the state of charge of the battery. If it is undercharged, remove the pipe plug and turn the adjustment screw clockwise one click. This will increase the charging voltage .3 volt. The vehicle should be driven and the battery re-checked several weeks later to determine if the voltage setting is keeping the battery charged. Careful battery checking is essential with transistorized regulator diagnosis. A defective battery can lead to false conclusions about voltage settings.

Integrated Circuit Type Regulators

These units are very compact with all transistors, diodes, and resistors sealed in a plastic case. Electrical connections to the regulator are provided by the manner in which the regulator is mounted on the alternator.

The regulator cannot be repaired or adjusted. If voltage regulation is unsatisfactory, the complete regulator must be replaced with a new one.

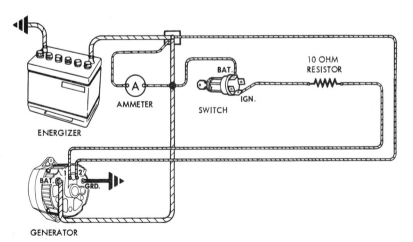

Fig. 23. Similar diagram again using 10 ohm resistor. Delco-Remy Div., General Motors Corp.

The alternators used with these regulators are different physically and electrically. The major electrical change is that no field brush is grounded. Both field brushes are insulated. One end of the field circuit is grounded in the regulator.

Provision is also made to supply battery voltage to the regulator to turn it on when the ignition switch is on. This voltage is sent through a 10 ohm current limiting resistor before it reaches the regulator. This is referred to as the supply voltage. Figs. 22, 23.

Operation of these regulators is started by turning on the ignition switch. This turns on the transistor in the regulator which sends current to the alternator rotor.

Voltage regulation is sensed by an internal regulator connection between battery and ground connections. This part of the regulator circuit is always on, but it draws so little current (3-5

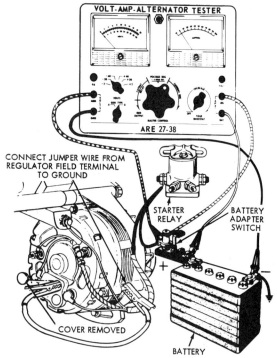

Fig. 24. **Connections for alternator output test—Integral Circuit Type.** Autolite Div., Ford Motor Co.

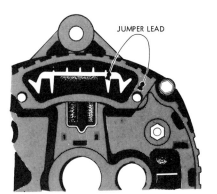

Fig. 25. Checking alternator output of integrated circuit type. Delco-Remy Div., General Motors Corp.

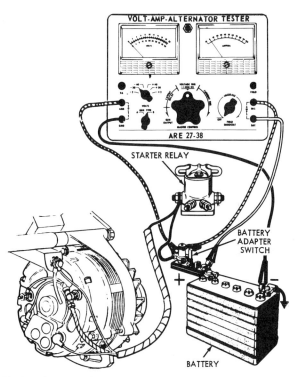

Fig. 26. Typical hook-up for voltage regulation test—transistorized regulator system (IC). Courtesy Autolite Div., Ford Motor Co.

milliamps) that there is not any discharge of the battery when the vehicle is shut off. However, because of this small drain, a battery drain test cannot be used. Note: a drain test involves connecting a voltmeter in *series* with the battery positive post and the positive cable. It is used to detect or diagnose battery discharging complaints.

Testing of this system involves the use of the same equipment as with conventional electro-mechanical regulators. The system should be checked only until the source of difficulty is located. All of these tests are not necessary and usually one or two will be sufficient. If the battery and wiring are good, the alternator should be tested for output. The alternator should produce its rated output plus 5 amperes for ignition and field current, at 2,000 rpm's. Note that the jumper wire is connected differently for the output test compared

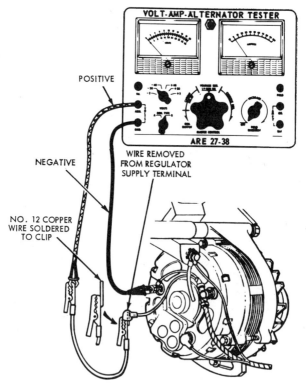

Fig. 27. Supply voltage test. Courtesy Autolite Div., Ford Motor Co.

to conventional alternators. The jumper wire is grounded to the frame of the alternator as shown in the illustrations Figs. 24, 25. If the alternator output is within specifications, a voltage regulator check can be performed. Fig. 26. The tester should show a current of 2 amperes or less, indicating a fully charged battery and the engine should be running at approximately 2,000 rpm's. If the battery is not fully charged, substitute a fully charged battery for this test. The jumper wire is not used. If the voltage is within specifications, (13.3 to 15.3) the regulator is not the problem. If the voltage is not up to specifications, then a supply voltage test should be made.

Supply Voltage Test

Fig. 27 shows the suggested method of measuring the supply voltage. The Delco unit supply voltage is measured at the number 1 terminal of the alternator. With the ignition switch turned on, a voltage reading should appear on the voltmeter. If no reading appears, there is an open in the supply circuit and a check must be made to locate this open. These tests are general and will locate most troubles very quickly. For exact procedures and specifications consult the manufacturer's service manual.

TRADE COMPETENCY TESTS

1. What checks are made to an alternator charging system that is not functioning properly?
2. What caution must be exercised when working around the battery and alternator?
3. How do you check and adjust belt tension?
4. Do you know how to make a light load battery test?
5. Why is it essential to eliminate any high resistance that may exist in the charging system?
6. How do you check alternator output, what equipment is necessary?
7. How do you cycle a regulator and why?
8. What is the difference in the charging rate when a voltage limiter operates on the upper set of contacts compared to operating on the lower set of contacts, why?
9. How do you test the field relay unit and what adjustments can be made?
10. What is the purpose of a field coil amperage draw test?
11. How do you check out a diode?
12. What tests can be made to a rotor?

CHAPTER 10

IGNITION
SYSTEMS

The operation of the gasoline engine is dependent upon the burning and expansion of the air-fuel mixture within each cylinder. The air-fuel mixture cannot burn or expand unless it is ignited by a spark produced by the ignition system.

The ignition system consists of a source of electrical energy (either the battery or charging system), ignition coil, condenser, distributor, ignition switch, low and high tension wiring, and the spark plugs. Fig. 1.

IGNITION SYSTEM

The function of the ignition system is to produce the high voltage current required for ignition and to direct the current to the spark plugs in the engine cylinders at the proper instant under all speed and load conditions. The ignition system has the job of taking 12 volts (or less) supplied by the storage battery or charging system and increasing it to the 5000, to 30,000 volts required to create a spark across the spark plug electrodes in the combustion chamber.

A typical ignition system must produce about 12,000 sparks for each mile that the vehicle is driven. About 200 sparks per second must be produced in a vehicle traveling 60 miles per hour. To realize what a tremendous job the ignition system has to perform it must be understood that each spark is the result of a complete cycle of events that transforms low voltage into high voltage and then delivers the high voltage to the proper spark plug at the right time. The ignition system is composed of two circuits, the primary circuit, and the secondary circuit, Fig. 2.

Primary Circuit

The primary ignition circuit receives low voltage current from

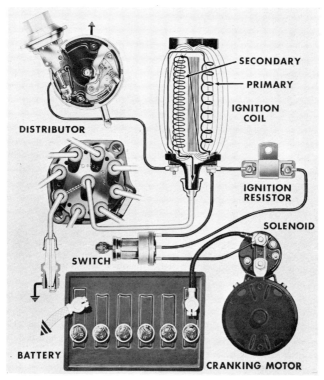

Fig. 1. Ignition system. Delco-Remy Div., General Motors Corp.

the storage battery or charging system. The circuit is composed of the ignition switch, resistance unit or resistance wire to the ignition coil, the primary winding in the ignition coil, the distributor breaker points, capacitor, and the low voltage wiring that connects these units.

The Secondary Circuit

The secondary ignition circuit consists of the secondary winding in the ignition coil, the coil to distributor secondary cable, the distributor cap and rotor, spark plug cables, and the spark plugs.

Ignition Wiring

The ignition system is wired with two types of wires. The primary circuit is wired with a low tension copper wire that has an

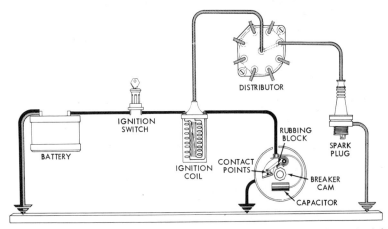

Fig. 2. Ignition system composed of two circuits: the primary circuit, to the left, consists of battery, resistance wire, ignition switch, primary winding in ignition coil, distributor contact points, capacitor, and low voltage wiring connections; the secondary circuit, at the right, includes secondary winding in coil, distributor, spark plugs, and cables.

oil and abrasion resistant covering. The terminals at the ends of the wire are usually soldered and the entire circuit is designed to offer low resistance to the flow of low battery or charging system voltage and current.

On the other hand, the secondary circuit wiring has a different job to do. The high tension ignition cables carry only a small amount of current but at a high voltage. Since about 1960, American vehicles have been equipped with resistance type secondary ignition cables in place of cables with a copper conductor. The electrical conductor in such cables consists of a multi-thread core impregnated with a carbon solution to give the desired conductivity, or a conductive rubber-like material. Both types of secondary wires act to suppress ignition radio noises. The cables have insulation that prevents leakage of high voltage, usually neoprene or rubber, and is designed to withstand the effects of heat, oil, and abrasion.

COMPONENTS OF THE IGNITION SYSTEM

Each of the components performs a specific function in its circuit. The ignition coil and the distributor each serve both the primary and secondary circuits.

Ignition Switch

When the ignition switch, Fig. 2, is turned on, it allows a low-voltage current to flow from the storage battery or charging system into the primary ignition circuit so that the engine can be started and operated. When the switch is turned off, the engine stops.

Ignition Coil

The coil is a pulse type of transformer that transforms or steps up the low voltage to the high voltage necessary to jump a spark across the gap at each spark plug.

The ignition coil, Fig. 3, is composed of a primary winding having about 200 turns of a relatively heavy wire, and a secondary winding of as many as 20,000 turns of a very fine wire wound in layers, each layer insulated from the others by waxed paper. The windings concentrate magnetic lines of force during operation by being wound over a soft iron core composed of thin strips of iron and enclosed with several layers of soft iron. This completes the

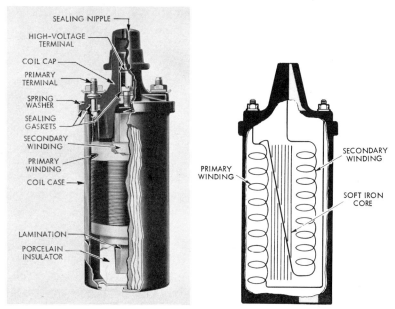

Fig. 3. Cutaway view (left) and internal wiring (right) of a typical ignition coil.
Delco-Remy Div., General Motors Corp.

magnetic circuit around the outside of the windings, reducing loss of magnetic lines of force.

Early ignition coil design had the primary coil wound on an iron core and the secondary wound over the primary coil, Fig. 3. The coil assembly is built into a metal case with a coil cap made of moulded insulating material which contains both primary and secondary terminals. One end of the secondary winding is connected to the primary winding inside the coil at the coil cap and the other end is connected to the center high tension terminal in the center of the cap. Most coils are oil-filled and hermetically sealed (airtight). The oil permits a rapid heat dissipation, provides greater insulation, and reduces the possibility of insulation failures. Other coils are filled with an asphalt base insulating material and hermetically sealed.

Ignition Coil Resistance Unit. One of the reasons for the 12 volt electrical system on automobiles in place of the 6 volt system is the need for better ignition in higher compression engines. The increased secondary voltages available from 12 volt systems are mainly the result of new ignition coil design which takes full advantage of the higher system voltage. The ignition coil has more turns of wire on the primary coil, more turns of wire on the secondary coil, and a higher number-of-turns ratio between the two as compared with 6 volt coils of the same size.

The greater number of turns of wire in the primary result in a higher inductance in the primary coil, which along with other changes, makes it possible for the coil to produce a higher secondary voltage output throughout the full speed range of the engine.

On vehicles with a 12 volt battery, the ignition system has a resistance in the primary circuit connecting the ignition switch with the primary coil winding, Fig. 1. The first vehicles with a 12 volt battery system used a separate resistance unit; today's vehicles all use a calibrated resistance (carbon core type) wire.

The purpose of the resistance is to limit to a safe maximum the amount of primary current flowing through the coil and distributor contact. When the engine is running the resistance reduces the battery voltage to the coil and distributor contacts to 7-8 volts. This reduced voltage protects the contact points at low engine speeds when the points are closed for longer intervals.

The resistance is bypassed during cranking, thus connecting the ignition coil directly to the battery. The direct connection permits maximum starting performance at low temperatures. The resistance is bypassed by means of a special terminal on the ignition switch or starting motor solenoid switch which is connected directly to the coil. This bypass makes full battery voltage available to the coil and keeps the ignition voltage as high as possible during cranking.

Capacitor

The function of the capacitor (condenser) is to reduce the arcing at the contact points, when the points first separate, by providing a place where the current can be stored until the points are completely separated. This action also aids in the rapid collapse of the magnetic field within the ignition coil so necessary for the development of high voltage in the secondary current.

The ignition capacitor is made up of two or more long sheets of tin foil separated from each other by an insulator (dielectic) in the form of waxed paper, Fig. 4. The unit is rolled into a cylinder and sealed in a small metal container. One sheet or plate of foil is connected to the metal case, and the other to a terminal wire projecting through the insulated cover on the case. Electricity cannot pass through the capacitor since there is no direct connection between the plates.

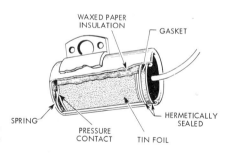

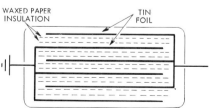

Fig. 4. Cutaway view of a capacitor (top) and a diagram of capacitor construction (bottom).

Ignition Distributor

The ignition distributor, Fig. 5, performs two major functions in the ignition system.

First, its breaker or contact points act as a switch to open and close the primary ignition circuit. When the points are closed, current flows through the ignition coil and builds up a magnetic field.

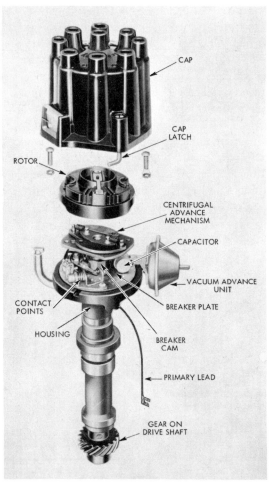

Fig. 5. Parts of distributor. Oldsmobile Div., General Motors Corp.

When the points are opened, current through the coil is stopped and the magnetic field collapses, creating a high-voltage current.

Secondly, the distributor distributes the high voltage current from the coil to the proper cylinder at the proper time to ignite the compressed air-fuel charge in the cylinder.

The distributor consists of a housing, a movable breaker plate upon which the contact points are mounted, a drive shaft with a breaker cam, a spark advancing mechanism, a rotor, and a cap. The distributor shaft and breaker cam are driven by the engine camshaft at one-half crankshaft speed. As the cam rotates, it opens and closes the contact points. The number of degrees of breaker cam rotation during which the contact points remain closed is known as the cam-angle or "dwell" period, Fig. 6. The cam has the same number of lobes as there are cylinders in the engine. Thus, in one revolution of the distributor cam (two revolutions of the crankshaft) the ignition coil produces a spark for each cylinder in the engine.

The contact point dwell period is important to the operation of the coil as it is during the period that the points are closed that current flows through the primary winding to build up its magnetic field. At low engine speeds the coil has sufficient time for maximum build-up. However, at high engine speeds the length of time that the points are closed may be too short for the coil to build up its maximum magnetic field. This could result in a loss of high tension voltage that would prevent the engine from developing full power. The contact dwell period increases as the point opening decreases and is reduced as the amount of point opening is increased.

Fig. 6. The rotating cam opens and closes the contact points. Amount of cam rotation while points remain closed constitutes "dwell" period.

Distributor with Dual Contacts. Some automobiles are equipped with a distributor having two sets of contact points. The arrangement of the dual contacts on the breaker plate creates an overlap between the opening and closing of the contacts, giving the primary coil a longer period of time (dwell period) to build up a strong magnetic field. Fig. 7.

The two sets of contacts are connected in parallel and are so positioned that one set of points closes the primary circuit to permit current to flow through the primary winding. The other set of points opens the circuit, causing the magnetic field to collapse and produce a high voltage spark. Immediately after the spark occurs the first set of points closes to complete the primary circuit, followed by the closing of the opposite set of points and the cycle is repeated.

Contact Points. The function of the contact points is to make and break the primary circuit at the proper instant to produce the necessary high voltage spark at the spark plugs. The contact points consist of two units: 1) a stationary contact connected to ground and 2) a movable contact attached to an insulated arm that pivots on a shaft mounted on the breaker plate, Figs. 5 and 7. The

Fig. 7. Distributors with dual contacts create overlap of opening and closing contacts; consequently, longer dwell period and stronger magnetic field result.

movable contact is connected to the coil primary winding. The movable contact arm has a rubbing block so that the arm will follow the distributor cam contour, which upon rotating makes (closes) and breaks (opens) the primary circuit. A flat spring on the arm closes the points. An adjustment is provided which permits moving the stationary contact to adjust the point clearance and dwell period.

While many materials, including some precious metals, have been tried as contact points, tungsten is almost universally used. The ignition contact performance is affected by contact spacing, bearing post friction and wear, spring tension, foreign material between the contact points, contact "bounce," oxidation, transfer of metal, contact alignment and rubbing block wear.

Proper contact point clearance is important, especially during starting and low speed operation. If the points have too little clearance arcing and burning occurs, this causes hard starting and poor low speed operation. If the points are set too wide, the cam angle or dwell period is too short to permit magnetic saturation of the coil at high speeds, resulting in a weak spark.

Spark Advance Mechanisms.

The high-voltage current from the distributor must produce a spark to ignite the fuel charge at all speed and load conditions. The timing of ignition and combustion must be regulated to produce the desired power with a minimum consumption of fuel. When ignition timing is advanced, the spark is made to occur earlier in the engine cycle, Fig. 8.

Factors Determining Ignition Timing. The combustion rate of the fuel, the engine speed and degree of compression, and the power developed are among the factors which determine ignition timing. Fuels vary in their rate of burning. Ignition should occur at an instant which allows complete burning of the fuel. The engine speed and load conditions determine the period of time over which the power stroke will occur. Therefore, ignition should be timed to match the engine speed and load conditions.

Idling. When the engine is idling, the spark is usually timed to occur in the cylinder just before the piston reaches top dead center. At low engine speeds, this gives the fuel mixture sufficient time to burn completely, and it permits the total pressure developed to be applied to the piston as it starts downward on the power stroke.

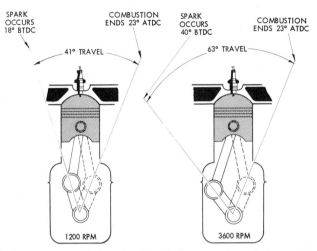

Fig. 8. Spark advance timing showing relation to engine rotation and speed.

Many engines today, in order to control exhaust emission levels as required by government regulations have the ignition timing set several degrees retarded so that the spark occurs after top dead center (ATDC).

Since the spark occurs later this permits more complete burning of the richer idle-air-fuel mixture. This causes a marked reduction in exhaust emissions at idle. It also requires a higher engine idle speed since retarded timing slows an engine. A wider throttle opening allows the engine to receive more air and thus has more time for combustion. Since timing is adjusted for emission control, the performance and economy of the engine will not be equal to non-emission engines. Other distributor modifications are made including a very precise centrifugal advance curve and a precise vacuum advance curve. These engines are specially redesigned to control emissions by reducing valve overlap. Combustion chambers are also changed to improve combustion.

The greatest change in the engine for emission control is during its low speed and idle range when a normally designed engine of the past was operating relatively rich. Special valves are sometimes used to control or reduce vacuum during periods of high manifold vacuum such as occurs during deceleration. Without these anti-backfire valves, high vacuum during deceleration would provide an over-rich mixture, and with retarded timing, backfiring in the intake manifold could take place.

At higher engine speeds, however, there is a shorter time interval available for the mixture to ignite, burn, and deliver its power to the piston. Therefore, if full power is to be obtained, the ignition system must distribute the high-voltage current to the spark plugs earlier in the engine cycle by advancing the spark.

Part Throttle. During part throttle operation, when maximum power is not demanded, compression pressures are lower and the rate of combustion is slower. Therefore, timing must be advanced for better combustion.

Full throttle at low speeds. During full or wide-open throttle at low speeds, when maximum power is demanded, a maximum fuel charge enters the cylinder so that higher compression takes place. The combustion rate is faster than during part-throttle operation at the same engine speed. Since less combustion time is required to produce maximum power, the ignition is advanced a smaller amount.

High Engine Speeds. As the engine approaches maximum speeds at full throttle, the timing must also be advanced. The timing during acceleration, however, is not advanced as far as at part-throttle operation. At maximum speeds, the throttle is fully open, but the time available for the power stroke to take place is reduced to a point where it is no longer possible to fill the cylinder with a full charge of air-fuel mixture. Compression is low because there is less mixture to compress. The rate of combustion is slower. Therefore, maximum timing advance is reached at this point.

Types of Spark Advance Mechanisms. Most distributors are constructed with both a centrifugal type advance mechanism and a vacuum controlled advance or pressure retard mechanism. Some distributors use only vacuum advance, employing both manifold vacuum and carburetor venturi vacuum.

Centrifugal advance. In many distributors, the centrifugal advance mechanism is located above the circuit breaker cam inside the rotor, Fig. 9 A. On others the centrifugal advance unit is located within the distributor housing below the breaker plate. Fig 9 B. The centrifugal type, Fig. 10, consists of an advance cam as part of the distributor shaft, a pair of advance weights, two springs, and a weight base (or weight-carrying) plate which is assembled to the dis-

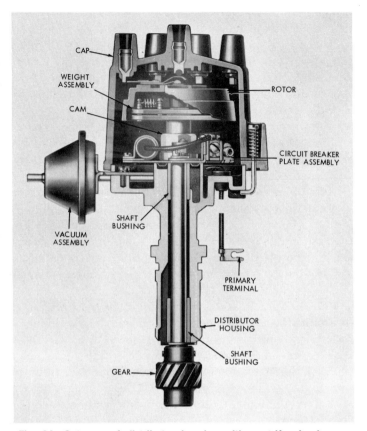

Fig. 9A. Cutaway of distributor housing with centrifugal advance mechanism *above* **circuit breaker cam.**

tributor cam. At idle speeds, the springs hold the advance weights, Fig. 10 A, so that there is no spark advance and the spark occurs in the cylinders according to the initial manual setting of the distributor. As the engine speed increases, centrifugal force causes the weights to gradually move outward against the spring tension, Fig. 10 B. Due to this motion the arms on the weights push against the advance cam, thus rotating the weight base' plate and the distributor cam ahead of its original position on the distributor shaft. In so doing, the spark is advanced and the distributor cam lobes open and close the contact points earlier in the compression stroke.

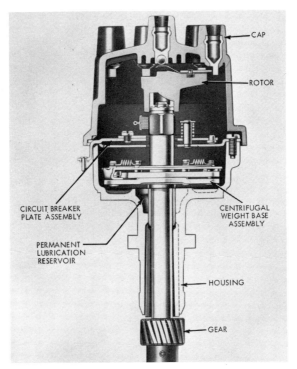

Fig. 9B. Cutaway of distributor housing with centrifugal advance unit *below* breaker plate assembly. Oldsmobile Div., General Motors Corp.

Vacuum Advance. Under part-throttle operation, there is a high vacuum in the intake manifold, as a result, a smaller amount of air-fuel mixture enters the cylinder. This mixture is less highly compressed and thus burns at a slower rate. Under such conditions, an additional spark advance beyond that already provided by the centrifugal advance mechanism will increase fuel economy.

The vacuum-advance unit consists of an airtight, spring-loaded diaphragm linked either to the distributor breaker plate or to the housing, Fig. 11. The airtight side of the diaphragm is connected by means of tubing to the carburetor air horn. This opening is on the atmospheric side of the throttle valve when the throttle is in idling position. During idle, no vacuum is imposed on the diaphragm, so the spring holds the distributor or breaker plate in the retarded position.

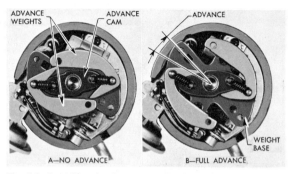

Fig. 10. Centrifugal advance mechanism viewed from the top of the distributor. In the full advance position, the weights have moved outward and rotated the base ahead of its original position. Buick Motor Div., General Motors Corp.

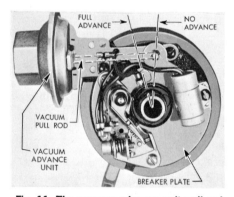

Fig. 11. The vacuum advance unit pull rod moves the breaker plate to automatically advance and retard the spark. Buick Motors Div., General Motors Corp.

When the throttle valve is opened slightly, the vacuum at the opening is sufficient to cause the diaphragm to compress the spring, and to rotate the breaker plate or distributor housing against the rotation of the breaker cam. This movement enables the contact points to open earlier on the compression stroke. The amount of throttle opening and the engine load determine the amount of intake manifold vacuum and, therefore, the amount of spark advance.

On some engines, the vacuum unit is connected directly to the intake manifold. With the engine idling, the high manifold vacuum results in full vacuum advance. When the throttle is opened for acceleration, or when the engine is under heavy load, manifold vacuum drops and the spring moves the breaker plate or distributor to the retarded position. As engine speed increases the manifold vacuum increases, advancing the spark.

There is usually some centrifugal advance beginning at engine crankshaft speeds of 900 rpm and above. The centrifugal advance will increase as engine crankshaft rpm increases. Vacuum advance will be added to the existing centrifugal advance depending upon throttle opening, Fig. 12. Thus, at part throttle operation, both mechanical and vacuum advance are present. At wide-open throttle position, there is usually no vacuum advance. The total ignition advance for any engine is the sum of centrifugal advance and vacuum advance.

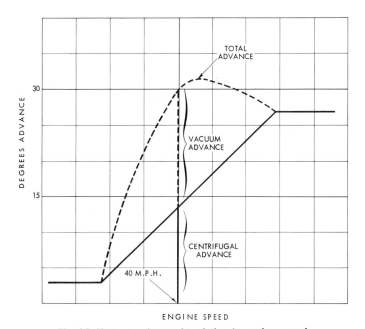

Fig. 12. Vacuum advance in relation to engine speed.

In yet another type of vacuum advance system the advance and retard movement of the breaker contact plate is controlled by the action of a vacuum actuated diaphragm working against the tension of two calibrated breaker plate springs, Fig. 13. The vacuum control unit is connected to the carburetor at two interconnected places, one connection being in the throat of the venturi and the other just above the closed throttle valve. A spark control valve located in the main carburetor body controls the vacuum (and the advance and retard) to the distributor under all speed and load conditions.

Some emission control engines have a dual advance and retard mechanism attached to the distributor. The retard diaphragm causes the ignition timing to be retarded approximately six degrees at idle speeds. Above idle, the retard unit does not influence timing.

Distributor Cap and Rotor. The function of the distributor cap and rotor is to take the high voltage current from the coil and connect it to the proper cap tower from where it goes to the corresponding cylinder. The distributor cap is usually made of a bakelite type insulating material with metal inserts cast into the cap towers to receive the spark plug wires. The metal inserts extend inside the

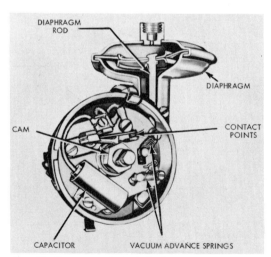

Fig. 13. Vacuum actuated diaphragm works against breaker plate springs to control advance and retard in breaker contact plate.

cap so that the rotor can provide a path between the center distributor cap coil terminal and the outer tower terminals at the time one of the spark plugs is ready to fire.

The rotor is made of insulating material and is mounted so that it rotates with the distributor cam. The rotor has a flat side which coincides with a flat side on the cam, keeping the rotor in proper relationship with the distributor cam. The rotor has a metal contact strip in contact with a carbon brush located in the center tower terminal which receives the high voltage wire from the coil. As the rotor revolves, it distributes the high voltage spark to the proper tower terminals and connected spark plugs.

OPERATION OF THE IGNITION SYSTEM

The construction and operation of the individual units which make up the ignition system have been described. To produce a high-voltage spark in the combustion chamber at the correct time and under proper conditions each unit must function in the correct relationship to the other units.

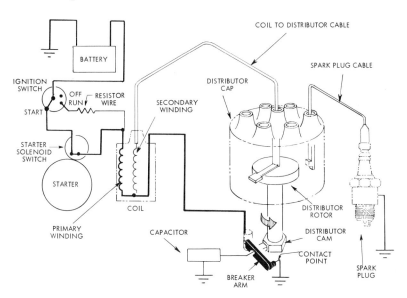

Fig. 14. Current flow in the primary ignition circuit during engine starting. While the ignition switch is in "start" position, current flows to the starter for cranking. Current bypasses the ignition resistor wire and flows directly from the starter switch and through the primary circuit.

When the ignition switch is turned to the "start" position, Fig. 14, a connection is made between the battery and the positive terminal of the ignition coil at the same instant that the starting motor begins to crank the engine. The completion of this circuit bypasses the resistance in the primary circuit, making the full battery voltage available to the coil during cranking. Once the engine starts, moving the ignition switch to the "on" position connects the resistance into the coil circuit thus limiting to a safe maximum the amount of primary current flowing through the coil and contact points.

When the contact points in the distributor are closed, Fig. 15, the battery or generator current flows through the primary winding of the ignition coil and through the contact points to ground. The flow of current through the primary windings of the coil creates a magnetic field around the coil windings, storing potential electrical energy in the coil. However, the current and magnetic field do not increase to their peak or full value instantly. It takes a small fraction of a second for this to occur; this is called build-up time. Fig. 16.

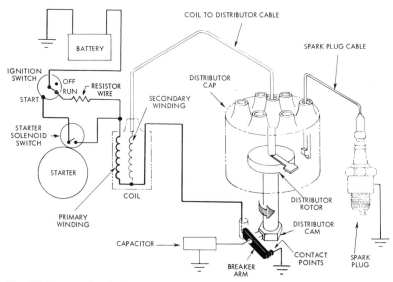

Fig. 15. Current flow in the primary ignition circuit while the engine is running. The ignition switch is in "run" position. Current now flows through the ignition resistor wire and then through the primary circuit and back to ground through the closed ignition contact points. Magnetic lines of force are built up in the ignition coil.

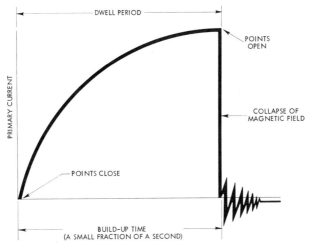

Fig. 16. Build-up time—time for flow of current with creation of magnetic field to build to peak or full value.

The reason for this build-up time is the reactance of the coil or the resistance of the coil to a change in current flow. It is a natural characteristic of a coiled wire to oppose any increase or decrease in the flow of current through the coil. If there is no current flowing, the coil will oppose the flow of current in it when connected to a source of voltage. This reactance is due to a self-induced voltage in the coil. While the magnetic field is being built up in the coil, the lines of force cut through the adjoining windings, inducing a voltage that opposes the battery voltage. The result is that it takes a small fraction of a second for the primary current in the coil to overcome the opposing voltage and reach its maximum magnetic strength, at which time the coil is said to be saturated.

When the distributor contact points begin to open, the current flowing in the primary circuit tends to continue flowing across the contact point gap. This again is due to reactance which not only opposed the build-up of current in the primary circuit but also opposes the stopping of current flow when the contact points open. As the contact points open the magnetic field within the coil starts to collapse, the lines of force cutting through the coil in the opposite direction from the coil build up. This again causes an induced voltage in the battery circuit and tends to keep the current flowing in the circuit. It is at this point that the capacitor comes into action.

The capacitor, being connected across (in parallel) the contact points, provides another path for the primary current. When the contact points open and the self-induced current tends to create an arc across the points, the capacitor absorbs the current until the contact points have opened sufficiently so that the arc can no longer occur.

Because of capacitor action, the flow of current in the primary comes to a sudden stop, Fig. 16. This causes a quick collapse of the magnetic field so that the lines of force readily cut through both the primary and secondary windings. The voltage induced in the primary may be as high as 250 volts and the secondary voltage may go as high as 25,000 volts. Fig. 17. The voltage actually developed is determined by the voltage required to cause the spark to jump across the spark plug gap, usually about 4000 to 6000 volts. The variations in voltage required are due to such variables as engine speed, compression, air-fuel mixture ratios, spark plug temperature, amount and shape of spark plug gap, etc.

Once the spark occurs, the energy stored in the coil in the form of magnetic flux drains from the coil through the secondary winding, sustaining the spark at the spark plug for several degrees of crankshaft rotation. After the spark occurs, the induced voltage in the coil decreases and the capacitor discharges back through the primary circuit, across the battery, and builds up in the opposite

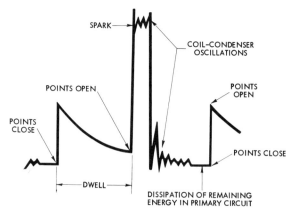

Fig. 17. Sudden collapse of magnetic field induces voltage in both coils.

plate of the capacitor. The current flow then discharges back in the opposite direction and recharges the opposite capacitor plate again. The current surges back and forth in the circuit, each time losing some energy in overcoming the circuit resistance until the oscillating action dies out, usually before the contacts close for the next spark build-up. One cycle from point opening to point closing at a speed of 30 miles per hour takes one one-hundredth of a second.

The high-voltage current developed in the secondary winding travels through the high-voltage cable connecting the coil secondary winding to the center of the distributor cap, through the rotor to the distributor cap segment in line with the rotor, from where it is conducted to the proper spark plug by the spark plug cables, Fig. 18. The high voltage jumps the gap between the spark plug electrodes producing the spark required to ignite the air-fuel mixture in the engine cylinder.

The use of the resistor type spark plug cables or resistor type

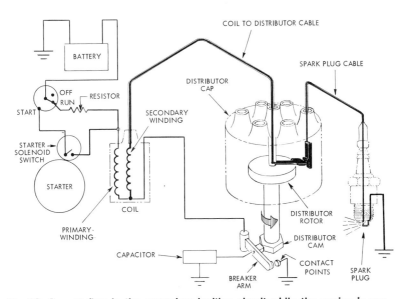

Fig. 18. Current flow in the secondary ignition circuit while the engine is running. The distributor cam opens the contact point, interrupting the flow of current in the primary circuit. The magnetic lines of force in the coil break down and induce a surge of high-voltage current in the secondary coil winding. The high-voltage surge travels to the distributor and through the rotor and spark plug cable to the spark plug. At the spark plug, the high-voltage current produces a spark by jumping the gap to the ground electrode.

spark plugs, because of their higher resistance to electrical flow, reduces the amount of surge which takes place. This helps to limit radio and television interference and reduces heat at the spark plug electrode so less spark plug electrode erosion takes place.

Spark Plugs

The spark plug, Fig. 19, provides a spark gap inside the engine cylinder. When the engine is operating, the high-voltage current produced by the ignition coil arcs across the gap and creates a spark

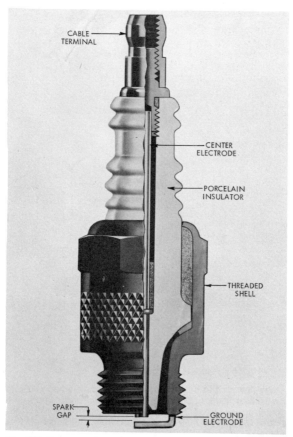

Fig. 19. Cutaway view of a spark plug. The electrodes provide the gap for the ignition spark.

that ignites the air-fuel mixture in the cylinder. The number of cylinders in an engine determines the number of spark plugs used.

Construction. The spark plug consists of three main parts: 1) a threaded metal shell with a ground electrode which is screwed into a hole in the cylinder head; 2) a porcelain insulator, and 3) the high-voltage or center electrode. Some spark plugs contain a special resistor built into the center electrode to eliminate radio and television interference. Others have a "booster gap" in the electrode that the spark must arc across before reaching the gap in the cylinder, reducing low temperature plug fouling encountered in some engines. The electrodes are made of nickel or nickel alloy to withstand the high temperatures encountered which may at times approach 1200°F. Spark plugs are usually adjusted to provide a gap of 0.030 in. to 0.035 in. between the electrodes. The spark plugs are assembled by means of gaskets and cement to provide a tight seal between the shell and the insulator.

Factors affecting spark plug operation. Spark plugs are designed to meet a wide variety of engine requirements, Fig. 20. Engine load

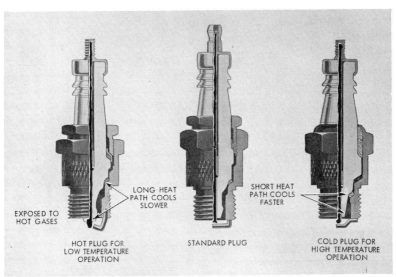

LONG HEAT PATH COOLS SLOWER

SHORT HEAT PATH COOLS FASTER

EXPOSED TO HOT GASES

HOT PLUG FOR LOW TEMPERATURE OPERATION

STANDARD PLUG

COLD PLUG FOR HIGH TEMPERATURE OPERATION

Fig. 20. There is a specific spark plug design for each type of engine operation.

and speed, air-fuel ratio, temperature, and type of fuel affect spark plug operation.

Spark plugs are classified according to a heat rating as "cold" or "hot," depending upon the length of the porcelain insulator within the spark plug shell. "Cold" plugs are generally used in heavy-load, high-speed operation where high temperatures are encountered. Lower speed, intermittent loading, and colder operating conditions require a "hotter" plug.

Certain additives in fuels, such as tetraethyl lead which is introduced into gasoline to change its combustion rate, will affect spark plug operation. When tetraethyl lead is used, oxides of lead will form at certain ratios and temperatures. At extreme temperatures, the oxides will be deposited on the porcelain insulator within the shell. Some conditions produce reverse effects where oxides are reduced and lead is deposited on the insulator. These deposits of oxides or lead can foul the plug. Fouling can cause misfiring and sometimes complete failure by shorting the plugs, preventing proper spark action. Fouling, shorting, and misfiring can be kept to a minimum by using spark plugs designed for the particular engine and operating conditions.

An important factor that affects the voltage required to jump across the spark gap is the polarity of the secondary system. Regardless of the polarity of the primary circuit, either positive or negative ground, the polarity of the secondary circuit is ALWAYS positive ground, and the spark jumps from the center electrode to the ground electrode. If the polarity is reversed (secondary circuit has a negative ground) a higher voltage will be required to cause a spark at the spark plug gap. This is because the center electrode is considerably hotter than the ground electrode and electrons flow much easier from a hot surface to a cold surface than from a cold to hot surface. Because electrons more readily leave a heated surface, less voltage is required to jump the spark gap.

TRANSISTORIZED IGNITION SYSTEMS

Each manufacturer will have a somewhat different arrangement for the use of transistors in the ignition system. Some are more complex than others. In every case, the end results are the same: prolonged ignition contact, spark plug life, and gap settings remaining fixed for a longer period of time. There is also a greater voltage delivered to the spark plugs at high speed, compared to the

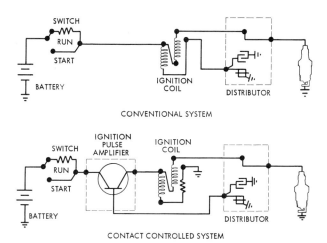

Fig. 21. With the development of transistorized ignition systems, greater variety and improvements are possible.

conventional system. Transistorized systems are a comparatively recent development; therefore, numerous changes and improvements are being made as time goes on and additional manufacturers enter the field. Fig. 21.

Two basic types of transistorized ignition systems will be discussed. The first type is a system which uses a set of conventional ignition contact points and the second is a system that has no contact points.

Contact-Point Transistorized Ignition

A close examination of the illustrations will help to see how the transistorized system differs from the conventional ignition system. The major change is in the path the primary current follows through the coil.

In a conventional system, primary current flows through the ignition switch and resistor, through the coil winding, into the distributor and to ground through the closed contact points. In this circuit the contact points carry full primary current. The design and function of these points is such that they can carry only a small amount of current without excessive arcing, which would reduce overall coil output and efficiency.

Notice that by using the contact points in the base circuit of a transistor that they need only carry a very small current. Also the

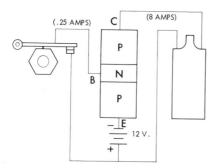

Fig. 22. Contact points arranged in the base circuit carry minimal current with virtually no surface wear.

emitter to collector circuit is connected to the coil primary and can supply almost twice the current as a conventional ignition system. A resistor is used in the coil primary circuit to control current flow and also to act as a voltage control in order to protect the transistor from excessive induced voltages. Fig. 22 shows that the contact points are carrying only the very small base current. The fact that the contact points conduct such a small current allows them to operate with virtually no wear taking place at the surfaces. The major wear point is at the cam and rubbing block. Electrically, these points would never require service. Mechanically, they are still subject to failure and this system does require service. Some manufacturers provide a specially polished breaker cam to reduce rubbing block wear. Contact point spacing is not a critical factor insofar as the transistor operation but point spacing would still affect ignition timing. The transistor coil is a special unit which is designed to

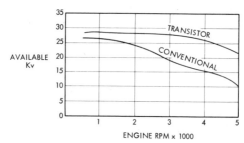

Fig. 23. Available voltage in transistorized system compared to conventional system. Ford Div.—Ford Motor Co.

carry the higher primary current flow available from the transistor. Otherwise the other ignition components are standard parts. A major advantage of the transistorized system is its ability to provide high voltage sparks at high engine speeds, Fig. 23.

The transistorized unit for these ignition systems is mounted in an aluminum heat sink. It is called the amplifier. Usually the amplifier will be located where it will not be subjected to temperature extremes and road splash. Exact location depends on the vehicle. Fig. 24. Within the amplifier are several resistors, capacitors, diodes, a zener diode, and the transistor. A schematic diagram of an amplifier operation is shown in Fig. 25.

Notice that the contact points when closed complete the emitter to base circuit of the transistor. This action makes the emitter to collector circuit operate which will supply current to the coil primary winding. D-1 is a zener diode which will break down when high voltages are applied to it to protect the transistor. These transient surges, as they are called, will thus by-pass the transistor.

When the contact points open, the transistor TR1 is turned off and this causes the coil primary current flow to stop. This action causes the rapid collapse of the coil magnetic flux to produce a high-voltage surge in the coil secondary winding which creates a spark across the spark gap.

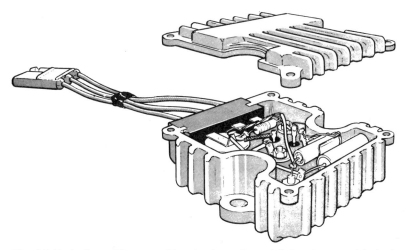

Fig. 24. Typical amplifier assembly: aluminum heat sink housing transistorized unit.

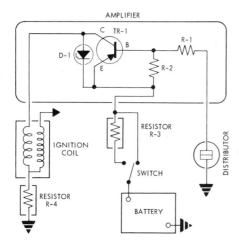

Fig. 25. Simplified diagram of amplifier circuitry. Delco-Remy Div., General Motors Corp.

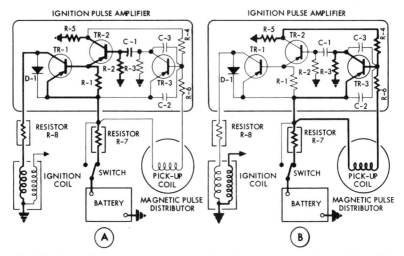

Fig. 26. A. Ignition system—internal wiring showing current flow with switch on and engine not running. B. Internal wiring showing current flow when spark plug fires. Heavy lines indicate current flow.

Some of these systems do not use the ignition capacitor in the distributor and some still do. Generally speaking, the capacitor function is part of the amplifier design. The contact points since they carry such low current values are not subject to arcing. Thus, the capacitor's other function, to speed up the coil magnetic field collapse is readily performed within the amplifier by the zener diode and a capacitor which is not shown in Fig. 25.

In Fig. 26 the circuitry for a somewhat different application of the transistor to the ignition system is shown. In particular, it should be noted that a distributor which has no contact points is used. Fig. 27 illustrates this type of distributor.

This distributor appears to be similar externally at least, to the standard unit. Internally, however, it is quite different. The standard set of contact points and breaker plate is replaced with a stationary permanent magnet and a rotating timer core. On the pole

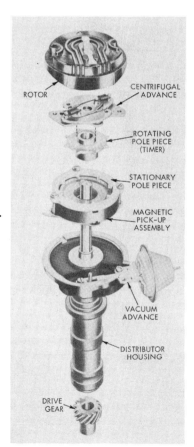

Fig. 27. Magnetic pulse distributor.

piece are internal teeth equal to the number of cylinders. The timer core also has teeth which correspond to the teeth on the pole piece.

Operating Principles. A wiring diagram showing the complete circuit for a typical ignition system is illustrated in Fig. 26A. Note that there are two separate resistors used in this type of circuit. These resistors may be separate units, or they may be in the form of resistance wire in the harness. The resistor connected directly to the switch is bypassed during cranking, whereas the other resistor is always in the circuit. On some applications, the bypass lead may be connected to the cranking motor solenoid instead of to the switch. The use of two resistors permits the required value of resistance to be bypassed during cranking.

In order to fire the spark plug, it is necessary to induce a high voltage in the ignition coil secondary winding by opening the circuit to the coil primary winding. In standard systems, this is accomplished by opening the distributor contact points. In this ignition system, this is accomplished as follows.

When the switch is closed, with the engine not running, current flows through a part of the circuit as shown in Fig. 26A. The current can be traced from the battery through the switch and resistor R-7 to the amplifier. Current then flows through transistors TR-1 and TR-2, resistors R-1, R-2, and R-5, and the coil primary winding and resistor R-8 to ground, thus completing the circuit back to the battery. It is important to note that under this condition, full current flows through the coil primary winding, and capacitor C-1 is charged with the positive voltage towards transistor TR-2.

When the engine is running, the vanes on the rotating iron core in the distributor line up with the internal teeth on the pole piece. This establishes a magnetic path through the center of the pickup coil, causing a voltage to be induced in the pickup coil. This voltage causes transistor TR-3 to conduct resulting in current flow in the circuit as shown in Fig. 26B.

The charge on capacitor C-1 causes transistor TR-2 to turn off, which in turn causes transistor TR-1 to turn off. This interrupts the circuit to the ignition coil primary winding, and the high voltage needed to fire the spark plug is induced in the coil secondary winding. These current flow conditions are shown in Fig. 26B.

The current flow conditions shown in Fig. 26B exist until the charge on capacitor C-1 has been dissipated through resistor R-2. When this happens, the system reverts back to the current flow conditions shown in Fig. 26A. The system is then ready to fire the next spark plug.

Resistor R-1 is a biasing resistor that allows transistor TR-1 to operate. Resistor R-4 is called a feedback resistor, and its purpose is to turn TR-3 off when TR-2 returns to the "on" condition. Zener diode D-1 protects transistor TR-1 from high voltages which may be induced in the coil primary winding. Capacitors C-2 and C-3 protect transistor TR-3 from high voltages which appear in the system. Resistor R-6 protects transistor TR-3 from excessive current in case the pickup coil circuit is grounded.

The above section has explained "what" happens in the ignition system, and has made no attempt to explain "why" the units function as they do. This is a long story, and is not considered to be necessary at this time.

The preceding types of ignition systems are examples of what has been done to improve ignition. Changes in the future will be very likely in the integrated circuits area. It would not be difficult to imagine the complete amplifier built into the distributor as the integrated regulator is on the alternator.

Distributor Modulator

To reduce engine emissions some vehicles are being equipped with a distributor vacuum modulator. This unit is an electronic component which allows no vacuum advance below 23 mph on acceleration. It also prevents distributor vacuum advance below 18 mph on deceleration.

The modulator is mounted inside the passenger compartment and consists of four basic units. They are a speed sensor, a thermal switch, an electronic control and a three-way solenoid valve.

Operation of the modulator is cancelled by the thermal switch at outside air temperature of 58°F. or lower. The speed sensor is operated by the speedometer cable. If the modulator unit malfunctions, it will cause the vehicle to operate as though the timing is retarded. Poor gas mileage and lack of power will be a basic symptom. Testing of these units consists of verifying proper vacuum at the distributor with a vacuum gauge connected to the large hose of

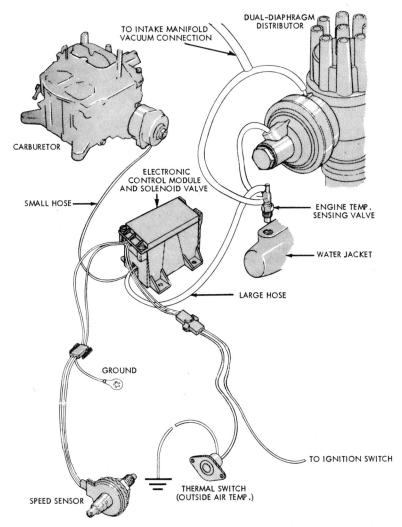

Fig. 28. Diagram of distributor modulator for emission control.

the electric module and operating the car with the driving wheels up off the road. Check the manufacturer's shop manual for specifications. Fig. 28.

TRADE COMPETENCY TESTS

1. Describe what is contained in the primary circuit. Secondary circuit.
2. How do the wires used in wiring the primary and secondary circuits differ?
3. Describe the construction of the ignition coil.
4. What is the purpose of the iron core in the coil?
5. What is the function of the ignition resistance wire?
6. How do 12 volt ignition coils compare with 6 volt coils?
7. Describe the construction of a capacitor.
8. What is the function of the capacitor in the ignition system?
9. What is the purpose of the distributor?
10. What is meant by the dwell period?
11. What material is used in the contact points?
12. What is the effect of excessive point clearance? Too little clearance?
13. Why must the spark be advanced on an engine?
14. How does the centrifugal advance system work?
15. Explain how the vacuum advance operates.
16. Explain how the ignition coil operates to produce a spark.
17. What is meant by the reactance of the coil?
18. How is the capacitor connected in the ignition circuit?
19. What is the voltage usually built up to in order to cause a spark at the spark plug?
20. What is meant by a cold plug? A hot plug?
21. Why should the polarity of the secondary circuit always be negative?
22. Explain how the transistor increases contact point life in a contact type transistorized system.
23. Describe a magnetic pulse distributor.

CHAPTER 11

IGNITION SYSTEMS SERVICE

Ignition failures and normal lowering of ignition system efficiency are probably the most common automobile troubles. A complete engine tune-up should be performed at 15,000 mile intervals or as often as needed to maintain peak performance and economy and prevent ignition failures. When an engine loses power, misfires, or does not run, check the ignition system first to make sure all units are in good working condition, Fig. 1.

Use test equipment to do a proper and scientific job of ignition tune-up. Even a minimum amount of equipment can help to locate ignition system troubles and make necessary repairs.

IGNITION TROUBLE-SHOOTING

Most engine trouble-shooting procedures start with tests that either establish the ignition system as the source of trouble or free the ignition system from further consideration. Before testing the ignition system, make sure the battery has enough charge to operate the cranking motor freely and that the fuel is reaching the carburetor.

When making ignition tests, avoid electric shocks by holding only the insulated portions of high-voltage cables. Avoid shorts by keeping tools off top of the battery. Avoid electrical burns by removing rings from the fingers.

If the engine does not run, the ignition system is at fault if:

1. There is no spark during cranking when a spark plug wire is held $\frac{1}{4}$ inch away from the engine.

2. The engine starts, but immediately stops when the ignition switch is released from the start position.

Ignition trouble occurs in three forms: the engine fails to start; the engine is hard to start; and the engine misfires.

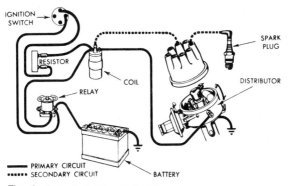

Fig. 1. A typical 12-volt ignition system showing units which must be checked if the engine does not start or run properly.

The following trouble-shooting chart lists a number of ignition troubles, their probable causes and their correction. Table 1.

IGNITION SYSTEM TESTING

The modern method of testing the components that make up the ignition system is with the oscilloscope. The oscilloscope checks the complete ignition system while the engine is running and shows the characteristics of the spark developed on a cathode ray tube. Most repair shops use this method of testing. However, some shops still have and use the older types of testing equipment which test the separate units of the ignition system.

TESTING IGNITION SYSTEM WITH AN OSCILLOSCOPE

The oscilloscope is an instrument that employs an entirely different method of testing engine ignition systems from that used in recent years. Until the advent of the oscilloscope, ignition test equipment was designed to test the individual units of the ignition system to locate ignition system troubles. The oscilloscope method of testing enables the operator to check the performance of the entire ignition system while the engine is running, taking into account the effects of compression and the other conditions under which the engine is operating.

The oscilloscope, Fig. 2, incorporates a cathode ray tube which electronically superimposes a visual trace or image of the total igni-

TABLE 1. IGNITION TROUBLE-SHOOTING CHART

CONDITION	PROBABLE CAUSE	CORRECTION
ENGINE WILL NOT START	1. BATTERY DISCHARGED	1. TEST AND RECHARGE BATTERY
	2. LOOSE CONNECTION OR BROKEN WIRES	2. EXAMINE ALL WIRES IN PRIMARY AND SECONDARY IGNITION CIRCUIT AND REPLACE AS NECESSARY. CLEAN AND TIGHTEN ANY LOOSE CONNECTION
	3. DEFECTIVE NEUTRAL SWITCH	3. TEST SWITCH AND REPLACE IF NECESSARY
	4. DEFECTIVE IGNITION SWITCH	4. TEST SWITCH AND REPLACE IF NECESSARY
	5. DEFECTIVE IGNITION COIL	5. TEST COIL AND REPLACE IF DEFECTIVE
	6. DEFECTIVE CONDENSER	6. TEST CONDENSER AND REPLACE IF DEFECTIVE
	7. DEFECTIVE DISTRIBUTOR CAP	7. EXAMINE CAP AND REPLACE IF CRACKED OR OTHERWISE DAMAGED
	8. DISTRIBUTOR CONTACTS POINTS IMPROPERLY ADJUSTED OR FAULTY	8. REPLACE CONTACT POINTS AND ADJUST DWELL
	9. IGNITION TIMING OFF	9. TIME IGNITION TO ENGINE
	10. INSUFFICIENT FUEL	10. CHECK FUEL SUPPLY
ENGINE IS HARD TO START	1. IGNITION TIMING OFF	1. RETIME IGNITION
	2. DISTRIBUTOR CONTACT POINTS IMPROPERLY ADJUSTED OR FAULTY	2. REPLACE CONTACT POINTS AND ADJUST DWELL.
	3. FAULTY CONDENSER	3. TEST CONDENSER AND REPLACE IF NECESSARY.
	4. LOOSE CONNECTION	4. CHECK ALL PRIMARY AND SECONDARY CONNECTION AND CLEAN AND TIGHTEN IF NEEDED.
	5. DEFECTIVE WIRING	5. EXAMINE ALL PRIMARY AND SECONDARY IGNITION WIRES AND REPLACE IF DEFECTIVE.
	6. FAULTY OR IMPROPERLY SET	6. CLEAN, ADJUST AND TEST ALL SPARK PLUGS. REPLACE AS NEEDED.
	7. LOW CAPACITY IGNITION COIL	7. TEST COIL AND REPLACE IF NECESSARY.
	8. FAULTY DISTRIBUTOR CAP OR ROTOR	8. EXAMINE DISTRIBUTOR CAP AND ROTOR AND REPLACE IF NECESSARY.
ENGINE MISFIRES	1. IGNITION IMPROPERLY TIME	1. RETIME IGNITION
	2. FAULTY SPARK PLUGS	2. CLEAN AND ADJUST SPARK PLUGS AND REPLACE AS NECESSARY
	3. LOOSE OR DEFECTIVE WIRING	3. REPLACE DEFECTIVE WIRES, CLEAN AND TIGHTEN ALL LOOSE CONNECTIONS
	4. DISTRIBUTOR CAP CRACKED	4. REPLACE DISTRIBUTOR CAP
	5. DISTRIBUTOR CONTACT POINTS IMPROPERLY ADJUSTED	5. CLEAN AND ADJUST DISTRIBUTOR CONTACT POINTS. REPLACE IF NECESSARY.
	6. POOR CYLINDER COMPRESSION	6. TEST ENGINE TO DETERMINE REASON FOR POOR COMPRESSION. RECONDITION VALVES. IF NECESSARY REPLACE PISTON RINGS.

Fig. 2. An oscilloscope gives analysis of entire ignition system taking into account operating conditions. Snap-On Tool Corp.

tion cycle on the face of the tube. The scope is capable of showing the ignition cycle patterns of both the primary and secondary circuits. With the engine running, definite and intermittent faults in the ignition cycle are clearly shown by the changes that occur in the normal image shape, readily indicating the exact defect involved.

Once the operator becomes acquainted with the basic patterns of the ignition cycle, any variations (which indicate troubles) become readily apparent. The basic patterns can be expanded on the face of the scope to present a full screen picture for each cylinder in succession or the patterns can be contracted so that the patterns for all the cylinders are shown, or all the cylinders can be superimposed one upon the other for a comparison of patterns between cylinders.

The various makes of oscilloscopes vary somewhat in their design and construction and in the pattern they project on the face of the cathode ray tube, Figs. 3 & 4. Although the patterns may vary, they all have the same three parts, namely: dwell, firing, and coil dissipation; but they are presented in a different order on the various makes of scopes.

The ignition cycle image illustrated in Fig. 4 gives a complete history of the ignition cycle for one cylinder in the primary circuit. On a six cylinder engine it represents 60 degrees of distributor cam

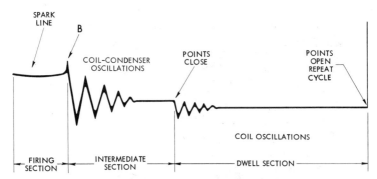

Fig. 3. Oscilloscope pattern of ignition cycle. At spark line contact points have opened and voltage rises as necessary to fire plug gap. Spark line indicates duration of arc across spark plug gap with arc end at "B."

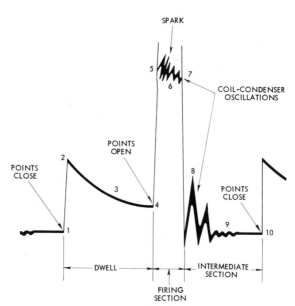

Fig. 4. A different oscilloscope pattern of the primary ignition cycle. The pattern begins with the points closing. The pattern has the same three parts: dwell, firing and coil oscillations. Snap-On Tool Corp.

travel, 45 degrees on an eight, and 90 degrees on a four cylinder engine. An explanation of the numbered pattern image is given below:

1. Here the distributor contact points close to begin the dwell period.
2. Current is flowing through the primary circuit building up a magnetic field within the coil.
3. Line starting at #2 and ending at #4 represents the contacts closed on dwell period.
4. At this point contact points open and magnetic field around coil windings collapses, causing a high voltage in the secondary circuit.
5. High voltage jumps across spark plug gap to produce spark.
6. Represents discharge of high voltage across distributor and spark plug air gap.
7. Spark ceases because of insufficient energy in coil to maintain spark.
8. Wavy line represents dissipation of remaining energy in primary and secondary circuit.
9. Line from end of oscillations to point where contact points close represents dissipation of energy remaining in primary circuit.
10. Contact points close and cycle starts over again.

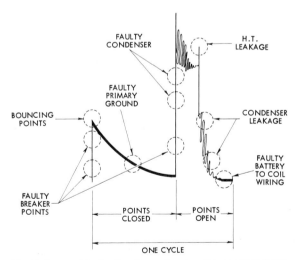

Fig. 5. A complete fault pattern showing the possible flaws in the primary circuit.

Regardless of which make of oscilloscope is used in making tests on an engine, a systematic test procedure must be followed. Each manufacturer of test equipment has developed a procedure to be used with his machine that will yield the most information in the shortest time. A check sheet is usually available to tabulate the test so that an intelligent analysis can be made.

However, an oscilloscope is not infallible and the mechanic can still make an incorrect diagnosis if he fails to make a thorough physical inspection of the parts being tested and unless he has a good command of basic knowledge of ignition system operation.

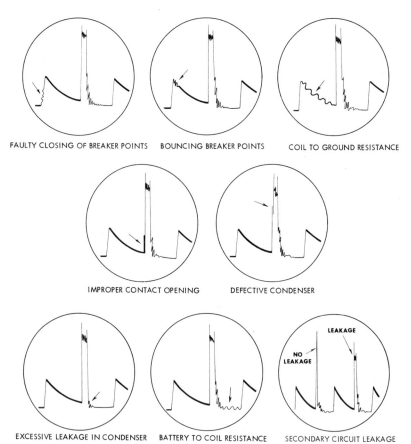

Fig. 6. Oscilloscope patterns of some common ignition system troubles. Snap-On Tools Corp.

Fig. 5 illustrates a primary composite fault diagram that shows where the most common ignition troubles will be found on the pattern image. Individual patterns of a number of common ignition troubles are illustrated in Fig. 6.

The oscilloscope is also capable of showing a secondary pattern as in the secondary circuit, Fig. 7. The secondary pattern usually gives more information about the real condition of the circuit than the primary pattern. In such patterns the primary phase of points close, coil build-up, and points open is inverted as compared to the primary pattern. The numbers on the pattern are similar to the numbers on the primary pattern and represent the same actions.

The oscilloscope will also test transistor type ignition systems. While there are several makes of transistor ignition systems on the market, they are one of two types: contact controlled and fully transistorized.

Most oscilloscopes have hook-ups for both type of systems. It will be found that the scope pattern produced by transistor ignition systems is not as irregular as that of the conventional ignition system. The firing, intermediate, and dwell sections of the pattern for all cylinders can be tested at the same time and compared. Malfunctions in the system can be seen by noting the variations in the scope patterns in the same way as with the conventional system.

TESTING IGNITION SYSTEM COMPONENTS

When an oscilloscope is not available, many repair shops have other equipment designed to test the individual parts of the igni-

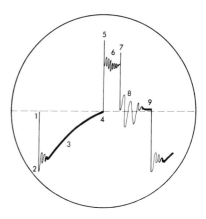

Fig. 7. Secondary pattern shown by oscilloscope. Numbers are same as in Fig. 4.

tion system to determine if they are functioning properly. The checking and testing of ignition circuits, ignition coil, capacitor and the testing and adjustment of distributors often require special equipment. Proper timing must also be set by means of special equipment. Gages are needed to check the spark plug gap. When using test equipment, you should always follow the directions for making connections. Failure to do so may give incorrect readings or even ruin the equipment. Comply with the automobile manufacturer's specifications regarding each unit and any necessary adjustments.

Checking Voltage Drop in the Primary Circuit

Loose or dirty connections and broken strands in stranded wire will increase the resistance to the current flow in the primary circuit and will cause a "voltage drop" below the required value. Any voltage drop in the primary circuit causes the voltage of the current flowing through the primary windings of the ignition coil to be lower than normal, reduces the voltage output of the coil, and thus causes weak spark at the plugs.

All terminals and connections in the ignition primary circuit must be clean and tight to insure that the voltage in that circuit does not lessen and drop below the voltage specified to produce a satisfactory spark at the spark plugs.

Voltage drop can be checked by connecting a voltmeter at certain points in the ignition primary circuit to measure the actual voltage in those portions of the circuit shown in Fig. 8. The voltage readings obtained are checked against the voltage readings provided by the vehicle manufacturer for those parts of the circuit. Voltage readings higher than those set as standard by the manufacturer indicate a high resistance in the portion of the circuit being tested and should be corrected by cleaning and tightening connections or by replacing any damaged wires or components.

Fig. 8 shows the voltmeter connections at three different locations. Only one meter is necessary. No connections need to be disturbed. The pointed prods on the voltmeter lead wires are tightly pressed against the terminals indicated and the meter read. The voltage readings shown in the caption below the illustration are typical of the voltage values specified by the manufacturer against which you check the readings you obtain.

IGNITION SYSTEMS SERVICE

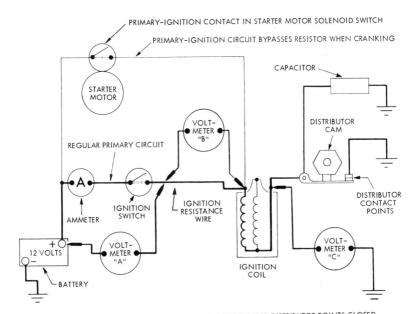

VOLTMETER "A" READING = 0.2 VOLTS WITH IGNITION SWITCH AND DISTRIBUTOR POINTS CLOSED

VOLTMETER "B" READING = 6.5 VOLTS MAX. 5.5 VOLTS MIN.—ENGINE HOT, IGNITION SWITCH AND END DISTRIBUTOR POINTS CLOSED

VOLTMETER "C" READING = 0.1 VOLTS WITH IGNITION SWITCH AND DISTRIBUTOR POINTS CLOSED

Fig. 8. Primary circuit voltage drop schematic. Remember a high resistance in any one part of the circuit will cause an abnormally low voltage in other portions. The defective part of the circuit will have an abnormally high reading.

Check the Secondary Ignition Cables

To keep the engine running at its highest efficiency, the high tension ignition cables should be checked whenever the engine is tuned up. The cables should be replaced at least every 30,000 miles or three years or whenever a cable has excessive resistance.

Replacement of cables becomes necessary because of aging of the insulation materials caused by heat, oil, grease, and electrical stresses which result in increased loss of voltage available to the spark plugs. The defects cannot usually be seen until they have reached the extreme stages of hard, stiff and often visible cracks in the cables. Often, due to rough handling when removing the cables, the carbon-like conductor separates to produce a gap. The separation causes arcing and burning of the thread and eventually an

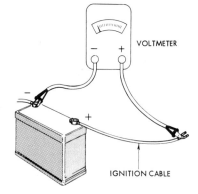

open wire. The boots and nipples on the spark plugs and distributor cap terminals are also subject to aging and will not normally last as long as the spark plug cables.

The oscilloscope is the fastest and simplest means of locating defective ignition cables. After the spark plugs have been serviced, the pattern on the scope will indicate if too high a voltage is required to jump the spark plug gap. If the voltage required is too high, check the towers of the ignition coil and distributor cap for corrosion, terminals not seated, improper gap between the rotor and insert in the distributor cap, and finally the cables. Always follow the manufacturer's instructions for the scope being used.

If a scope is not available the cables can be checked for continuous circuit with a voltmeter. Connect a battery and voltmeter to the cable as shown in Fig. 9. An indication of voltage on the meter means that the cable has no gap in the carbon-like material and should perform properly. The amount of voltage indicated has no significance.

An ohmmeter can be used to test high tension spark plug wires also, Fig. 10. Each manufacturer will have a slightly different specification but a general value of 8,000 ohms per foot is reasonable for resistance type spark plug wire.

Secondary cables can also be tested for punctures and cracks while the engine is running with a probe (test point), one end of which is grounded to the engine. With the engine running, disconnect one spark plug wire and prevent the cable end from grounding. Move the test probe along the entire length of wire. If the wire

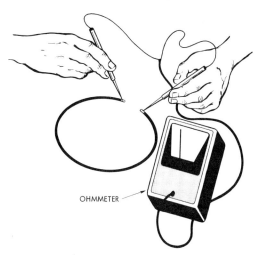

Fig. 10. Testing suppression wiring by an ohmme-ter. This is an ideal instrument for this purpose.

has a puncture or crack, a spark will jump from the wire to the test probe. Check each of the spark plug wires, including the second-ary coil wire, and replace any cracked, leaking or faulty cables.

When replacing ignition cables, twist the boot or nipple to loosen it from the spark plug or distributor cap and pull off the cable, holding it by the boot or nipple and terminal. *Do not jerk or pull on the cable since this tends to break the carbon conductor.*

When installing cable, the firing order of the engine must be taken into consideration since routing of the cables to cylinders which fire in sequence could cause cross firing of the cylinders. Cross firing has the effect of changing the spark timing in the affected cylinders. For cylinders that fire in sequence the wires should not be located parallel to each other since wires parallel by only a few inches can develop cross fire due to the induced field which builds up in one cable as the current flows in the other. Insulated metal or fiber brackets should be used to hold the cables in relation to each other and away from manifolds and other metal objects.

Check Ballast Resistor

While the resistor type distributor to coil primary wire is now used in place of a ballast coil, a number of vehicles still use the ballast coil; therefore, it is well to know how to determine if the coil is faulty. The same test procedure can apply to the resistor wire. Occasionally, when starting an engine, the engine will start but fail to keep running once the ignition switch or starter switch is released. When this happens one possible source of trouble is the ballast resistance or resistor wire in the primary ignition system.

If the resistor is completely burned out, it causes an open circuit in the primary winding, and the engine will not continue to operate after it has been started. Resistance can change in the resistor due to a number of factors; therefore, it is well to check the unit if trouble exists in the ignition system.

The resistor can be checked with an ohmmeter to see if it meets manufacturer's specifications. Comparing voltage drop with a new unit will show if the unit is faulty. A quick test of the ballast resistor to determine if it is at fault is to bypass the resistor momentarily with a jumper wire.

Test Coil and Capacitor

In the case of a coil or a capacitor, it is impractical to make any repairs. Therefore, the unit must be replaced if defective. In many cases it is essential that a coil tester be used; the coil may function properly under certain circumstances, and yet fail under others. The same situation may exist with a capacitor. An internal breakdown may occur only under certain load conditions.

Coil Test. A coil is tested for resistance and continuity of the primary and secondary windings on a meter type tester. Some coils will perform satisfactorily when cold but break down when warm. Hence, a coil should always be warm before testing. Some testers check the output voltage, while others check the current reading in milliamperes of the spark as well. Generally the voltage and the current are checked against the readings of a "master" coil.

An ohmmeter can also be used to test a coil if a special tester is not available. Two ohmmeter readings, one for primary circuit resistance and the second one for secondary resistance, are necessary. To check primary circuit resistance, disconnect the coil primary wires. Use the low scale of the ohmmeter and place each lead on a primary terminal. A good coil should have less than 4 ohms resistance as a general rule. If the resistance is very high, an open circuit

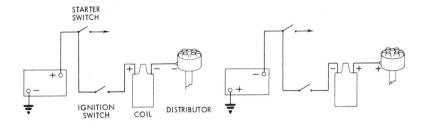

NEGATIVE GROUND SYSTEM   POSITIVE GROUND SYSTEM

Fig. 11. Methods of connecting ignition coil to assure negative polarity at center spark plug electrode.

is indicated. A reading of less than 1 ohm would indicate a possible shorted primary winding.

The secondary resistance is checked by inserting an ohmmeter lead into the secondary terminal of the coil and placing the other ohmmeter lead on a coil primary terminal (either one). A good secondary winding should have less than 10,000 ohms resistance.

When installing a coil be sure that it is connected in the ignition circuit so that a negative voltage exists at the center spark plug electrode, Fig. 11. Coil polarity can be checked on an oscilloscope where it shows up as an inverted pattern. It can also be checked with a voltmeter where reversed polarity causes the pointer to move in the

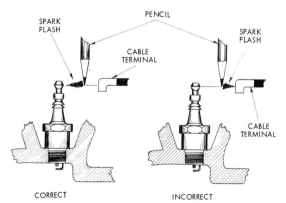

Fig. 12. Checking coil polarity with a pencil.

reverse direction. When neither a scope nor a voltmeter are available, a simple test can be made with a pencil. Remove a terminal from a spark plug and place a pencil between the terminal on the wire and the spark plug terminal, Fig. 12. Crank the engine and if the spark flashes between the cable and the pencil, the polarity is wrong. Correct polarity can be established by switching the primary wires at the coil terminals. While most engines have negative polarity at the center spark plug terminal, there may be some that do not. Be sure to check the engine specifications if there is any doubt.

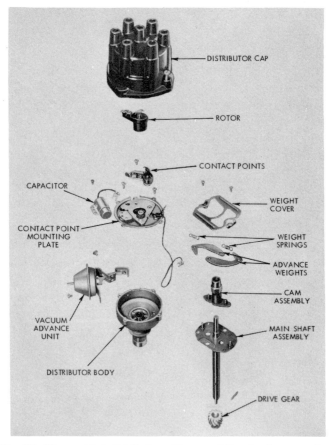

Fig. 13. Diassembled distributor with a centrifugal advance unit above the cam and contact point assembly. Chevrolet Div.—General Motors Corp.

Capacitor Test. Capacitor testers as a rule give three types of readings—capacitance in microfarads, leakage, and series resistance. Replace the capacitor (condenser) if tests show that it is defective. When in doubt and if you do not have the means of measuring its capacitance, replace the capacitor since it is relatively low in cost. However, before replacing a capacitor examine the contact points to determine if operating conditions have caused excessive arcing or metal transfer. Either condition indicates an incorrect capacitor capacity. An under-capacity capacitor causes transfer of material from the stationary (negative) point to the moveable (positive) point. Over-capacity capacitor causes transfer of metal from the positive to the negative point. Since conditions within an engine vary with engine speed, a capacitor with a rating near the low end of the acceptable microfarad capacity would more nearly meet the requirements of a vehicle usually driven at highway speeds and a capacitor near the high end of acceptable microfarad rating for city stop and go driving. Some shops save and identify the capacity of used capacitors and are able to install a capacitor which will match the coil characteristics as described above. Generally, selective purchase of automotive capacitors is not possible.

Distributor

The disassembly of a distributor varies in accordance with its construction. Some distributors have the centrifugal advance unit mounted above the cam and contact point assembly while on others the advance unit is mounted within the distributor housing below the cam and contact point plate, Fig. 13.

The disassembly of the distributor is readily apparent and the rotor, contact points, capacitor, vacuum advance unit, and contact point plate should be removed. Check the amount of clearance between the distributor shaft and bushing as shown in Fig. 14. If the clearance exceeds 0.006 inch, either the bushing, distributor shaft, or both should be replaced. The new bushings are sized to fit the distributor shaft with the proper clearance by pressing a burnishing tool through the bushings.

Check the action of the centrifugal advance weights, which should move freely without binding. Remove the springs and weights carefully and check the weights' hinge pins for wear. Some distributors have a plate which is slotted for movement of guide pins located on the centrifugal weights which should be checked for

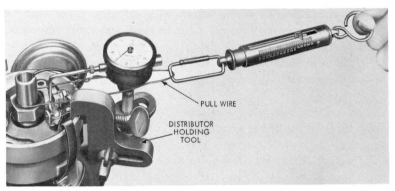

Fig. 14. Checking distributor shaft and bushing clearance. Plymouth Div.—Chrysler Corp.

wear. Replace worn parts since any appreciable wear in those parts changes the characteristics of the spark advance.

After the necessary repairs have been completed, reassembly of the distributor is the reverse of the disassembly procedure outlined. Be sure to lubricate the bushings and the hinge pins on the advance unit with a light grease. When installing the distributor drive gear on the shaft, use a new retaining pin.

Contact Points

The condition of the ignition contact points is very important to the proper functioning of the ignition system. A number of faults occur in the contacts, making periodic attention a necessary part of ignition service.

Contact Points Analysis. The color of the ignition contact points will often serve as a clue to the cause of their failure or cause of their high resistance. After operating for some time, the ideal color of the point material is grey, indicating that the contacts are operating under normal conditions, Fig. 15. If the contact surfaces are blue, the cause is usually excessive heating due to high resistance, arcing across the points due to a defective condenser, high voltage due to an improperly adjusted voltage limiter, and improper alignment. If the contact surfaces are black it is an indication that oil, oil vapors, or grease are getting onto the point surfaces somehow. This could be the result of over-lubrication of the distributor cam

CONDITION	CAUSED BY
	Any discoloration other than a frosted slate grey shall be considered as burned points.
 **EXCESSIVE METAL TRANSFER OR PITTING**	Incorrect alignment. Incorrect voltage regulator setting. Radio condenser installed to the distributor side of the coil. Ignition condenser of improper capacity. Extended operation of the engine at speeds other than normal.

Fig. 15. Contact point analysis. Causes for poor conditions. Ford Div.—Ford Motor Co.

or oil seepage between the distributor shaft and bushing.

The contacts sometimes develop a high spot on one point and a crater or depression on the other, caused by electrolytic action transferring metal from one point to the other, Fig. 15. A small amount of pitting in several thousand miles is normal and does not affect distributor operation. However, excessive pitting is harmful and causes arcing and voltage loss. Excessive pitting could be the result of unusual vehicle operation, such as extremely low speeds or high speed operation or an unbalanced primary circuit which sometimes can be corrected by changing the condenser to one of higher or lower capacitance. If the high spot or mound is on the negative point, change to a condenser of lesser capacity, Fig. 15. If the mound is on the positive point, change to a condenser of greater capacity. Keep in mind that coils and condensers (capacitors) have to operate as a balanced electrical team. Always use the correct coil and capacitor for the vehicle.

Replace Contact Points. Examine the contact point surfaces and if they are deeply pitted or are blue or black in color they should be replaced. Contact points are relatively inexpensive and should not be dressed (filed or honed) except in an emergency or as a temporary measure when new contacts are not available.

To remove the contacts disconnect the condenser and primary leads within the distributor and remove the screws securing the

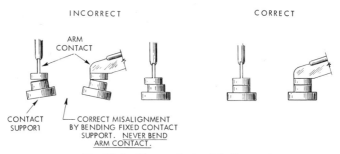

Fig. 16. Ignition contact point alignment.

base of the contact set to the breaker plate. Remove the contact point assembly.

Install the new set of points, making certain that they are properly positioned on the breaker plate. Install the screws and tighten. Reconnect the condenser and primary wires.

Check the alignment of the contact points with the points closed, Fig. 16. Align the contact points so that they meet squarely by bending the stationary contact as needed. Never bend the moveable contact.

Check Contact Point Spring Tension. Fig. 17 illustrates how contact point spring tension is measured. The measurement must

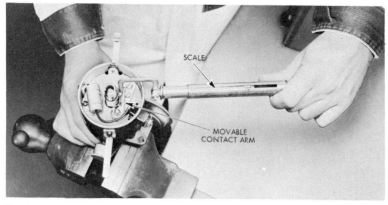

Fig. 17. Checking contact point tension with a scale. Chevrolet Motor Div.— General Motors Corp.

be taken as near to the contact as possible and the pull exerted at right angles to the face of the points, otherwise a true reading will not be obtained. Before checking the tension make sure that the contact point moves freely in its pivot. A typical specification for contact point spring tension is 17 to 20 ounces.

Contact point spring tension is important to the operation of the ignition system since, if the tension is too great, rapid wear of the rubbing block and cam will result. Moreover, at high speeds the contacts will close so violently that they will bounce, in effect reducing the coil saturation period. If the contact point spring tension is too little, the rubbing block will not follow the contour of the cam at high speeds. This will also reduce the coil saturation period.

Some contact point sets provide a means for adjusting the spring tension, such as the screw that holds the spring in position and a slot in the end of the spring. Re-positioning the slot with respect to the screw will change the spring tension.

After making the necessary adjustments check the cam surface for roughness. Place a small amount of high temperature lubricant on the cam surface or lubricate the felt cam lubricator to reduce rubbing block wear.

Adjust Contact Point Gap. Contact point gap (dwell angle) is important to the operation of the engine. The clearance can be checked with a feeler gage (new points only) or a dial indicator, on the engine while it is running with the aid of a dwell meter, or on a distributor testing machine. The clearance must be adjusted whenever new points are installed or the old points cleaned.

To adjust the contact points on most distributors, crank the

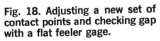

Fig. 18. Adjusting a new set of contact points and checking gap with a flat feeler gage.

engine so the distributor cam rotates until the rubbing block is on the high point of the distributor cam lobe. Loosen the stationary contact plate screw, and with new points set the contact gap to specifications using a flat feeler gage, Fig. 18. A flat feeler gage should not be used with used points, particularly if the point surfaces are

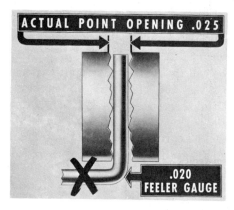

Fig. 19. A flat feeler gage will not permit accurate point clearance adjustment when points are rough or pitted.

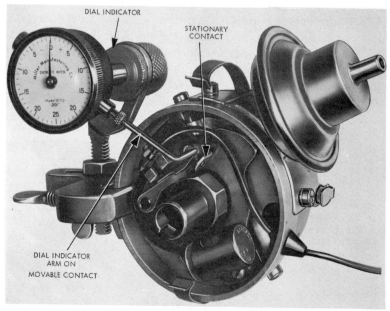

Fig. 20. Measuring contact point gap with a dial indicator.

rough or pitted, since it would be impossible to get an accurate adjustment, Fig. 19. The amount of contact point opening can also be checked with a dial indicator as illustrated in Fig. 20.

Equipment for checking the contact point dwell is commonly used while the distributor is mounted in a distributor tester, Fig. 21. The distributor is mounted on the machine and operated at a recommended speed to make the test. A dwell meter indicates the length of time the contact points are closed, and is calibrated in terms of the dwell or cam angle. The amount of dwell is specified in degrees and is directly related to the contact point gap, and any change in contact point gap setting will change the dwell angle reading. After removing the cap and rotor, cranking the engine, and determining the dwell, adjust the point opening, replace the cap and rotor, and recheck the dwell with the engine idling.

Fig. 21. Checking the dwell period or cam angle on a distributor tester. The tester will check centrifugal spark advance and vacuum advance as well.

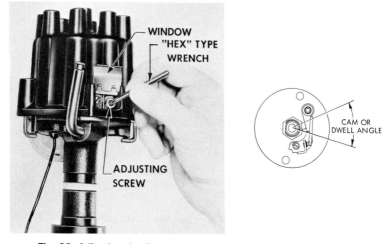

Fig. 22. Adjusting dwell angle through window in distributor cap.

On distributors with a window in the cap, set the dwell angle with the engine running or with the distributor mounted on a distributor tester. Raise the window and adjust the screw with a hex wrench until the correct angle is obtained. If no dwell meter is available, turn the screw clockwise until the engine begins to miss; then reverse it one half turn.

Inspect Distributor Cap and Rotor

Remove the distributor cap and rotor and wipe clean with a cloth. Inspect the cap for visible cracks, carbon tracks, and burned and corroded terminals. Examine the center carbon brush terminal; if damaged or worn, replace the cap.

Clean the rotor. Replace the rotor if it is damaged or otherwise impaired.

Check Distributor Advance

All distributors are provided with some means of advancing or retarding the ignition timing under certain load and speed conditions. Most distributors have a centrifugal as well as a vacuum advance mechanism. It is possible for the initial timing of the distributor at idle speed to be correct but at other speeds to be incorrect.

When the spark advance is exactly right at all speeds, the distributor is said to be "on its advance curve." If at one or several points the spark advances too far or is retarded, the distributor is said to be "off its advance curve."

The advance and retard operating characteristics are built into the distributor and can best be checked on the engine with a timing light equipped with an advance meter.

Check Advance on the Engine. Clean the timing marks on the crankshaft pulley or vibration damper and the pointer. Connect the timing light to the number one spark plug. With the engine running at idle and the distributor vacuum line disconnected, point the timing light directly towards the timing pointer to determine if the initial timing is correct. Gradually increase the engine speed and notice the distributor advances throughout the total advance range.

The specifications for distributor advance are given in terms of distributor shaft speeds. Starting with the engine at idle, slowly increase the engine speed, and at the speeds indicated in the specifications check the amount of advance on the meter. Check the amount of advance at all speeds indicated in the specifications and if the advance characteristics are not correct make corrections by increasing or decreasing the spring tension on the advance weights.

The actual maximum amount of advance (but not the advance curve) can be checked with a timing light that does not have an advance meter. After the initial timing is checked, the engine is speeded up and the maximum advance is indicated by the timing marks on the flywheel pulley or vibration damper.

Check Advance on the Test Bench. Modern distributor test benches, Fig. 21, are provided with means of checking not only maximum spark advance, but the degree of advance at any speed, or at any vacuum as well. These machines permit the spacing of contacts electrically, and will show any variation in timing between cylinders that occurs with a bent shaft, inaccurate cam, or worn bearings. The test bench provides a means of timing a second set of contacts in relation to the first set on dual point distributors. Each make of test bench comes with complete detailed instructions covering how the tests are made.

To check the operation of the centrifugal advance, the distributor is mounted on the test bench and operated at the recommended speeds to check the spark advance curve. A stroboscopic neon light flashes at the edge of the protractor each time the contact points open. As the centrifugal unit advances the spark timing (points opening) the light advances on the protractor, indicating the number of degrees of advance. Changing the spring tension on the distributor advance weights by bending the spring hangers changes the advance pattern.

Such testers also have a device capable of developing sufficient vacuum to test the operation of the vacuum advance unit. With the distributor mounted on the machine and in operation, a specified amount of vacuum should advance the spark a specific number of degrees. To change the pattern of advance change the diaphragm spring tension on some distributors by adding or removing washers.

Setting Ignition Timing

A timing light is used to set ignition timing. Marks on most engines are found on the vibration damper or pulley with a pointer located on the timing chain cover. On some older engines the timing marks are found on the flywheel. A small opening with a pointer is located on the front side of the flywheel cover.

Place a chalk mark on the specified number of degrees of advance. The timing light is always connected to No. 1 spark plug and the battery if of the battery-powered type. With the distributor vacuum line(s) disconnected, start the engine and operate at a slow idle. Aim the timing light directly at the timing mark pointer. The timing flash should occur at the instant the chalk mark directly faces the pointer, Fig. 23. If not, loosen the distributor clamp bolt and rotate the distributor clockwise or counterclockwise until the correct setting is obtained. Tighten the distributor clamp bolt. As engine speed is increased, the timing light should indicate a gradual spark advance if the advance mechanism is operating.

Some cars will use the retard diaphragm as shown in Fig. 24. It is very important to follow specification on these engines. When setting timing both vacuum lines must be disconnected and plugged. The distributor vacuum control valve is a temperature switch installed at intake manifold water passage. The engine when idling with retarded timing will tend to overheat. This valve will sense the rise in coolant temperature and turn off the vacuum supply to the retard unit. When this occurs the timing is advanced which allows the engine to speed up slightly and allow better cooling. When the engine cools down, the switch will again supply manifold vacuum

Fig. 23. Setting ignition timing.

TIMING LIGHT   POINTER   TIMING MARKS

to the retard unit. Many unusual combinations will be found that utilize this switch. Always be absolutely sure the vacuum lines are correctly installed. A check of the retard unit can be made by noting whether the timing retards as the vacuum line is attached.

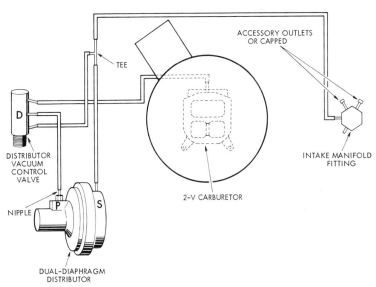

ACCESSORY OUTLETS OR CAPPED

TEE

D

DISTRIBUTOR VACUUM CONTROL VALVE

INTAKE MANIFOLD FITTING

NIPPLE

P   S

2-V CARBURETOR

DUAL-DIAPHRAGM DISTRIBUTOR

Fig. 24. Use of retard diaphragm on some cars.

Initial Timing. If the distributor has been removed and the exact position of the rotor shaft is not known when reinstalling, turn the crankshaft to top dead center for No. 1 cylinder. Top dead center can be found by first removing No. 1 spark plug. Place a thumb over the spark plug hole. Be sure to keep fingers out of the spark plug holes. Slowly turn the crankshaft until compression can be felt against the thumb. Continue turning the crankshaft until the TDC timing mark lines up with the timing mark pointer.

Next, install the distributor with the rotor pointing toward the No. 1 spark plug cap terminal when the distributor cap is in place. Rotate the distributor until the points are just ready to open. The engine is now ready to fire No. 1 cylinder. If the spark plug cables have been removed, install them in correct firing order in the direction of rotor rotation.

Firing Order. The firing order of the engine is determined by the manufacturer. A typical six cylinder firing order is 1 5 3 6 2 4. This would not apply to a V-6 engine. V-8 engines have several different firing orders. To install spark plug wires in the correct firing order requires several steps. First, locate from specifications the cylinder numbering sequence, such as left bank odd numbers. Next the proper firing order must be obtained also from specifications. Locate #1 as described earlier in this section. Then note the direction of rotation of the distributor rotor. Install each wire according to the firing order in the direction of rotor rotation. The timing should be reset by using a timing light after the engine is started.

When installing new spark plugs, be sure to install plugs of the correct heat range. Another important factor when replacing spark plugs is the length of the spark plug threads. The length is known as the "reach" of the plug. Plugs must have the proper reach. If the threads extend too far into the combustion chamber, they can become glowing hot and cause preignition.

TRANSISTOR IGNITION SYSTEM SERVICE

Service to the components of a transistorized system is the same as for conventional systems. The switch, coil (special), distributor, contact points, if used, timing, wires and spark plugs are serviced as described earlier. It is not possible to service the amplifier unit at all. If ignition trouble is indicated by failure to start, or missing, all the conventional components should be checked first. If all units are satisfactory, check to be sure the amplifier is grounded properly by using a jumper. Because each type of amplifier system is different, a service manual for the particular system should be used to make a complete step by step check of the system.

TRADE COMPETENCY TESTS

1. Why is it logical that a tune-up operation be performed on an engine every 15,000 miles?

2. What distance should a normal spark jump from the end of the spark plug wire to ground?

3. How can you determine if failure of the vehicle to start is due to trouble in the ignition system?

4. How does the oscilloscope method of testing ignition systems differ from other methods of testing?

5. What are the three phases of the ignition cycle that all scopes show in the image pattern?

6. How would you test coil polarity with a pencil?

7. What tests should be made on a capacitor to determine its condition?

8. What causes high spots or craters to develop on the grounded contact point? On the breaker arm?

9. Why is it important that the ignition contact points be properly aligned?

10. What is the importance of having the ignition contact points properly spaced?

11. How do you check and set contact gap spacing when the engine is not running?

12. How would you adjust the contact points when the engine is running?

13. How do you change the advance pattern setting of the centrifugal advance mechanism?

14. What method is considered the best way for checking secondary ignition cables?

15. What are the characteristics of an engine when the ignition timing is advanced too much? retarded too much?

16. How is the initial timing set when the engine is running?

CHAPTER 12

AUTOMOTIVE ELECTRONICS

SEMI-CONDUCTORS

Semi-conductor devices such as diodes and transistors are being used frequently in the automotive electrical system. In order to acquaint the automotive technician with these electrical units, this chapter will present fundamental information about the construction and operation of diodes and transistors.

Semi-conductor is the name applied to a certain group of elements. Some elements, usually metals, have less than four electrons in the outer ring and are able to share or lose these electrons easily. This property of losing electrons easily is characteristic of a conductor. Conversely, some elements have more than four electrons in the outer ring. These are classified as insulators because they do not lose electrons readily.

When an element has only four electrons in its outer ring it can behave as a conductor or an insulator. This is where the term semi-conductor is appropriate.

When a crystal of one of these semi-conductor materials is "doped" or treated chemically, it can be made to behave in a rather unusual manner, electrically. Silicon, germanium, and indium are elements commonly used in diodes and transistors.

In Fig. 1, a number of silicon atoms are combined in a crystalline form. Note that every atom is sharing an electron from another atom. This is known as covalent bonding. Since each atom has eight electrons in its outer ring, the crystal is a good insulator.

When the crystal of silicon is doped by adding a very small amount of another element it can be unbalanced in electrons.

In Fig. 2, phosphorus has been added to the silicon crystal. Phosphorus has five electrons in its outer ring and as a result there is an

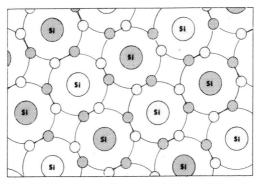

Fig. 1. Silicon atoms in a crystal. Each electron is shared with another atom. This is covalent bonding.

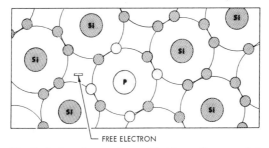

FREE ELECTRON

Fig. 2. A phosphorus atom added to a silicon crystal. Phosphorus has an extra electron which is not bonded and moves around. This is N or negative.

extra electron in the silicon crystal. This electron is free to move about and the material is referred to as N or negative type material.

In Fig. 3, the same type of silicon crystal has been doped with the element boron which has three electrons in its outer ring. Notice that there is an empty space where an electron should be part of a covalent bond. This empty space is known as a "hole." Since it is short one electron it becomes positive with respect to the N type material. A piece of material that is short an electron is known as P or positive type material.

When a crystal of material is formed or grown in the laboratory, it can be doped so that part of the crystal is N type and part is P

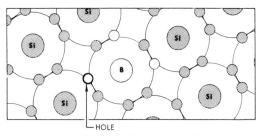

Fig. 3. Boron added to a silicon crystal. Boron is short one electron and an opening or hole is left. This is P or positive electrically.

Fig. 4. A diode. This is basically a junction of P and N material in a crystal.

type material. This is a solid piece of material; not two pieces put together. This crystal can then be sliced into very thin pieces, which will contain P and N type materials. This is the basic part of the diode and transistor. The center of this small piece of crystal is known as a P-N junction. A diode is a P-N junction.

Let us now examine the P-N junction to see how it operates, Fig. 4. It is known that unlike electrical charges attract, and that like charges repel each other. A P-N junction is composed of one half electrons and one half "holes" or, to make things easier to understand the "hole" can be thought of as being a positive charge. (It is, however, not a positive charge. It is merely an empty space into which an electron could move.) If the P-N junction is made up of two types of material of opposite electrical polarity, it is logical to think that the electrons would move across the junction and fill the holes.

In fact, a small number of electrons does move across and fill holes. When this occurs, however, the electrons that are leaving cause a positively charged particle (one which has lost an electron) to be left behind. This positive ion, as it is called, attracts electrons away from the junction area. The holes also produce ions with a negative charge. This negative charge tends to hold the holes

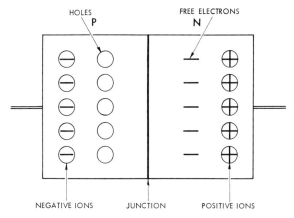

Fig. 5. Electrical balance in a diode.

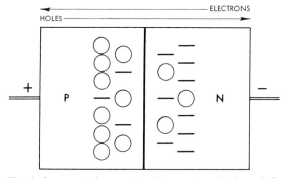

Fig. 6. A current changes the balance in a diode and the holes and electrons move to the junction and the diode becomes a conductor.

away from the junction area. These forces then tend to keep the junction area void, Fig. 5.

When a charge of electricity is connected to a P-N junction, notice what takes place, Fig. 6.

Electrons will now move from the negative material across the junction and through the positive type material and back to the battery. The P-N junction is now of a low resistance and is acting as a conductor. The positive charge applied to the P type material has forced the holes to move toward the junction and the negative

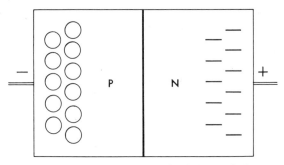

Fig. 7. A reverse voltage moves the holes and electrons away from the junction and the diode becomes an insulator.

charge applied to the N type material has forced the electrons to the junction also. Under these conditions the P-N junction becomes a conducting unit. Note that as an electron enters the crystal one will also leave so the total number of holes and electrons that was originally in the crystal is still there. There is merely a movement of electrons which is called a forward "bias."

Notice what occurs if the battery voltage is reversed or the junction is given reverse bias. As shown in Fig. 7, the positive charge will pull the electrons in the N type material away from the junction, and the negative charge will attract also the holes away from the junction. Since the junction now is void, it becomes a high resistance and acts as an insulator. (It does conduct a very small amount of reverse current, but it is so slight that it is not considered at all for automotive purposes.) These phenomena should make it apparent that the term "semi-conductor" is appropriate for the P-N junction diode.

DIODES

A diode is a P-N junction mounted within a case as in Fig. 8. The silicon junction is placed in a metal case with a lead wire attached to one side of the crystal or junction. The other side of the junction rests on the metal case. The lead wire is insulated from the case by glass insulation. This insulation also provides hermetic sealing of the diode to keep out moisture. The "getter" material is designed to remove impurities within the diode and also insulate the silicon wafer from the sides of the case.

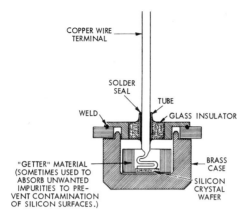

Fig. 8. Cross section of a diode mounted for use.

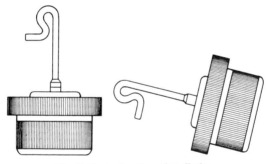

Fig. 9. Typical automotive diodes.

The automotive diode is called positive or negative but this merely denotes its function in the electrical unit such as the alternator. The difference between the two types of diodes is the position of the P-N junction in the case.

Heat is generated while the diode is operating and it is usually mounted in an aluminum part called a heat sink. The heat sink allows the heat produced by the diode to be dissipated over a larger area and thus prevents damage due to overheating. The diode is pressed into position in the heat sink or soldered to a combination printed circuit board and heat sink. Fig. 9 illustrates a typical

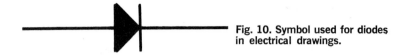

Fig. 10. Symbol used for diodes in electrical drawings.

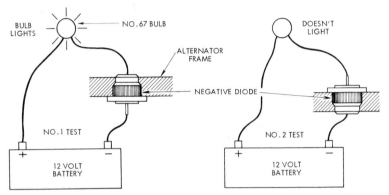

Fig. 11. Testing a diode. Current should only flow in one direction. Reversing the diode should cause the light to go out.

automotive diode. Fig. 10 shows the electrical symbol for a diode. The arrow indicates the direction of current flow in automotive circuits. Actually the electron flow is opposite the direction of the arrow but in automotive circuits the conventional method is to have current flow from positive to negative. Electron movement is from negative to positive.

Diodes can be either shorted or open. Testing a diode can be accomplished with either a low voltage test light, a diode tester, or an ohmmeter. A good diode will light a test lamp in one direction only, Fig. 11. On an ohmmeter, a diode should give one high resistance reading and one low resistance reading if it is in good condition. Diode testers should be used according to the manufacturer's instructions, Fig. 12.

Diodes should be handled carefully so as not to damage them physically. When soldering a diode (during installation), grip the lead with a pair of long-nosed pliers to prevent soldering heat from damaging the diode.

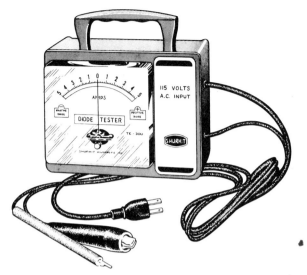

Fig. 12. Commercial diodes testers should be used according to the manufacturer's directions.

It is a good practice to replace all diodes if one has become defective because the other diodes may have become weakened and may fail in a short time.

Diodes that are pressed into an aluminum heat sink should be removed with a diode press. This is a tool similar to a "C" clamp which has special adapters to facilitate easy removal and replacement of the diodes without damaging the aluminum frames.

TRANSISTORS

A transistor is a special form of the P-N junction. Note that in Fig. 13, the transistor contains two P-N junctions instead of one as with the diode. With an understanding of the P-N junction it should not be too difficult to also understand the basic operation of a transistor.

The basic transistor is made up of three sections of a crystal so that two sections are P type and the middle section is N type material. This is known as PNP transistor. An NPN transistor would be composed of two N type sections and the middle would

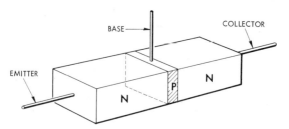

Fig. 13. A transistor is a special type of PN junction. Basically it is two junctions in one.

be P type material. PNP transistors are frequently used in automotive electronic devices.

The transistor has three terminals or leads which are named emitter, base, and collector. These are new terms to automotive technicians and should be thoroughly understood to comprehend the transistor operation.

In a transistor, the middle material is extremely thin, about .001″. The outer material is somewhat thicker, about .005″. With proper bias applied to the transistor and its circuitry completed, the transistor can operate as a conductor of fairly low resistance and can be controlled, or turned on and off, by an extremely small electrical current. When the transistor is off it has high resistance and does not conduct electrical current.

The transistor has two circuits: the emitter to base circuit and the emitter to collector circuit. The base circuit is the control circuit of the transistor. The collector circuit carries the major portion of the electrical current. Fig. 14.

As shown in the illustration, if the base circuit is complete, then the collector circuit will be conducting electrons or current. Examining the action of the P-N junctions reveals that with the base circuit closed the + bias will cause electrons or holes to move across the P-N junction establishing a flow from emitter to base. This is a very small flow because of the very small size of the center section. As a result, the electrons tend to move across the very thin base material and out the collector end of the transistor. In effect, the base material is conducting a very small current, but because it is doing so, a large collector current will result. The inertia of the electrons causes most of them to flow straight across to the collector side.

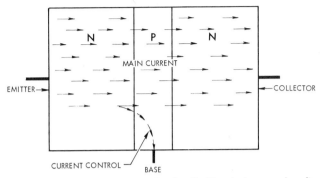

Fig. 14. Transistors have two circuits. Emitter to base and emitter to collector. The base circuit only carries a small flow of current.

When the base circuit is opened, the transistor will stop conducting and no current will flow to the collector circuit. The junction is then effective and acts as a high resistance again until the base circuit is completed once again.

A transistor can easily be turned on and off by various methods. It is capable of switching on and off at speeds of 2000 times per second. Keep in mind also that there are no moving parts and thus no mechanical breakdowns possible. The major enemy of semiconductors is excessive heat. During their operation the movement of the electrons generates a considerable amount of heat which, if it is not properly conducted away, will cause failure of the diode or transistor.

To better understand how the transistor operates notice that the base circuit can be manipulated by a set of contact points or a mechanical switch as shown in Fig. 15. Note the use of the transistor symbol.

Another method used to control the transistor is to reverse the voltage to the base circuit. With reverse bias at its base the transistor functions as a non-conductor and is turned off as shown in Fig. 16.

Transistors have many uses in electrical units on the automobile. The greatest use of the transistor has been with the alternator charging system and the ignition system. Other components use transistors such as radios and sequential flashers, with other kinds of applications being introduced constantly.

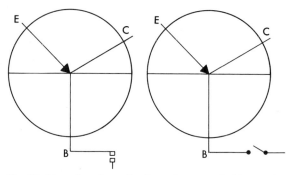

Fig. 15. A transistor base circuit can be controlled by a switch or contacts.

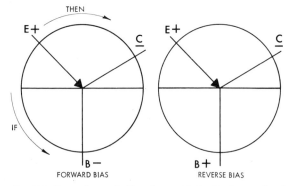

Fig. 16. Reversing polarity of current to the base circuit (reverse bias) shuts off flow through the transistor.

For detailed explanations of the transistor used in the charging circuit and the ignition system, refer to the appropriate chapters (Chapter 8, AC Charging Systems, Chapter 10, Ignition Systems).

ZENER DIODE

The zener diode is a special form of diode which for all practical purposes operates exactly as a P-N junction diode.

The zener diode, however, has one peculiar operating characteristic which makes it worthwhile to mention at this time. A zener diode will conduct reverse bias voltage and current when its particular zener value is attained. This unique ability to respond to a

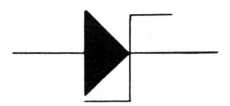

Fig. 17. A zener diode is often indicated by this symbol. Zener diodes serve special functions in automotive circuits.

particular size voltage enables the zener diode to function as a voltage sensing unit in conjunction with a couple of transistors. The zener diode is one of the most important parts of the electronic circuitry.

The difference in the zener diode is that it has a larger area, somewhat different construction techniques, and other small differences to enable it to operate reliably in a reverse zener region. If the reverse current is not properly controlled by a series resistance or some other means, the zener diode would be ruined due to excessive heat. When operated in a properly designed circuit, the zener diode functions very well to limit the amount of voltage at the proper zener level with extremely tight precision.

The symbol for a zener diode is shown in Fig. 17. Frequently, no special designation is used in circuit diagrams, however. When the operation of the transistorized circuitry is studied, particularly in Chapter 10, the function of the zener diode will be readily understood.

INTEGRATED CIRCUITS (IC)

In recent years, the application of electronic devices has grown considerably. One major development which has contributed significantly to greater use of electronic devices is the application of integrated circuits or IC's. Fig. 18.

In the past, noise, vibration, varied temperatures, and cost had ruled out the use of much automotive electronic gear.

One of the techniques used to produce transistors was a first step toward the development of IC's. In 1955 crystals were grown in the laboratory with controlled amounts of impurities. By slicing these crystals apart a handful of transistors were available. Subse-

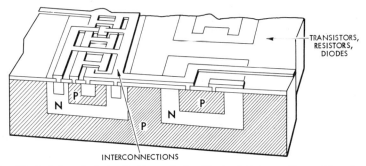

Fig. 18. An integrated circuit. Formed of a block of P type silicon with a layer of N type. Through manufacturing processes diodes, transistors, and other electrical components are formed and interconnected in the single block.

quently, further processes were developed which allowed the growth of complete electronic circuits which were very small and contained all the units such as transistors, diodes, resistors, and capacitors. With all these components formed into one integral piece, the integrated circuit was developed. The IC's are not expensive, have no moving parts or connections, and require no service.

Integrated circuits are part of the micro-miniaturization that is moving across the electronics field. Much of the research and development came from space efforts of the United States Government.

Several manufacturers are now using alternator voltage regulators which are IC's that are built into or otherwise attached directly to the alternators. Integrated circuits are also being applied to ignition systems and to various electrical components such as automotive air conditioning controls, turn signal sequential flashers, electronically controlled fuel-injection systems, and anti-skid braking devices, to mention a few.

Since the IC units are more efficient than conventional systems and are sealed so that they are not affected by moisture, weather, aging, and vibration, it is obvious that eventually they will be used wherever possible by the automobile industry.

In conclusion, this chapter should have clarified what the role of electronics is and will be in the automobile. The discussion of the P-N junction should provide adequate understanding of the principles of operation of such units as diodes and transistors.

Service to these components when necessary will involve locating and subsequent replacement only. No other service is possible. With the basic material in this chapter, new electronic devices should not be frightening or awesome to the technician, but welcomed as a development which will enable better overall service and operation of the vehicle.

TRADE COMPETENCY TESTS

1. What is P type material? What is N type material?
2. How does the P-N junction operate?
3. What are the two basic types of diodes named?
4. How is a diode tested?
5. What are the basic components of a transistor?
6. How does a transistor operate?
7. What are the three terminals of a transistor?
8. What is special about the zener diode?
9. Explain what an IC is.

CHAPTER 13

LIGHTS AND ACCESSORIES SYSTEMS

The purpose of the lighting system is to make the vehicle visible at night, to light the road ahead for the driver, to transmit signals to drivers of approaching and following vehicles, and to illuminate the interior of the vehicle and instrument dials for the driver and his passengers.

In addition to lights certain accessories such as a horn, windshield wipers and window defrosters are necessary for the safe operation of an automobile. Other accessories such as a heater, power-operated seats and windows, cigar lighter, radio, etc., while not essential for vehicle operation, are widely used on many vehicles.

LIGHTING SYSTEM

Headlights

The headlights are the sealed beam type for maximum light distribution on the road. Other lights on the vehicle have small incandescent bulbs mounted in sockets. The bulbs are filled with an inert gas and may contain single or double filaments. Depending upon their design the bulbs may have one or two contacts in the base and are known as single- or double-contact bulbs. The filaments turn white-hot and give off light when current flows through them. The use of inert gas in the bulb prevents the filaments from being oxidized.

The lighting system receives its current from the charging circuit at a point between the charge indicator and the generator or alternator. When the generator or alternator is not charging, or is charging less than the current being used by the lights, current for the lighting system comes from the battery. If an ammeter is used it shows discharge at this point. If the generator or alternator is charging at a rate sufficient to supply all of the electrical needs, including the lights, the excess current charges the battery.

Since the light circuit is connected into the charging circuit between the charge indicator and the generator or alternator, the battery, its ground connection, and the portion of the battery and charging circuit through the charge indicator (including the indicator) are all a part of the lighting system. This system consists of a number of parallel circuits, each of which is provided with at least one switch. Each of the separate lighting circuits has a portion of its circuit in common with all the other lighting system circuits. The general practice is to branch off from the main lighting circuit at whatever point is most convenient.

The lights used in an automotive vehicle vary considerably in the amount of current used. In general, the headlight circuit is the main circuit and generally uses heavier wire than is used for the other lights. Resistance to current flow decreases as wire thickness increases. If thicker than normal wires are used in the headlight circuit the resistance normally provided by the wiring is decreased, the voltage across the lamp filament increases, current flow through the filament increases, and the life of the lamp will be reduced.

Most headlight circuits are designed to have a voltage drop of about 0.7 volts; the lengths of the wires involved, in some instances, determine what gage wire is used. Usually, the circuit voltage (measured parallel to the lamp bulbs) should be about 13.2 volts. Under this condition, the candle power (brightness) will be normal, and the bulb life will be normal (about 460 hours). If by use of larger wires the voltage across the light socket is raised, the candle power increases and the bulb life is reduced.

The lighting system circuits are protected from overload by means of a safety device. This may be a fuse, a thermal circuit breaker, a fusible link, or a combination of those units. These protective devices are actuated by high amperage. They do not protect the lamp bulb from high voltage.

The headlight circuit is the main lighting circuit and carries the greatest current load. This circuit usually runs along one side of the vehicle to the headlights on that side. Just before the wiring reaches the headlights, a parallel or branch circuit is led to the headlights on the other side of the vehicle.

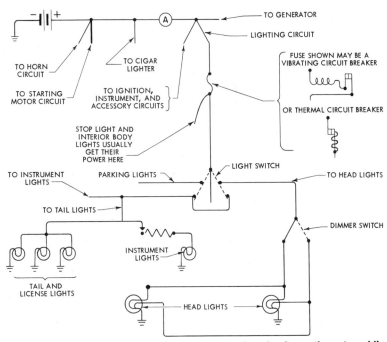

Fig. 1. The lighting circuit and its relationship to other circuits on the automobile.

All headlights have a *high* and a *low* beam. The low beam generally branches off the main headlight circuit at a foot-operated dimmer switch. As the switch is depressed, one headlight circuit is switched off and the other is switched on. The fuse or other protective device is located in a part of the circuit that is common to both the high and low beam branches of the main lighting circuit.

Nearly all vehicles have a light switch mounted on the instrument panel; the switch has two ON positions. When the switch is all the way in, the lights are off. When the switch is moved into the first position, the parking lights, the tail lights, and the license plate lights are on. When moved to the extreme out position, the headlights, tail lights, and license plate lights are on.

Many headlight switches are constructed with a rheostat to control the intensity of the instrument lights. Turning the knob of the headlight switch brightens or dims the instrument panel lights. On some switches, turning the knob to the extreme right or left will turn on the interior lights. When the vehicle is equipped with vacuum-actuated headlight covers, the vacuum switch used to operate the headlight covers is also incorporated in the headlight switch. Pulling the switch knob to the extreme out position will cause the covers to open.

Fig. 1 illustrates the elements of a lighting system circuit and the relationship of the lighting system to other circuits on the vehicle.

Headlights

The sealed beam headlight consists of a lens, a glass reflector with a vaporized aluminum reflecting material deposited on its inner surface, and one or two filaments assembled into a permanently sealed unit, Fig. 2. During assembly the unit is filled with an inert gas. Headlights with one filament have the filament set off-focus near the center of the reflector. The two-filament type sealed beam headlight has its filaments arranged to give two separate headlight beams, depending upon which filament is burning. Because the unit is sealed against dirt, moisture, and corrosion there is little decrease in the amount of projected light throughout its life.

The lens consists of fluted or concave prisms in the glass front to re-direct, bend and spread out the light beam ahead. The light reflected by the reflector is controlled by the flutes and prisms in the headlight lens to give the best possible road illumination with-

Fig. 2. Sealed beam headlight.
Chevrolet Div. — General Motors Corp.

Fig. 3. Distribution of light from the high beam of a sealed beam headlight.

out objectionable glare, Fig. 3. Sealed beam headlights may have a metal shield over the filaments. The shield enables the headlights to project more light farther down the road while shielding stray lights and therefore reducing glare for approaching vehicles.

Three glass projections are equally spaced around the perimeter of the lens. These projections are carefully ground at the factory to provide a mounting point for an aiming device for proper aiming of the headlights.

To provide improved road illumination for night driving, automobiles today are equipped with four headlights paired horizontally or vertically on each side of the vehicle. When mounted horizontally, the outboard lights have two filaments each, one for low beam and the other for high beam. Both outboard lights have a numeral 2 molded in the glass lens. Locating tabs molded in the glass allow mounting of the lights in the outboard light support frames only. The low beams (numeral 2 lights only) are used for city driving and when meeting oncoming traffic on the highway.

The two inboard headlights have a *single,* high beam, off-focus filament, and are marked with a numeral 1 molded in the glass lens. These lamps also have locating tabs molded in the glass lens that allow mounting in the inboard headlight support frame only.

When driving on the high beam, the numeral 1 lights provide the high-intensity light that "reaches" down the highway (Fig. 3); the numeral 2 off-focus filament lights provide the closer light that illuminates the side of the road, ditches, etc. A red indicator lamp on the instrument panel shows when the high beam is on. When driving on the low beam, the numeral 1 headlights are off; illumination is provided by the low beam filaments of the numeral 2 headlights.

On vehicles with the headlights mounted vertically on each side of the vehicle, the numeral 1 headlights are mounted in the lower position and the numeral 2 headlights in the upper position.

Glare. Any light source produces glare if it appreciably affects the vision of an observer looking toward it. However, glare from a light source is not a constant quantity. The intensity of light which affects vision at night would not appear bright in the daylight.

Glare from automobile headlights is caused by a strong beam of light shining into the eyes of the oncoming driver or pedestrian. Glare can be largely eliminated if the strong light rays can be kept below the eye level of the approaching driver, and if the intensity of light which does strike the eye is kept below the glare value.

With the early headlight designs, a part of the light beam was reflected upward. This created a curtain of light between the driver and the road in adverse weather. The design of the sealed beam headlight reduces the amount of uncontrolled and misdirected light, minimizing the amount of glare from the headlights.

Automatic Headlight Dimmer. Some automobiles are equipped with a four unit electronic headlight dimmer, which automatically chooses the correct headlight beam. A light-sensitive plate within a phototube converts oncoming light to current. This current is then amplified to activate a power relay with two pairs of contact points. The current, dependent upon the amount of oncoming light, then determines which set of contacts are closed and consequently which beams are used. A foot switch is also provided for auxiliary use.

Directional Signal Light

Directional signal lights are controlled by a manually operated switch mounted on the steering column. When the switch lever is moved to indicate a turn, a flasher switch causes the front and rear lights to flash on and off on the side of the car nearest to the direction of turn, at a rate of about 60-120 times per minute. While the signal lights are flashing, a signal indicator bulb on the instrument

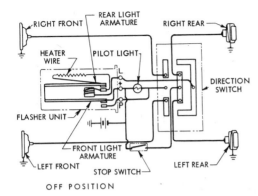

Fig. 4. Typical directional signal wiring diagram.

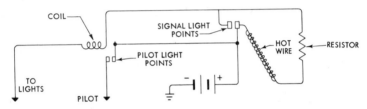

Fig. 5. Internal circuit of a directional signal flasher switch.

panel also flashes, producing a small arrow of light to indicate to the driver the direction for which the signal has been set. Fig. 4 illustrates the manner in which the control and flasher switches are connected in a typical directional signal light circuit.

The flasher switch employed in the control contains two sets of contacts actuated by the flow of current (Fig. 5). Both contacts are open when the hand-operated switch is off. When turned on, current enters at the wire marked " + " and flows through the "hot wire," "resistor," "coil," and signal lights to ground. The resistor impedes the flow of the current to the extent that it is not strong enough to light the lights or energize the coil. The "hot wire" expands, however, allowing the signal light contact points to close. The resistor and "hot wire" are then shunted out of the circuit, and sufficient current flows through the coil to light the lights. The coil is energized, closing the pilot light contact points. Each pilot light and signal light flashes simultaneously. As soon as current stops flowing through the "hot wire," it cools, contracts, and opens the signal light contacts, causing the circuit to collapse until the "hot wire" again heats up and the cycle is repeated.

Emergency Warning Light. Vehicles presently being manufactured have a hazard warning switch, sometimes called the *emergency warning flasher switch,* mounted on the steering column opposite the directional signal switch. When the switch is turned on, all of the directional signal lights will flash. The directional signal light circuit is used; however, another flasher unit is generally incorporated because of the difference in circuit resistance when four lights are used rather than two lights.

Cornering Lights. Many automobiles have cornering lights installed at the side of each front fender to illuminate the side of the road toward which the automobile is turning. The lights operate through the directional signal lever switch through a relay at each light that holds the circuit in the ON position as long as the turn signals are on. As the steering wheel is straightened after the turn, both the cornering and directional lights are turned off.

Back Up Lights

The back up lights consist of two lights mounted at the rear of the vehicle, either in the body or the rear bumper. Whenever the ignition switch is turned to the ON or the ACC position and the shift lever is moved to the reverse position, the backup switch connected to the shift lever turns on both white lights to illuminate the area at the rear of the vehicle. On vehicles with an automatic transmission the back-up switch is incorporated in the cranking circuit's neutral switch. On vehicles with a manually-shifted transmission, a separate back-up switch connected to the shift lever is provided. Fig. 6 illustrates a typical back-up light circuit.

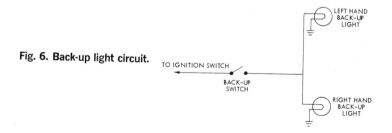

Fig. 6. Back-up light circuit.

TO IGNITION SWITCH

BACK-UP SWITCH

LEFT HAND BACK-UP LIGHT

RIGHT HAND BACK-UP LIGHT

Parking and Stop Lights

The parking lights consist of a parking light mounted on each side at the front of the vehicle (either in the fender, on the bumper, or at the ends of the grill), two tail lights, and a license plate light. The parking lights are controlled by the light switch on the dash which activates the tail and license lights also on the first stop.

Each front parking light has a dual filament bulb, and serves as a parking and directional signal light. Each rear light also contains a dual filament bulb and serves as a combination tail light, directional signal light, and stop light.

The stop lights are controlled by either a hydraulic switch mounted on the master cylinder or by a mechanical switch operated by the brake pedal. The hydraulic switch is closed to turn on the stop lights by hydraulic pressure when the brakes are applied. For the mechanical switch, the stop light switch is connected to the brake pedal and the circuit to the stop lights is closed the instant the brake pedal is depressed. Fig. 7 illustrates typical parking and stop light circuits.

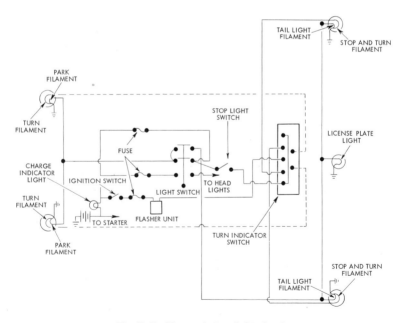

Fig. 7. Parking and stop light circuits.

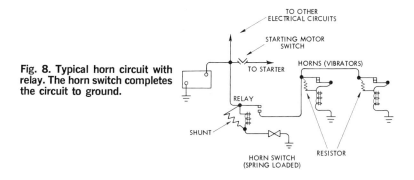

Fig. 8. Typical horn circuit with relay. The horn switch completes the circuit to ground.

Other Lights

Numerous other lights will be found on the automobile: the instrument panel lights, courtesy light in the front compartment, dome light, glove compartment light, radio panel light, and others. Each of these lights is connected in parallel with the main lighting circuit and is turned on or off either by the headlight and parking light control switch or by a separate switch. Spring loaded jamb switches are employed to automatically turn on and off the dome, pillar, trunk, glove compartment and courtesy lights in the interior of the vehicle. Switches are mounted in a hole drilled in the door jamb or close to the edge of the glove compartment opening so that opening and closing the door will activate the switch.

ACCESSORIES

Certain accessories are necessary for the safe operation of a vehicle. Other accessories, while not absolutely necessary, contribute to the comfort and convenience of the vehicle's occupants.

Horns

The horn circuit consists of a matched pair of horns, a relay, a storage battery, a horn ring on the steering wheel, connecting wires and a ground return circuit. See Fig. 8.

The horn consists of a diaphragm that is caused to vibrate by an electromagnet to produce an audible sound. See Fig. 9. When the electromagnet is energized, it pulls on an armature attached to the diaphragm. Movement of the armature flexes the diaphragm and opens a set of contact points. This opens the electromagnet circuit

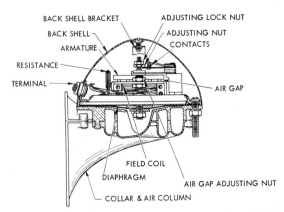

Fig. 9. A cross section of a diaphragm type horn. Both contacts and air gaps are points of adjustment. Delco-Remy Div.—General Motors Corp.

and the diaphragm returns to its original position, closing the contacts. The cycle is repeated many times per second. The higher the pitch of the horn, the greater the number of cycles (vibrations). A resistor is connected across the contacts and in series with the electromagnet winding to reduce arcing at the contact points and prolong their life.

To keep the current flow through the horn (switch) contacts at the steering wheel at a minimum amount, a relay is used between the battery and the horn, Fig. 8. When the horn ring is depressed, the current from the battery flows through the relay coil winding. The magnetism created in the iron core pulls the armature down, closing the circuit between the battery and the horn.

Many horn circuit relays have a shunt resistor connected in parallel with the relay coil as shown in Fig. 8. When the magnetic field of the relay collapses (horn circuit is opened), a high voltage is induced in the horn switch circuit. This high voltage can cause a disagreeable electric shock. The purpose of the shunt is to provide a path for this current, thus eliminating the possibility of an electric shock from this source. The shunt usually consists of a short length of very fine wire.

Horn Relay-Buzzer (Theft Deterrent System). Some vehicles are equipped with a buzzer built into the horn relay which operates when the ignition key is in the switch and the driver's door is

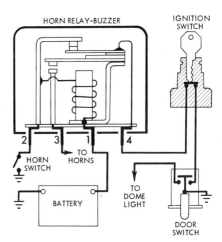

Fig. 10. A schematic of a typical horn relay—buzzer. Chevrolet Div. —General Motors Corp.

opened. The buzzer sounds to remind the driver to remove the keys from the ignition when he is leaving the car. Fig. 10 is the wiring schematic of the combination horn relay and buzzer circuit.

When the key is fully inserted in the ignition switch, the number 4 terminal of the relay is connected to ground through the door jamb switch when the driver's door is opened. Current flows from the battery through the relay coil winding, the buzzer contacts, the ignition switch and door jamb switch to ground. The magnetism created by current flowing through the coil causes the buzzer contacts to open, which opens the coil winding circuit, and the contacts then re-close. This cycle is repeated many times per second to give the buzzing sound. Removing the key or closing the door will open the circuit and shut off the buzzer.

Windshield Wiper

The windshield wipers in use on present day vehicles are generally electrically operated, although windshield wipers used in the past have been operated by vacuum and are still used on some vehicles. Electric windshield wipers are of either the one-, two-, or three-speed type, or are equipped with a rheostat-type switch and have variable speed. Electric windshield wipers operate at a uniform speed regardless of the speed of the engine or vehicle, Fig. 11.

The windshield wiper consists of a 12-volt electric motor and a gear train that causes a crank arm to rotate, Fig. 11. The drive link-

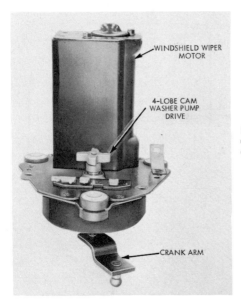

Fig. 11. Windshield wiper motor. Chevrolet Div.—General Motors Corp.

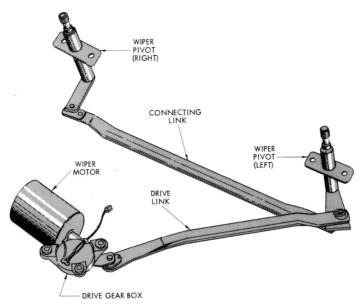

Fig. 12. Dual windshield wiper operating mechanism. Plymouth Div.—Chrysler Corp.

age is connected to the crank arm so that rotation of the crank arm imparts a reciprocating movement through the linkage to the pivots. See Fig. 12. The pivots in turn move the wiper arms back and forth across the windshield.

Windshield wipers are classed as being of either the depressed or non-depressed type. In the depressed type the wiper blades, when in the at-rest position (not in use) are located off the windshield below the trim molding. In the non-depressed type, the blades in the at-rest position are located $1\frac{1}{2}$ to 2 inches above the windshield trim molding.

Some depressed-type wiper blades are concealed by a cover panel when not in use. The wiper blade cover panel is operated by a vacuum actuator attached to a control assembly which pivots the cover panel up and forward before the blades will operate. The same vacuum source that operates the headlight covers is also used to operate the wiper blade cover. The wiper switch electrically energizes a solenoid, which in turn actuates the vacuum control switch.

WINDSHIELD
WIPER MOTOR

WASHER PUMP
ACTUATOR

4-LOBE CAM

CRANK ARM

Fig. 13. Windshield washer unit attached to a windshield wiper motor. Chevrolet Div.—General Motors Corp.

Windshield Washer

On many vehicles the windshield wiper has a windshield washer attached as an added accessory. See Fig. 13. The washer is a positive displacement pump consisting of a rubber bellows, bellows spring, and valve arrangement assembled in a casing attached to the wiper gear box, Fig. 14. The washer is operated by a 3- or 4-lobe cam attached to the wiper motor shaft. Operation of the washer is controlled both electrically and mechanically by a relay assembly and ratchet wheel arrangement.

When only the windshield wiper is operating, the plunger arm attached to the bellows is held in the locked-out position by an eccentric on the ratchet wheel. When the pushbutton on the wiper control is pushed in to start the washer the relay coil becomes energized, pulling the armature away from the ratchet wheel. This permits the ratchet arm to become operative and rotate the ratchet wheel, causing the eccentric to release the plunger arm for pumping action.

As the wiper motor cam revolves, each lobe of the cam pulls the plunger arm and attached bellows back on the suction stroke. With each stroke the bellows fills with water from the supply bottle under

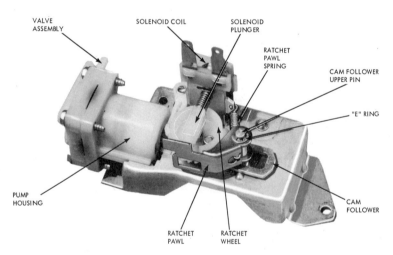

Fig. 14. Windshield washer pump mechanism. Chevrolet Div.—General Motors Corp.

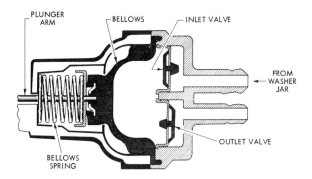

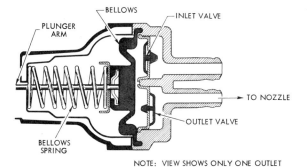

NOTE: VIEW SHOWS ONLY ONE OUTLET

Fig. 15. Operation of the windshield washer pump bellows on intake and exhaust strokes. (In newer models the bellows has been replaced by a piston-type pump.) Pontiac Div.— General Motors Corp.

the hood. See Fig. 15. As the high point of the cam lobe is passed, the compressed spring within the bellows pushes on the bellows, forcing the water out of the outlet valve onto the windshield. Each revolution of the cam produces four pump strokes and each pump stroke advances the ratchet wheel one tooth. The pump operates through one revolution of the ratchet wheel (about 21 teeth), after which the eccentric on the ratchet wheel again is in position to lock out the plunger shaft and pump bellows.

Electric Motors

Numerous electric motors are used throughout the automobile to operate many of the accessories. Power seats, power windows, heaters, and defrosters are all operated by small electric motors. For all practical purposes the electric motors are constructed and operate in exactly the same manner as the starting motor and generator (while being motorized).

Power Windows. Power windows are operated by reversible electric motors with an internal circuit breaker and a self-locking, rubber coupled gear drive. Each window has a separate electric motor connected to a gear drive and operates the regulator mechanism in the same manner as a manually-operated window regulator. Each power window can be controlled by either a master switch located on the left front door or by an individual switch on the respective door of the vehicle.

In addition to the circuit breaker, a relay is used in the circuit which prevents the operation of the power windows until the ignition switch is turned on.

Power Seats. The four-way or six-way power seat adjuster is actuated by an electric motor. The motor is energized by a multi-type control switch. The entire circuit is protected by a circuit breaker. In some installations a relay is used in the circuit to prevent operaton of the seat adjuster until the ignition switch is turned on.

On all installations a motor operates the gear drive train which supplies power through flexible cables to the individual slave units

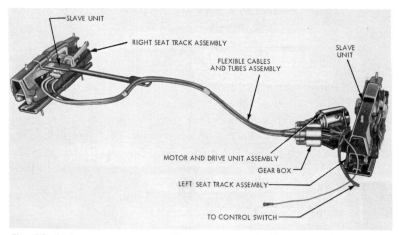

Fig. 16. A six-way power seat adjuster motor and drive assembly. Plymouth Div.—Chrysler Corp.

located in the seat tracks, Fig. 16. Solenoids are used to activate the cable which will drive the mechanism to give the desired movement. When the selected switch is operated, current flows to the gear box (transmission) solenoid, which controls the called-for seat movement. Energizing the solenoid coil results in the solenoid plunger dog engaging the proper gear mechanism to drive the control cable. The same switch action also produces a current flow through the motor control relay to the motor field coils. The current flows through the relay and closes the contacts between the relay power source and the armature motor lead wire, causing the motor to operate.

The seat is raised or lowered by turning a gear nut either to the left or the right depending upon which way the seat is to be moved. The cable turns a pinion which engages the seat rack to move the seat forward or backward.

Heater and Defroster Motors. The heating and defrosting system

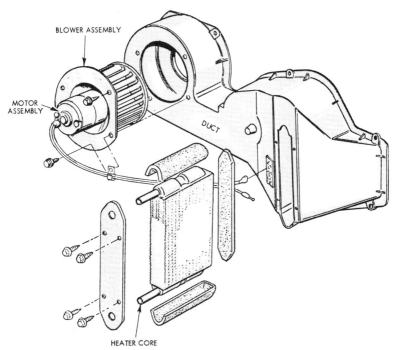

Fig. 17. Heater assembly. Ford Div.—Ford Motor Co.

uses one or two electric motors to give a forced air effect, usually blending fresh outside air with heat produced by the heater radiator core. An axial flow blower is usually employed and is attached directly to the motor shaft, Fig. 17. A two or three speed switch incorporated in the circuit provides air control by regulating blower speed. When only one motor is used, a damper is used in the main duct to direct the air to the proper duct for defrosting and/or heat-

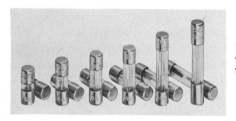

Fig. 18. Fuses employed in automotive electrical circuits. Littlefuse, Inc.

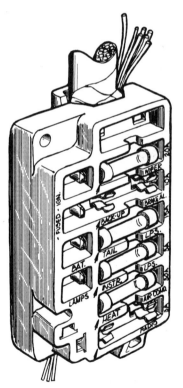

Fig. 19. Typical fuse block, generally mounted near the underside of the instrument panel. Chevrolet Div.—General Motors Corp.

ing. The electrical circuit to the heater and defroster motors is usually protected by a fuse.

Fuses and Circuit Breakers

Automotive vehicles employ fuses, circuit breakers or both in the lighting, accessory, and horn circuits for the purpose of preventing an excessive current flow which might damage the wiring, instruments, or electrical units. Fuses are designed to burn out when an overload occurs in any of the circuits they protect. Circuit breakers are not damaged by an overload.

Fuses. Fuses used in automotive vehicles consist of a glass enclosed strip of alloy metal which has a low melting point. The fuses vary in size and capacity and are rated according to the amount of current (amperage) they can safely carry (Fig. 18). When an excessive amount of current flows through a circuit, the overload heats the fuse, causing the alloy metal strip to melt. This breaks the continuity of the electrical circuit, and stops the flow of current. After the trouble which caused the fuse to burn out has been corrected, the fuse must be replaced to complete the circuit again.

Fuses are generally mounted in a fuse block (Fig. 19) that holds all or nearly all the fuses employed on the vehicle. The fuse block is usually located at some point under the instrument panel.

Circuit Breaker. Some automotive vehicles employ one or more circuit breakers in place of fuses to protect the wiring and electrical units. The circuit breaker is a current-limiting relay, designed to reduce the current flowing through a circuit to a safe value when it exceeds what is intended for the circuit.

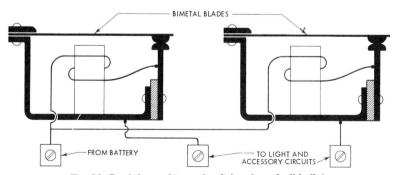

Fig. 20. Dual thermal-type circuit breaker—fusible link.

TABLE 1. FUSIBLE LINKS

Location	Color	Protects
Battery terminal of starter relay to main wire harness	Red	Complete wiring
Battery terminal of horn relay to main wire harness.	Pink	Horn circuit
Accessory terminal of ignition switch.	Brown	Electric tailgate, instrument panel switch, cigarette lighter, all accessories from fuse panel, electric windshield wiper.
Ignition terminal of ignition switch to wire harness.	Yellow	Alternator field voltage, fuel and temperature indicators, park brake warning light.

Although automotive vehicles in the past employed a vibrating or lock-out type circuit breaker (no longer used) many present-day vehicles have one or more thermal-type circuit breakers connected in the wiring system. The thermal-operated circuit breaker employed on a number of vehicles has a coil winding on an iron core, the winding being connected in series with a set of contact points and a bimetal blade (Fig. 20). When excessive current flows through the circuit breaker, the iron core becomes magnetized and tends to hold the points closed. The magnetic effect offsets, temporarily, the tendency of the bimetal blade to curl with the heat to open the contacts. The bimetal blade becomes excessively hot and, as a result, less susceptible to the magnetic pull of the iron core. As a result, the bimetal blade curls rapidly the moment the points open. With the points open, the flow of current in the circuit stops. As the bimetal blade cools, the points close and current once more flows through the circuit; the iron core again becomes magnetized, holding the points firmly together. This magnetic force assures a firm contact even though the bimetal blade may not have sufficiently cooled in the intervening time.

Fusible Links. A fusible link is a special wire placed in the wiring harness. It has a special non-flammable insulation which will bubble or blister if the wire link is overheated by excessive current flow through it. The fusible link is used to prevent major damage in case a short circuit, grounded or overload condition exists.

An example of the location and function of fusible links follows in Table I.

TRADE COMPETENCY TESTS

1. What is the purpose of a fusible link and how does it protect the circuit?

2. What effect does wire size have on the life of a light bulb? Why?

3. How is the sealed beam type of headlight bulb constructed?

4. What is the function of the reflector in the headlight? Of the lens?

5. What is the difference between a #1 and a #2 sealed beam headlight?

6. How does the flasher unit operate in controlling the turn indicator lights?

7. What keeps the cornering light burning steadily while the turn indicator lights are flashing?

8. How are the stop lights controlled?

9. Can you trace the flow of electricity from the battery to the headlights?

10. What is a jamb switch and where is it used?

11. How does a vibrator horn operate?

12. How does the windshield washer operate?

13. What is the purpose of a fuse?

14. How do thermal type circuit breakers operate to protect the circuit?

CHAPTER 14

LIGHTS AND ACCESSORIES
SYSTEMS SERVICE

State and federal laws require that the lighting system be kept in a safe operating condition. While the lighting system is remarkably free from troubles occasionally they do develop and light bulbs occasionally burn out and must be replaced. For maximum safe illumination for night driving headlights should be checked periodically to see that they are aimed properly. They should also be checked whenever a headlight is replaced or after a front end collision.

LIGHTING SYSTEM TROUBLES

When a circuit breaker is used in a headlight circuit and the lights flicker from bright to dim, the circuit breaker is opening and closing the circuit as a result of a grounded or shorted wire in that particular circuit. Try switching from high beam to low beam to isolate the short or ground. If the condition exists in both circuits, the trouble will be in a branch of the circuit which is common to both the high and low beams, such as the tail lights or license plate light. Fig. 1 is a typical wiring diagram of the front lighting and engine compartment wiring. Fig. 2 is a typical diagram of the body and rear lighting wiring.

If one light in a circuit does not light but the others do, the fault is usually in the bulb itself. When a new bulb is installed but still does not operate, there is a break in the circuit. Lights that burn out prematurely usually indicate a high voltage in the circuit. Clean and tighten all electrical connections in the particular circuit, including the battery cable connections. When replacing burned out bulbs, make certain that the replacement bulbs carry the same code number as the original or that the replacement bulb can readily be interchanged with the original.

Replacement of Sealed Beam Headlights

To remove a sealed beam headlight from the vehicle, first remove the screws holding the headlight trim ring or trim panel. Fig. 3. Then remove the retaining ring either by unscrewing the screws or by unhooking the spring and clip. Next, pull the headlight unit forward and disconnect the wiring assembly plug. Connect the wiring plug to the new headlight and place in position, being certain to locate the glass tabs in the positioning slots. Replace and refasten the retaining ring. Align the headlight and replace the trim ring.

Light Bulb Replacement

The method of replacing bulbs other than the sealed beam headlights varies with the construction of the light assembly. Bulbs are replaced either from the front of the light assembly after the lens is removed, or from the rear without removing the lens.

Replace Bulb from Front. To replace a light bulb, examine the assembly to see how the lens is secured, Fig. 4. If the lens or its frame is held in position by screws, the lens must be removed in order to replace the bulb. Remove the screws from the retaining ring and remove the retaining ring and lens. To remove the spring loaded bulb, press in on the bulb, turn to the left, and pull the bulb out. Install the new bulb, and reassemble the light, using a new gasket if necessary.

Note: On light assemblies with a removable lens, the gasket may deteriorate with age and weathering. Where this occurs, moisture may get by the gasket to corrode the bulb socket. Corrosion may be present on the base of the bulb as well as on the walls and terminals of the bulb socket. Extreme corrosion can short out the socket or cause intermittent operation.

Slight corrosion can be corrected by scraping or sanding the socket to remove the rust and corrosion. Extreme corrosion may necessitate replacement of the entire lamp housing. Corrosion of this type will often be found in older cars with signal lights mounted in, or below the level of, the bumpers.

Replace Bulb from Rear. On some lights employed on automotive vehicles, the light bulb is not accessible from the front and is replaced by removing the light socket and bulb from the rear of the

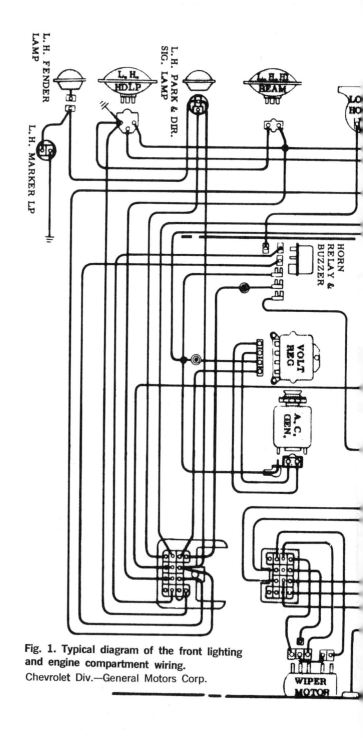

Fig. 1. Typical diagram of the front lighting and engine compartment wiring.
Chevrolet Div.—General Motors Corp.

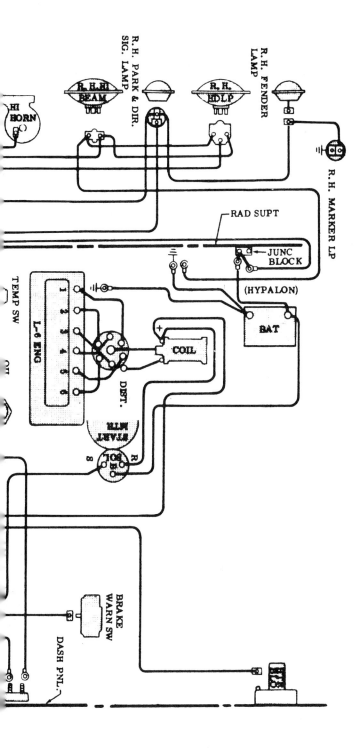

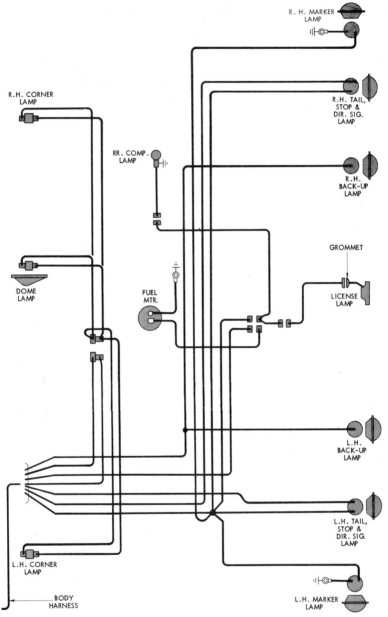

Fig. 2. Typical wiring diagram of the body and rear lighting. Chevrolet Div.—
General Motors Corp.

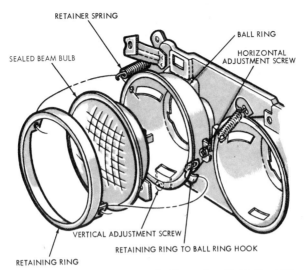

Fig. 3. Replacement of a sealed beam headlight. Ford Div. —Ford Motor Co.

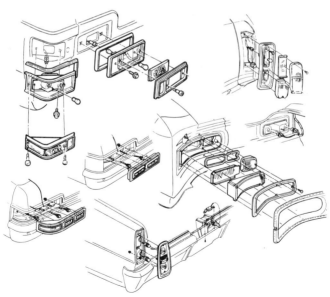

Fig. 4. Various designs of rear light assemblies on which the lens must be removed to replace the bulb. Chevrolet Div.—General Motors Corp.

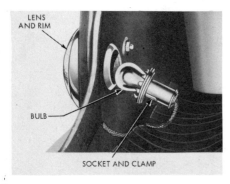

Fig. 5. A button-type rear light receptacle.

lamp assembly. Various methods of mounting the light socket on the body may be employed.

Fig. 5 illustrates a button type socket and receptable. The receptacle is removed by pushing it to one side to free it from the lamp body, then pulling it away from the lamp body. To replace, push in until it snaps into place. In another design, the bulb receptacle must be pushed in slightly and twisted to the left to remove the receptacle. Another form of construction employs retaining fingers or clips to hold the bulb receptacle in place. The bulb receptacle can be removed by moving the retaining fingers or clips to one side.

To replace the bulb in light assemblies designed for replacement from the rear, examine the light to determine which form of construction is employed. Remove the receptacle and bulb from the lamp. To remove the bulb from its socket, press in slightly on the bulb, twist to the left, and pull the bulb out of the socket. Install the new bulb and replace the receptacle.

Replacement of Fuses and Circuit Breakers

Fuses should be replaced only after the trouble in the circuit has been corrected. Circuit breakers need not be replaced unless they have been damaged by overload.

Replace Fuse. Remove the burned out fuse from the fuse clip. Make certain that the fuse clips are clean, and install a new fuse having the same number as the fuse being replaced.

Check Circuit Breaker. Although circuit breakers seldom break down, an overload on the circuit breaker may cause the points to become burned or pitted or may "draw" the temper from the return spring. If the temper of the return spring is lost to the extent

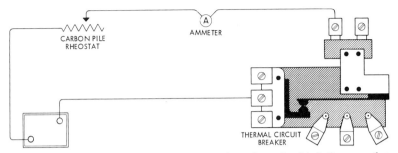

Fig. 6. A rheostat and ammeter are connected as shown to check the operation of a thermal circuit breaker.

that the circuit breaker does not operate properly, the unit should be replaced.

Thermal circuit breakers can be checked for proper operation with a battery, ammeter, and carbon pile rheostat. Connect the ammeter and carbon pile rheostat in series with the battery and thermal circuit breaker as shown in Fig. 6. The ammeter and rheostat should each have a capacity of 50 amperes.

Adjust the rheostat to indicate on the ammeter the rated current value of the circuit breaker (42 amperes on some types). The circuit breaker should start vibrating in three minutes or less.

Adjust the rheostat to reduce the current flowing through the circuit breaker to 75 percent of the rated value ($31\frac{1}{2}$ amperes on circuit breakers with a 42 ampere maximum rating). The circuit breaker should remain closed indefinitely at this current value.

If the circuit breaker does not operate as specified, it should be replaced. Circuit breakers are not adjustable, and no attempt should be made to alter the calibration by bending the bimetal blade.

Checking Switches

The operation of a switch can be checked by using a jumper wire to by-pass the switch. A voltmeter can be used to determine if current is present at the switch. A switch that fails to operate properly must be replaced.

Headlight Alignment

The alignment of headlights involves two steps: the checking of headlight alignment and the adjustment or aiming of the headlights.

The procedure for the checking of headlight alignment varies with the type of equipment you have to work with. Regardless of the means employed to check headlight alignment, the method of making the adjustment is the same.

The headlights of an automobile should be checked for aim periodically, but particularly after a front-end collision, to maintain the maximum road illumination and safety that the headlights were designed to provide. Regardless of which method is used for checking the headlights, the vehicle must be at curb weight, i.e., with gas, oil, and spare tire, but no passengers. (Some manufacturers recommend that the driver and a passenger be seated in the front seat during headlight alignment.) The tires must be uniformly inflated to the specified air pressure, and the vehicle should be rocked to take the "set" out of the springs. If the vehicle regularly carries an unusual load in the rear compartment or tows a trailer, these conditions should be approximated when the headlights are checked. Some states have special requirements (loading allowance) for aiming headlights which must be known and followed to secure correct alignment.

Aiming Screen. The alignment of headlights with an aiming screen requires a space large enough so that the vehicle can be placed with the headlight lens 25 feet from a light-colored vertical screen or wall. The floor where the testing is to be done should be as level as possible. If the floor is not level, the slope in the floor

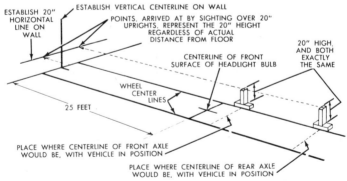

Fig. 7. Proper method for developing a wall-type headlight aiming screen. Ford Div.—Ford Motor Co.

should be fairly constant. Otherwise, the operation is complicated for cars of different wheel bases.

To align the headlights place the vehicle in position facing a screen with the headlight lens 25 feet from the screen. Prepare two uprights which stand exactly 20 inches high. Place the uprights alongside the points where the front and rear tires on one side of the car rest on the floor. Sight along the tops of both uprights to establish a point on the screen. See Fig. 7. Repeat the procedure for the other side of the vehicle. Draw a horizontal line through the two sighted points on the screen. This line represents the 20-inch height projected to the screen regardless of the actual measured distance of the line from the floor (i.e., the line drawn on the screen may not measure 20 inches from the floor when measured with a rule).

Measure the distance from the floor to the center of the No. 1 (high beam) headlight. Subtract 20 inches from this measurement. The result (dimension *B* in the upper diagram of Fig. 8) is then transferred to the screen. Measuring from the 20-inch reference line, dimension *B* is marked off on the screen at two places. The line drawn through the two points (and parallel to 20-inch reference line) represents the height of the horizontal centerline of the No. 1 headlights.

Draw another line two inches below, and parallel to, the horizontal centerline. The No. 1 headlights will be centered vertically on this line.

Sight through the center of the rear window and over the center of the hood to establish the centerline of the vehicle on the screen. Draw vertical lines on the screen to the right and left of the centerline of the car, at a distance equal to half the center-to-center distance (dimension *A*) between the two headlights, as shown in the upper diagram of Fig. 8. The No. 1 headlights (the high beam headlights) are adjusted to this diagram.

Adjustment. The headlights should be adjusted so that the highest intensity portion of the light occurs at the points indicated by the two diagrams in Fig. 8. To aim the high beam (No. 1) headlights, remove the headlight trim ring. Turn on the headlights and switch to high beam. Both the No. 1 and the No. 2 headlight high beams will be on. Cover the No. 2 lights when making the No. 1 headlight adjustments.

Move the light beam to the right or left by turning the horizontal adjusting screw (Fig. 9) so that the highest light intensity is *cen-*

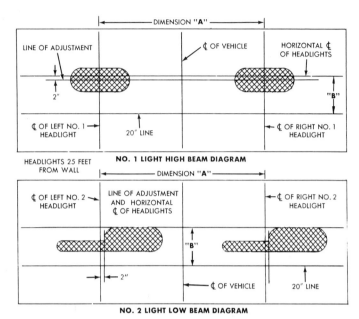

NO. 1 LIGHT HIGH BEAM DIAGRAM

NO. 2 LIGHT LOW BEAM DIAGRAM

Fig. 8. Correct position for No. 1 headlights (top) and No. 2 headlights (bottom) on aiming screens. Ford Div.—Ford Motor Co.

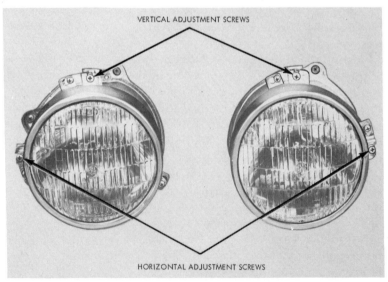

Fig. 9. Headlight adjustment screws are identified. Plymouth Div.—Chrysler Corp.

tered on the vertical centerline. Adjust the light beam up or down by turning the vertical adjusting screw (Fig. 9) so that the light intensity is *centered* on the line drawn two inches below the horizontal centerline, as shown in the upper diagram of Fig. 8.

Once the No. 1 (high beam) headlights are adjusted, switch the dimmer to low beam and adjust the No. 2 headlights. To adjust the No. 2 headlights (the low beam headlights) a new chart may be required depending on how the headlights are mounted relative to each other. Dimension *B* will change if the No. 2 headlight is mounted below instead of alongside the No. 1 headlight. Thus, the No. 2 headlights are adjusted as shown in the lower diagram of Fig. 8. Note that in adjusting the No. 2 lights, the adjustment is made directly to the horizontal centerline (instead of to a line 2 inches below the centerline). Adjust the lights so that the uppermost part of the low beam is flush with the horizontal centerline. Adjustment of the No. 2 headlight low beams automatically adjusts the No. 2 headlight high beams.

The beam pattern of earlier type head lights may be of different shape, depending on the contour of the reflector and the design of the lens. However, all lights of a particular type should have the same light pattern on the screen. If the pattern varies, the bulb is out of focus due to filament sag, or a defective lens or reflector.

Aiming Device. Fig. 10 illustrates an aiming device for sealed beam headlights. Headlights can be aligned with this device without turning the lights on. The aimers are installed on each headlight and held in place by means of a plunger-operated suction cup. The headlight has three accurately ground projections on the lens which serve to align the aimer on the headlight. The two arms extending forward are checked for horizontal alignment with a piece of string.

Correct horizontal aim is obtained by turning the proper headlight adjustment screw until desired alignment is secured between the string and arms of the aimer. Vertical aim is obtained by turning the vertical aim adjustment screw until the bubble in the level built into each aimer aligns with the desired markings.

CHECKING THE HORN

In some cases where the horn fails to sound, a wire is disconnected; it is always good practice to check for a disconnected or loose wire before making further checks. Establish a good ground

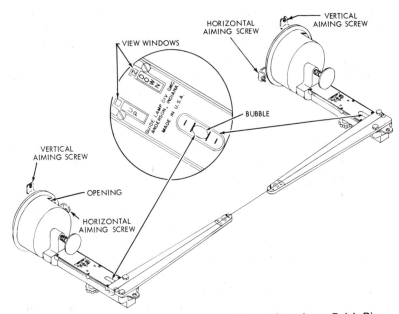

Fig. 10. Adjusting horizontal and vertical aim with a safety aimer. Buick Div.— General Motors Corp.

for the horn by means of a jumper wire. After grounding the horn with a jumper wire, press the horn ring. If the horn now sounds, the horn is not properly grounded. Remove the horn from its mounting brackets and clean away rust or paint to assure a good ground.

If the horn still does not sound, disconnect the main feed wire at the horn relay and ground it momentarily. Note whether or not a spark occurs as the wire is grounded. If no spark occurs, an open circuit exists between the end of the wire that was grounded and the battery. Make the necessary repairs to the circuit.

If a spark occurs when the feed wire is grounded, the circuit supplying current to that point can be considered satisfactory. Touch the feed wire to the horn terminal of the relay. If the horn now sounds, replace the horn relay. If the horn still does not sound, connect a jumper wire from the main feed wire to the terminal of the horn. If the horn now sounds, an open circuit exists between the relay and the horn.

If, when the main feed wire was connected through a jumper

directly to the horn, it did not sound, the fault is in the horn itself. Repair or replace the horn.

The continuous sounding of the horn can be the result of a short to ground in the relay-to-horn button circuit, or of stuck contact points in the relay.

CHECKING WINDSHIELD WIPER MOTOR

If the windshield wiper motor fails to operate check the wiring to the motor, including the switch. If electricity is present at the switch, use a jumper wire to by-pass the switch. If the motor now operates, the trouble is in the switch. Replace the switch.

If jumping the switch has no effect, use a voltmeter to determine if current is reaching the wiper motor. If the motor is getting electricity and still does not function, replace the wiper motor assembly. If the motor itself operates properly, it will be necessary to inspect

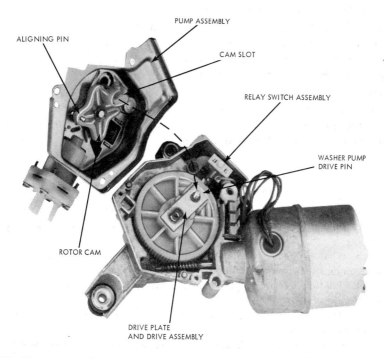

Fig. 11. Partially disassembled wiper and washer pump assembly. Chevrolet Div. —General Motors Corp.

the gear box assembly for worn and defective parts. Fig. 11 illustrates a partially disassembled wiper and washer mechanism.

Windshield Washer

The windshield washer pump assembly, Fig. 11, can be separated from the wiper motor for service. Before removing the washer assembly make sure the hoses are not cracked, broken, or plugged. Be sure the spray nozzles are clear and that the screen on the intake hose in the fluid container is clean and in the solution. It is usually best to replace a defective washer unit rather than trying to repair it. The cost of installing a rebuilt, or even a completely new, unit is often considerably less than the labor costs to repair the defective unit.

CHECK ELECTRIC MOTORS

Before condemning any electric motor make sure that electricity is reaching the motor (there is a complete circuit). This may be checked by disconnecting the wire at the motor and attaching a voltmeter. If there is no reading, check the switch as well as the ground. The switch can be checked by using a jumper wire to bypass the switch, or by connecting the jumper wire directly from a source of electricity to the motor. Check the motor ground by connecting a jumper wire between a good ground and a clean spot on the motor housing. If the motor is found to be defective, it is usually better to replace the motor rather than to attempt to repair it.

TRADE COMPETENCY TESTS

1. Describe the procedure for replacing sealed beam headlights.
2. How is a bayonet type light bulb socket removed from the lamp housing?
3. What methods are employed to secure the socket receptacle to the body on lights where the bulb is accessible from the rear only?
4. What devices are employed in the wiring system to protect the system from overload?
5. How do thermal-type circuit breakers operate to protect the circuit they are connected to?
6. What is meant when it is said that a vehicle must be at curb weight?
7. When aligning headlights, what is the acceptable loading allowance in most localities?

8. When aligning the headlights with an aiming screen, how far must the vehicle be from the screen?

9. In sealed beam headlights with dual filaments, which headlight beam is employed to align the headlight?

10. What is the purpose of the 20″ uprights in laying out an aiming screen?

11. What provisions are incorporated in sealed beam headlights for aiming the light bulb?

12. How is the safety aimer device mounted on the headlights to assure accuracy in alignment?

13. How is a horn circuit checked when the horn fails to sound?

14. How can a switch be checked for proper operation?

CHAPTER 15

INSTRUMENTS
AND GAGES

Several type of gage and signaling devices are used on automotive vehicles to indicate the operating condition of the engine oiling system, electrical system, cooling system, and the amount of fuel. Speedometers are used to indicate both distance traveled and speed in miles per hour.

The instruments supplied with most cars and trucks are intended to be used only as a means of indicating to the driver the operating condition of the vehicle. They are not intended as accurate meters that could be used for testing purposes.

The ignition switch is usually connected in the circuits of electrically operated instruments so that when the ignition switch is turned off the instruments are inoperative.

It is not advisable to attempt repairs on most instruments used on automotive vehicles. Instruments such as ammeters, fuel gages, and temperature indicators are inexpensive, and it is usually wise to replace them as a complete unit. Other instruments, such as the speedometer, contain delicately calibrated mechanisms which can be repaired. However, they require specialized skills and should be sent to specialty shops which do such work.

Instrument Voltage Regulator

Some vehicles use a voltage regulator in the instrument circuit to regulate the variable voltage from the battery and charging system (input voltage) to a constant 5 volts output to the indicating devices. Note: the instrument voltage regulator is not to be confused with the voltage limiter of a DC generator regulator. The voltage regulator, Fig. 1, is a simple device consisting of a bimetal arm, a heating coil and a pair of contacts.

In operation, when the ignition switch is turned on, current flows

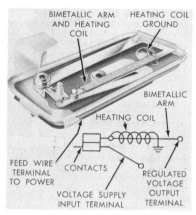

BIMETALLIC ARM AND HEATING COIL

HEATING COIL GROUND

BIMETALLIC ARM

HEATING COIL

FEED WIRE TERMINAL TO POWER

CONTACTS

VOLTAGE SUPPLY INPUT TERMINAL

REGULATED VOLTAGE OUTPUT TERMINAL

Fig. 1. The constant voltage regulator limits the instrument voltage to an effective 5 volts. The regulator consists of a heating coil and a bimetal arm which bends with the heat to open the contacts. Ford Div.—Ford Motor Co.

through the heating coil and heats the bimetal arm, causing it to bend and open the contacts. Opening the contacts stops the flow of current in the coil. The bimetal arm cools, permitting the contacts to re-close to start the cycle over again. The rapid making and breaking of the contacts causes a pulsating voltage with an effective average value of 5 volts that is supplied to the fuel, oil, and temperature gages. Although the pulsations are quite rapid, the gages are so constructed that a steady reading is assured.

Charge Indicator

Both a properly operating generator or alternator and a fully charged battery are necessary for continued operation of the vehicle. In an automobile, the fact that the generator or alternator is charging or discharging is indicated by means of a charge indicator light on the instrument panel or by means of an ammeter.

Charge Indicator Light. On most automobiles the charge indicator consists of a red light on the instrument panel that flashes on when the alternator or generator is not charging. See Fig. 2.

On vehicles using an alternator in the charging system, when the ignition switch is turned on, battery current flows through the charge indicator light bulb (and resistor connected in parallel with the light) and then through the field coil within the alternator rotor. Since the circuit is completed to ground through the field coil, the red light flashes on. However, the current flowing through the field coil is now great enough to establish a magnetic field, which allows the alternator to start charging.

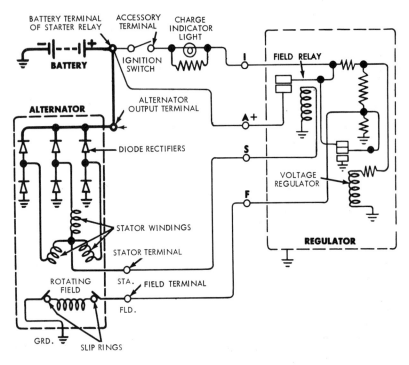

Fig. 2. Charge indicator light in an alternator charging circuit. Ford Div.—Ford Motor Co.

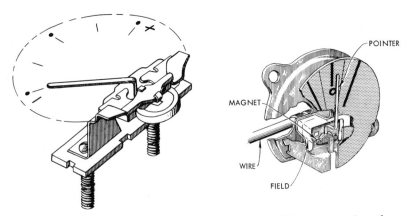

Fig. 3. Left, construction of a moving vane ammeter. Right, construction of a loop type ammeter.

As the alternator builds up voltage, the field relay contact points close. The battery current can now flow directly to the field coil (through the relay contact points) without going through the resistance unit and bulb. Therefore, the light will no longer glow.

In vehicles equipped with a direct current generator, the red charge indicator light is connected in parallel with the cutout relay contact points. With the ignition switch ON and the cutout points open, the charge indicator light glows, indicating that the generator is not connected to the battery. Once the engine is started and the generator starts charging, the cutout relay points close. This bypasses the warning light, which goes out, indicating that the generator is charging.

Ammeter. The ammeter performs an important function in keeping the driver constantly informed about the performance of the generator and battery circuit.

The ammeter, Fig. 3, indicates the direction of flow of current. Ammeters offer practically no resistance to the flow of current and are always connected in series in the charging circuit. When the battery is being charged by the generator, the ammeter pointer will indicate on the positive ($+$) side of the scale the strength of current flowing into the battery. Current being used for the lights, the engine, or the other electrical accessories reduces the amount of current flowing to the battery. If the battery is being discharged under such conditions, the ammeter will indicate on the negative ($-$) side of the scale the strength of current flowing out of the battery. The ammeter will show little or no charging rate when the battery is fully charged.

Operating Principles

Ammeters commonly used in automotive vehicles are the moving vane type or loop type.

Moving Vane Type. The moving vane type ammeter, Fig. 3, left, has two terminals and consists of a frame to which is attached a permanent magnet, a heavy conductor between the two terminals, and a pivoted vane to which an armature and pointer are attached. The armature is positioned between the poles of the permanent magnet, so that a pointer mounted on the armature points to zero when no current is flowing through the instrument. As current passes through the heavy conductor in either direction, a magnetic field is built up around the conductor. This overcomes the effect of the permanent

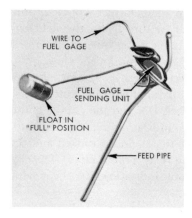

Fig. 4. Fuel gage sending unit. Buick Div. —General Motors Corp.

magnet, thus giving a reading proportional to the strength of the current passing through the instrument.

Loop Type. The loop type ammeter, Fig. 3, right, consists of a magnet and pointer assembly. No terminals are used on this type. When current flows through the wire assembled through a loop in the back of the instrument, a magnetic field is created around the wire. This causes the pointer assembly to move in proportion to the strength of the magnetic field.

Fuel Gage

Knowledge of the fuel supply is vitally important to the driver or the mechanic. This is supplied by the fuel gage system.

The fuel gage is electrically operated and consists of two units, a float-type "sending" unit actuated by the fuel level in the tank and a "receiving" unit mounted on the instrument panel.

Sending Unit. The tank unit consists of a float controlled rheostat or variable resistor, Fig. 4. It is mounted on top of the tank with the float and float arm extending into the tank. The float always follows the level of the fuel in the tank. The position of the float determines the amount of electrical resistance within the sending unit, and hence the amount of electricity sent to the fuel gage. The fuel gage on the instrument panel, by sensing the amount of electricity received, registers the level of fuel in the tank.

Receiving Unit. Two different types of fuel gages may be used, a thermostatic type or an electromagnetic type.

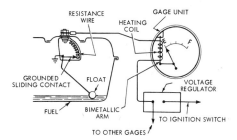

Fig. 5. Thermostatic fuel gage circuit. Plymouth Div.—Chrysler Corp.

Thermostatic Fuel Gage

The thermostatic gage consists of a bimetallic arm attached to a pointer and a heating coil, Fig. 5. When the fuel tank is empty, the sliding contact in the tank unit, which is controlled by the float, is at the end of the resistance wire. Because of the larger resistance only a small amount of current is sent to the heating coil of the fuel gage. The heat developed causes a slight bend in the bimetallic arm of the gage, deflecting the pointer to the "E" (Empty) position. When the tank is filled the float rises with the fuel level in the tank, and moves the ground contact toward the beginning of the resistance wire. With less resistance in the circuit, more current will flow through the heating coil of the receiving unit, which creates more heat around the bimetallic arm. The increasing current (and heat) increasingly bends the bimetallic arm and deflects the pointer to the "F" (Full) position on the gauge. The use of bimetal in the fuel gage eliminates fluctuation due to the surging of fuel in the tank and the float bobbing on the surface of the fuel.

Electromagnetic Fuel Gage

This type of receiving unit has two magnetic circuits, each with a coil to produce a magnetic field. One coil is grounded internally and exerts a constant pull on the pointer toward the empty mark when the ignition switch is turned on, Fig. 6. The other coil is grounded through the tank unit and exerts a pull on the pointer toward the full side. The tank unit contains a resistor and a sliding contact which moves as the float moves. A strong magnetic field is induced in the variable coil when the level of fuel in the tank rises, and the field weakens as the level drops. The gage is calibrated to indicate the amount of fuel left in the tank.

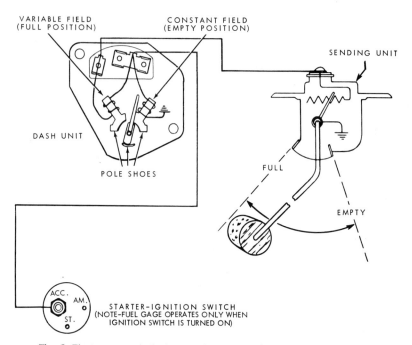

Fig. 6. Electromagnetic fuel gage circuit. Plymouth Div.—Chrysler Corp.

Oil Pressure Indicating Light

Whenever the engine is operating it is essential that sufficient oil is supplied to the various engine bearings. Excessive leakage or failure of the oil pump to function will cause loss of oil pressure and oil circulation. The oil pressure, therefore, is important because without proper oil circulation, bearings and other internal engine parts would not receive adequate lubrication.

Today's automobiles are equipped with a red indicator light on the instrument panel which lights when the oil pressure drops below a safe value. The light should light when the ignition switch is first turned on, and should go out when the engine starts and the oil pressure builds up. This indicator is connected in series between the oil pressure switch (sending unit) and the ON terminal of the ignition switch. Fig. 7 illustrates a typical oil pressure indicating light circuit.

The pressure switch is connected into the engine oil pressure

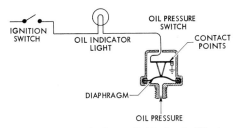

Fig. 7. Oil pressure indicator light circuit. Diaphragm actuated contacts will close when oil pressure drops below a safe level.

system. The switch is mounted on (screwed into) the cylinder block and consists of a diaphragm, spring, linkage, and contact points. When the engine is not operating, the contacts in the pressure switch are closed. Thus with no oil pressure, current flows from the ON terminal of the ignition switch through the light bulb and through the oil pressure switch contact points to ground, causing the bulb to light.

When the engine starts the oil pressure begins to rise. When the pressure has risen to approximately five pounds per square inch the oil pressure, acting on the diaphragm in the switch, opens the contact points. This breaks the circuit and causes the red light to go out. As long as sufficient oil pressure is maintained, the indicator lamp will remain out. If at any time the oil pressure in the system drops below five pounds per square inch, the switch contacts close and the oil pressure warning light comes on.

Oil Temperature Warning Light

In addition to the oil pressure warning system, a few cars have an oil temperature warning system. The oil temperature warning system alerts the driver to high operating temperatures which might damage the engine.

The oil temperature switch is connected in parallel with the oil pressure switch; both switches activate the same warning light. Fig. 8. A flasher unit is included in the oil temperature switch circuit so that the signals from the two switches can be distinguished.

The oil temperature switch has a thermostatically controlled set of contact points which closes when the oil temperature reaches 315°F. This completes the circuit; current flows through the flasher

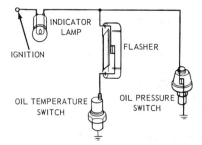

Fig. 8. Oil temperature light circuit is parallel to the pressure circuit. Both activate the same instrument panel warning light. A flasher unit is included in the oil temperature circuit to identify the signal. Ford Div.—Ford Motor Co.

unit and the temperature switch contact points to ground. The flasher unit contains a bimetal element which alternately opens and closes the circuit, causing the warning light to flash on and off until the oil temperature drops to below 315°F.

Temperature Indicator

Automotive vehicles are equipped with a temperature indicating device which is either a gage that shows the approximate temperature of the engine coolant or a warning light that lights when the engine becomes too hot. The temperature indicator fills a real need since too high a coolant temperature could damage the engine and too low a temperature would deprive the engine of power.

Temperature Indicating Light. A temperature indicating light system consists of a sending unit that is sensitive to coolant temperature changes, and an indicating light (or lights) mounted on the instrument panel. Fig. 9.

The temperature indicating light is controlled by a sending unit which consists of a bimetallic arm that connects the lights to ground. When the engine is first started, a green or blue (cold) light flashes on, the circuit to ground being completed by the bimetallic arm in contact with the cold terminal on the sending unit. As the engine heats up, the bimetallic arm bends, breaking the circuit to the green light (at approximately 125°F.) and causing the lights to go out.

Further heating of the arm causes the arm to bend still more until (at about 245°F.) the arm makes contact with the hot terminal and the red light flashes on, indicating that the engine is overheating. Some engines have no green light, utilizing only the red light to indicate excessive engine temperature.

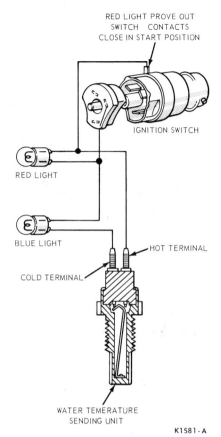

Fig. 9. Engine temperature warning light circuit. Sending unit is a plug screwed into the water jacket. It contains a bimetal element that bends with extreme heat to contact the "hot" terminal and ground the warning light circuit. Ford Div.— Ford Motor Co.

When the ignition switch is first turned on, a set of contacts in the ignition switch causes the red light to flash on momentarily, indicating that the light is operative.

Temperature Indicating Gage. Some vehicles are equipped with a temperature gage that indicates the approximate temperature of the engine coolant. The circuit consists of a sending unit mounted in the cylinder head and a gage mounted on the instrument panel, Fig. 10, left.

The sending unit contains a small disc of sintered material that is sensitive to temperature change. This material has a low electrical resistance when hot and a high resistance when cold. The material is enclosed in a sealed bulb that screws into the cylinder head. The

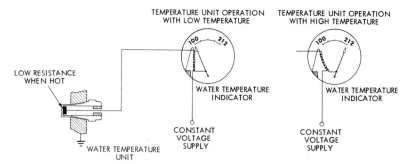

Fig. 10. Bimetallic engine temperature circuit. Left, operation at low temperature. Right, high temperature lowers resistance of sending unit and causes increased current flow through heater coil. Bimetal strip bends with heat and moves pointer to "hot" side of scale.

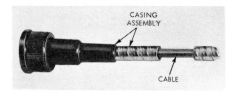

Fig. 11. **Speedometer drive cable and casing.** A.C. Spark Plug Div.—General Motors Corp.

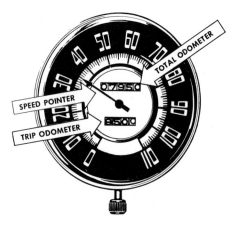

Fig. 12. **Typical speedometer face.** A.C. Spark Plug Div.—General Motors Corp.

extreme end of the bulb is in contact with the coolant so that the bulb is quite sensitive to the coolant temperaure.

The temperature gage located on the instrument panel is of the bimetallic type with a heater coil. When the engine is cold the high resistance of the sending unit permits little current flow in the gage circuit, and the gage reads on the "cold" end of the dial. When the engine reaches its normal operating temperature the decreased resistance of the sending unit allows more current to flow through the gage circuit, causing the heater coil to become hot. This bends the bimetallic arm which is linked to the pointer, so that the gage reads at the "hot" end of the meter scale, Fig. 10, right.

Balanced coil temperature gages are also used with such sending units. The changes in current strength modify the magnetic pull of the receiving unit coils, causing the gage pointer to indicate the temperature of the engine coolant on the dial.

Speedometer

The speedometer is, of course, an essential instrument on modern automobiles. Engineering improvements introduced year after year have made possible greater speeds with smoother and quieter operation.

With high speeds easily reached the driver must observe safe driving speeds under all weather, road and traffic conditions. The modern car can be driven at 50, 60, or 70 mph as easily as at 20 or 30 mph. In fact, without a speedometer to indicate vehicle speed, it is difficult to accurately estimate the actual speed of a car.

Traffic laws restrict road speeds for the safety of the public. Good drivers watch the speedometer and drive at safe speeds, not only for their own safety, but for the safety of others on the road as well.

All passenger car speedometers are driven by a flexible shaft. The flexible cable is enclosed in a casing or housing, Fig. 11. A gear attached to one end of the shaft is meshed with a gear assembled on the transmission main drive shaft. The other end of the drive cable is connected to the speedometer head. When the cable revolves, it actuates the mechanism in the head (usually 1,000 rpm indicates a speed of 60 mph).

Speed is indicated on the speedometer face, Fig. 12, by a pointer in miles per hour. The distance traveled is registered on an odometer

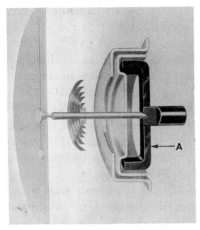
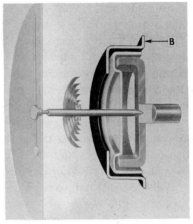
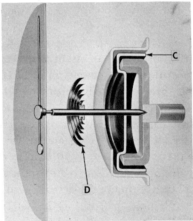

Fig. 13. Speed indicating mechanism of a speedometer. A, permanent magnet driven by flexible drive shaft. B, stationary field plate completes magnetic circuit. C, non-magnetic speed cup, attached to pointer shaft, is actuated by eddy currents created by rotating permanent magnet. D, hairspring controls pointer deflection. A C Spark Plug Div., General Motors Corp.

which records up to 99,999 miles. Some speedometers are equipped with a trip odometer which registers distances traveled up to 999.9 miles. Trip odometers are built with a reset stem so that they may be reset to zero whenever desired.

Most speedometers contain a permanent magnet, Fig. 13A, which rotates at the same speed as the drive cable. A non-magnetic

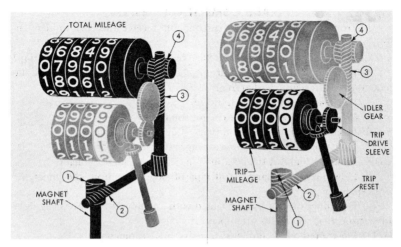

Fig. 14. Odometer mechanism in typical speedometer. A.C. Spark Plug Div.—
General Motors Corp.

speed cup, Fig. 13C, to which the pointer shaft is attached, floats
on bearings. A field plate, Fig. 13B, completes the field to produce
eddy currents by the rotating magnet. This exerts a definite pull on
the speed cup, causing it to move in direct ratio to the speed of the
revolving magnet (representing car speed). As the speed of the
vehicle increases the rotating magnet increases the magnetic drag
and pulls the speed cup and pointer farther around, indicating
faster speed. A finely calibrated hairspring, Fig. 13D, is adjusted in
relation to the magnetic pull to indicate true speed. The hairspring
also serves to pull the speed cup and pointer to zero when the vehicle is stopped.

As seen in Fig. 14, the odometer is driven by the same shaft
which drives the magnet in the speed-indicating portion of the instrument. A series of gears are driven through a worm gear cut on
the magnet shaft as shown at 1, 2, 3, and 4 in Fig. 14. The odometer
face consists of five wheels, each numbered with digits from 1 to 0.
A complete revolution of any one wheel turns the next left-hand
wheel one-tenth of one revolution.

The trip odometer (Fig. 14) is driven by an idler gear and a trip-
drive sleeve on the trip-odometer shaft. In most instruments, the
right-hand wheel registers in tenths of a mile.

TRADE COMPETENCY TESTS

1. From where do electrical instruments receive the current that energizes them?

2. What is the purpose of the voltage regulator in instrument operation?

3. How does the charge indicator light operate to indicate that the generator or alternator is charging?

4. What does an ammeter indicate?

5. What two types of ammeters are commonly used?

6. What are the two common types of electric fuel gages?

7. How does an oil pressure warning system light operate?

8. How are high oil temperatures indicated on some vehicles?

9. How does the balanced coil type of gage differ from the bimetallic arm type of gage?

10. How does the sending unit used with a temperature indicating light differ from that used with a temperature gage?

11. What method is employed to drive a speedometer?

12. What causes the speedometer pointer to move to indicate vehicle speed?

13. What is an odometer?

INDEX

A

"A" circuit, DC generator 135, *136*
AC (*see* Alternating current)
Accessories 341
  electric motors 347
  defroster 349
  heater 349, *349*
  power seats 348, *348*
  power windows 348
  horns 341, *341, 342*
  relay-buzzer 342, *343*
  windshield wiper 343, *344*
  windshield washer *345*, 346, *346, 347*
Advance mechanisms
  centrifugal 267, *268, 269, 270*
  distributor 312
  engine advance 313
  test bench check 313
  spark 265, *266*
  vacuum *270, 271, 272*
Air gap (AC) *237, 238,* 239, *239*
Aimer, safety *366*
Aiming screen 362, *362*
Alignment, headlights 361, *362, 366*
  adjustment 363, *364*
  aiming 362, *362, 364*
Alternating current
  AC charging system
    (*see* Charging systems, AC)
Alternator
  assembly 250
  construction 194, *194, 195, 196*
    end frame *194,* 197
    rotor 194, *196*
    stator 194, *196*
  disassembly 245, *246*
  operation 197, *198, 199*
  output 207, *207, 208*
    check 227, *228*
  principles 192, *193*
  service 243
    brushes 248
    brush holders 248
    diode test *244,* 245
    field coil amperage draw 243, *243*
    rotor test 247, *248*
    stator test 247, *249*
  test conclusions 229
Alternator regulator 209
Alternator voltage limiter 209, *210, 212*
  with field relay 213, *214, 215, 217*
Ambient temperature
  voltage chart *154, 230*

Ammeter *25,* 27, *27*
  loop type *372,* 374
  moving vane type *372,* 373
Ampere 9
Amplifier
  assembly *284*
  circuitry *283*
Armature 80, *80, 85*
  generator 126, *126*
  lap wound *132*
Armature,
  effects of current
    in 133, *133*
  repairs
    open circuit 114
    resurfacing commutator 115
    tests 113, 169
    ground 114, *114,* 169, *170*
    short circuit 114, *115,* 169, *170, 171*
Assembly (*see* name of individual unit)
Atom 1
  boron *320*
  helium *3*
  hydrogen *2*
  oxygen *4*
  phosphorus *319*
  silicon *319*

B

"B" circuit in DC generator 136, *136*
Back up lights 339, *339*
Ballast resistor 301
Basic electrical units
  ampere 9
  ohm 9
  volt 9
Battery
  in charging system 158
  connections, cleaning 158
  construction of *33*
    cables 67
    cable clamps *63,* 64, *64, 65*
    case *36,* 37, *37*
    cells 33
      arrangement of 38, *38*
    electrolyte 37, 45
    (*see also* Electrolyte; Specific
      gravity)
    elements 35, *36*
    plates 34, *35, 36*
    separators 35, *36*
  defects 76
  dopes 51

Battery—*continued*
  operating principles
    charge 32, 40, *41*
    discharge 32, 40, *41*
    self-discharge 43
  power output 44
  ratings tests
    five-ten second voltage test 44
    SAE twenty-hour rating 43
    zero test 44
  replacing 68, *69*
  servicing 64
    corrosion *63*, 64, *66*
  sizes 39
  state of charge 48
  temperature effects 42, *42*, 49, *49*
  testing 53
    cadmium cell probe 58, *59*, *60*
    capacity 60, *61*
    421 battery 62, *63*
    open circuit voltage 55, *56*, *58*
    specific gravity 54
    state of charge 53
  water consumption 189
  warranty 39
Bench output test, DC
  generator 178, *179*
Bendix drive 91, *91*, *93*, *96*
  inspection 120
Brake lights 340, *340*
Brushes 81
  alternator 248
  DC generator 127, *127*, 173, 175, *176*
  neutral point 133, *134*
  test 118
Brush holders
  alternator 248
  DC generator 173, *174*
  test 118, *119*
Brush spring tension 119
  on DC generator 173, *175*
Build-up time 274, *275*
Bulb, light replacement *359*
  from front 355
  from rear 355, *360*
Bushing
  clearance in ignition
  distributor *306*

C

Cable clamps *63*, 64, *65*
Cables
  battery 67
  secondary ignition 299, *300*, *301*
Cadmium cell probe test 58, *59*, *60*
Cap, distributor 272, 312, *312*
Capacitor (ignition) 261, *261*
  test 302, 305

Capacity test 60, *61*
Case, battery *36*, 37, *37*
Cells, battery
  arrangement of 38, *38*
Centrifugal advance 267, *268*, *269*, *270*
Changing battery 68
Charge, electrical
  like *7*
  unlike *8*
Charge indicator 371
  light 371, *372*
Charging, battery 32, 40, *41*, 69
  boost charging 72
  fast charging 70, *71*
  modified fast and slow
    charging *74*
  overcharging 74
  preparation 69
  slow charging 72, *73*
Charging DC generator *138*
Charging circuit control, DC 139, *141*
Charging systems
  AC 191, *192*
    diagnosis 225, *226*
    service 224
  DC 123
Chemical reaction in
  battery 40, *41*
Circuit breakers 351, *351*
  replacement 360, *361*
Circuit resistance tests 108, 229
Circuits
  amplifier *284*
  charging control 139, *141*
  DC generator 131, 135, 136,
    136, 157
  electrical
    diagram symbols *30*
    parallel 12, *13*
    series 11, *12*
    series-parallel 14, *14*
  grounded
    field coils 117, *117*, 164, *166*
    generator 169, *170*
  horn *341*, 342, *342*
  ignition
    primary 256, *258*, *273*, *274*
      voltage drop test in 298, *299*
    secondary 257, *258*
    transistorized 284, *285*
  instrument 370
  integrated 329, *330*
  internal motor 86, *86*
  lighting (*see also* Lighting system)
    body *358*
    engine compartment *357*
    front *356*
    rear *358*

Circuits—*continued*
  open
    armature 114
    field coils 116, *116*, 164, *165*, *166*
    voltage test 55, *56*, *57*, *58*
  parallel 12, *13*
  regulator resistor 150
  relay buzzer 342, *343*
  resistance tests 108, 229
  series 11, *12*
  series-parallel 14, *14*
  short
    armature 114, 115
    field coils 165, *167*
    generator 169, *170*, *171*
  starting motor, *86*, *87*, 92
  symbols *30*
  transistor *327*
Cleaner, terminal *66*
Clearance
  bushing in ignition *306*
  pinion 121, *121*
Coils 22, *23*
  ignition 259, *259*
  polarity *303*
  resistance unit 260
  test 302, *303*
Commutator
  in DC generator 171, *172*
  resurfacing 115
Commutator end frame 81, 127, *128*
  in DC generator 174
  inspection 120
Conductor 5
  diode as *321*
  magnetic effect when parallel 21, *21*, 22
Contact points
  ignition *263*, 264, *282*
    alignment *308*
    analysis 306, *307*
    distributor with dual contact 264, *264*
    dwell 311, *311*
    gap adjustment 309, *309*, 310
    replacement 307
    spring tension 308, *308*
  regulator in DC generator 187
Control, DC charging circuit 139, *141*
Control system, DC generator 139
Cornering lights 339
Corrosion of battery 64, *66*
Courtesy lights 341
Covalent bonding *319*
Current
  flow in DC generator 131
  induction in DC generator 129, *129*
  reverse bias *328*

Current draw test, solenoid 110, *111*
Current regulator in generator 146
Current regulator test DC generator 186
Cutout relay 141, *143*
  in DC generator 183, *185*

D

DC (*see* Direct current)
Defroster motor 349
Diaphragm, retard *315*
Dimmer, headlight 337
Diode 201, *202*, *321*, 322
  automotive type *333*
  conducting properties 321, *321*
  cross-section *333*
  electrical balance 320, *321*
  insulating properties 322, *322*
  PN junction in 320, *320*
  symbol for *324*
  testing *244*, 245, 324, *324*, *325*
Diode, zener 328, *329*
Direct current
  DC charging circuit
    control 139, *141*
  DC charging system 123
  DC generator *130* (*see also* Generator DC)
Directional signal light 337, *338*
Disassembly of starting
  motor 112, *113*
Discharge of battery 32, 40, *41*
Distortion of lines of force *82*
Distributor
  advance 312
    engine 313
    test bench 313
  bushing clearance *306*
  cap 272, 312, *312*
  disassembly *304*, 305, *306*
  ignition 262, *262*
    with dual contacts 264, *264*
  magnetic pulse *285*
  modulator 287, *288*
  rotor 272, 312
  shaft *306*
  tester 311, *311*
Dopes, battery 51
Double contact point voltage regulator
  151, 152, *152*, *153*
Drive end plate, DC generator 128, 175
Drive housing 81
  inspection 119
Drives
  Bendix 91, *91*, *93*
  gear reduction *89*
  overrunning clutch 90, *90*
  starting motor 89
Dry charge battery 75

Dwell angle in ignition system *311, 312*
Dwell period *264*

E

Electrical circuits, (*see* Circuits)
Electrical measurements
  meters 22, 24
    ammeter *25*, 27, *27*
    ohmmeter *29*, 30
    shunt *25*, 26
    voltmeter *26*, 28, *28*
  units
    ampere 9
    ohm 9
    volt 9
Electric Motors
  checking 368
Electrical nature of matter 1
  charges *7, 8*
  circuits 11
    parallel 12, *13*
    series-parallel 14, *14*
  power 10
Electricity, static 6
Electrolyte
  adjusting 51
  mixing 50, *50*
  temperature effects 49
  (*see also* Specific gravity)
Electromagnetic fuel gage 375, *376*
Electromagnetism 19, *119*
Electromotive forces 10
Electron Theory 1
  flow 4, 5, *6, 7,*
  potential 4, 5, 7
Elements, battery 35, *36*
Emergency warning light *338,* 339
Emission control 266, 272, 287, 288
  (*see also* Distributor modulator)
End frame assemblies in alternator
    194, 197
Externally grounded DC generator
    135, *136*
Externally mounted transistorized
    regulator 218, *219*

F

Feeler gage *309, 310*
Field coils
  amperage draw check (on alternator)
    243, *243*
  DC generator 125, *125*
  ground circuit 117, *117,* 164, *166*
  open circuit 116, *116,* 164, *165, 166*
  repair, replacing 117
  short circuit 165, *167*

Field relay
  AC adjustment 240, *240, 241, 242*
  on alternator voltage limiter 213,
    214, 215
  testing 233, *234*
  voltage limiter setting 241
Five-ten second voltage test 44
Flasher, emergency *338,* 339
Flat Feeler gage *309, 310*
Flaws, ignition *295*
Flow
  electron 5, *7*
  water *6*
421 battery test 62, *63*
Frame, DC generator 124, *125*
Freezing of electrolyte 49
Fuel gage, (*see* Meters)
Full-wave rectification 202, *203, 204,*
    205, 206
Fuses *350,* 351
  replacement of 360
Fusible links 352, *352*

G

Gages (*see* Meters)
Gap
  contact point adjustment 309, *309*
Generator, DC
  assembly 176, *179*
  charging properties *138,* 161, *162*
  circuit 157
  construction of 124, *124,* 134, 135,
    135
    armature 126, *126*
    brushes 127, *127*
    field coils 125, *125*
    frame 124, *125*
    pole shoes *125*
  control system 139
  disassembly 163, *164*
  externally grounded ("A" circuit)
    135, *136*
  inspection 159
  installation 180, *180*
  internally grounded ("B" circuit)
    136, *136*
  motorizing test 177
  operation of 128, 137
    current flow,
      continuous 131
      one direction 131
    current induction 129, *129*
  output test 160, *160*
  polarizing 136, 177
  repair
    armature 169
      grounded circuit 169, *170*
      short circuit 169, *170, 171*

Generator—*continued*
  brushes 173, 175, *176*
  brush holder 173, *174*
  brush spring tension 173, *175*
    cleaning 163
  commutator 171, *172*
  commutator end plate 174
  drive end plate 175
  field coils 163, *165*
  grounded circuit 164, *166*
  open circuit 164, *165, 166*
  short circuit 165, *167*
  tests
    bench output 178, *179*
    charging 161, *162*
    generator output 160, *160*
  types 137
Generator, DC regulation 144, *145, 146*
  units of 140, *141*

H

Headlights 332, 335
  adjustment 363, *364, 365*
  aiming 362, *362, 364*
  alignment 361, *362, 366*
  sealed beam *335, 336*
    replacement of 355, *359*
Heater motor 349, *349*
Helium atom *3*
Horn 341, *341, 342*
  checking 365
  circuit *341*, 342, *342*
  relay-buzzer 342, *343*
Housing
  drive 81
  starter 78, *80*
Hydrogen atom *2*
Hydrometer *46*, 47, 54, *54*

I-J-K

Idling, engine 265
Ignition capacitor 261, *261*
Ignition coil 259, *259*
Ignition distributor 262, *262*
  with dual contacts 264, *264*
Ignition resistor 96
Ignition switch 259
Ignition system 256, *257*
  circuits
    primary 256, *258, 273, 274*
    secondary 257, *258*
  components of 258
    capacitor 261, *261*
    coil 259, *259*
    coil resistance unit 260
    distributor 262, *262*
      with dual contacts 264, *264*

  spark advance mechanism
    265, *266*
  switch 259
  operation of 273, *276, 277*
  service
    transistor 316
  testing 291
    individual components 297
      ballast resistor 301
      capacitor 302, 305
      coil 302, *303*
      contact points 306, *307 (see also*
        Contact points)
      distributor *304*, 305, *306*
        advance 312
        cap and rotor 312, *312*
      ignition timing 314, *315*
        firing order 316
        initial timing 316
      secondary ignition cables
        299, *300, 301*
      voltage drop in primary circuit
        298, *299*
    with oscilloscope 291, *293*, 2⁰,̓
  transistorized 280, *281, 282*
    circuitry 284, *285*
    contact-point ignition 281
    operating principles 286
Ignition timing
  idling 265
  vacuum advance 269
Ignition trouble-shooting 290, *292*
Ignition wiring 257
Indicator
  AC charge 242
  engine temperature
    gage 379, *380*
    light 378, *379*
  oil pressure 376, *377*
  oil temperature 377, *378*
Induction
  of current in DC generator 129, *129*
  of voltage in alternator 199, *199*
  magnetic 19
Inertia drives (*see* Drives, Bendix)
Intrument circuit 370
Instrument lights 341
Instrument voltage regulator 370, *371*
Instruments, measuring (*see* Meters)
Insulator
  diode as *322*
Integrated circuits 329, *330*
Interior lights 341
Internal motor circuits 86, *86*
Internally grounded DC generator
  136, *136*
Internally mounted transistorized
  regulators 218, *219*

L

Lap wound armature *132*
Left hand rule 20, *20,* 82, *82*
  for coils 23, *23*
Light
  charge indicator 242
Light, distribution
  glare 337
  from sealed beam headlight *336*
Lighting system 332, *334*
  back-up lights 339, *339*
  cornering lights 339
  directional signal 337, *338*
  emergency warning 339
  headlights 332, 335
    sealed beam *335, 336*
  instrument lights 341
  indicator lights (*see* Indicator)
  parking lights 340, *340*
  stop lights 340, *340*
Lighting system service 354, *356, 357*
Light bulb replacement
  from front 355, *359*
  from rear 355, *360*
Light load test of battery 226, *226*
Lines of force 79, *80*
  distortion of *82*
Locked resistance test 107, *108*

M

Magnet
  bar *16, 18*
  horseshoe *16, 17*
Magnetic effects of parallel conductors
    21, *21, 22*
Magnetic field (*see also* Magnetic lines
    of force)
  current thru armature *85*
  current thru field coils *85*
  shifting of *85*
  in simplified series type motor *85*
Magnetic induction 19
Magnetic lines of force
  (fields) *16, 17,* 18, *18*
  around bar magnet *16, 18*
  in coil *20, 23*
  around horseshoe magnet *16, 17*
  in parallel conductors 21, *21, 22*
  in wire *19*
Magnetic pulse distributor *285*
Magnetic permeability 19
Magnetism 15
  electro- 19
  molecular arrangement *18*
  theory of 15
Matter, electrical nature 1

Measurement of electricity (*see* Meters)
  units 9
Meter, parts 24
Meters
  ammeter *372,* 373
    loop *372, 373,* 374
    moving vane *372,* 373
  charge indicator 371, *372*
  flat feeler gage *309, 310*
  fuel gage
    types
      electromagnetic 375, *376*
      thermostatic 375, *375*
    units
      receiving 374
      sending 374, *374*
  ignition testing
    dial indicator *310*
    distributor tester *311*
    feeler gage *309, 310*
    tension scale *308*
  odometer 382, *383*
  ohmmeter *29,* 30
  oil pressure light 376, *377*
  oil temperature warning light 377,
    378
  speedometer *380,* 381, *382*
  temperature indicator 378
    gage 379, *380*
    light 378, *379*
  voltage regulator 370, *371*
  voltmeter *26,* 28, *28*
Modulator, distributor 287, *288*
Motorizing test on DC generator 177
Motors
  characteristics 88
  electric 368
    defroster 349
    heater 349, *349*
    power seats 348, *348*
    power windows 348
    windshield wiper 367, *367*

N

Neutral point location of brushes 133
Neutral safety switch 97, *97*
Neutral switch test 111, *112*
No load test 103, *104*

O

Odometer 382, *383*
Ohm 9
Ohmmeter *29,* 30
Ohm's law 9
Oil pressure indicating light 376, *377*
Oil temperature warning light 377, *378*
Open circuit voltage test 55, *56, 57, 58*

Operation of systems (*see* name of system)
Oscilloscope
  patterns
    common troubles 296
    complete fault 295
    primary ignition cycle 294
    secondary 297
    testing ignition system with 291, *293, 294*
Output
  alternator 207, *207, 208*
  checking 227, *228*
Overrunning clutch drive 90, *90*
  inspection 120, *121*
Oxygen atom *4*

P-Q

PN junction
  diode 320, *320*
  transistor *326*
Parallel circuit 12, *13*
Parallel conductors
  magnetic effect 21, *21, 22*
Parking lights 340, *340*
Patterns, oscilloscope (*see* Oscilloscope Patterns)
Permeability, magnetic 19
Pinion clearance 121, *121*
Plates, battery 34, *35, 36*
Polarity
  DC generators 136
  ignition coil *303*
  regulator 155
Polarizing generator 177
Pole shoes, DC generator *125*
Pollution (*see* Emission control)
Power, electrical 10
Power output, battery 44

R

Ratings of battery (*see* Battery, ratings)
Rectification
  full-wave (six stages) 202, *203, 204, 205, 206*
Regulator
  alternator 209
    with field relay 213, *214, 215, 217*
    voltage limiter *210, 212*
  DC generator 144, *145, 146*, 181
    adjusting 181, *184, 185*
    current 146
    double contact point voltage *151*, 152, *152*
    inspection 181, *182*
    testing 181
    units 140, *141*

voltage in 148
  transistorized (alternator) 250
    externally mounted 218, *219*, 250
    integrated circuit *250*, 251, *251*
    testing *252, 253*, 254
    internally mounted *220*, 221, *221, 222*
Regulator contact points
  cleaning 187
Regulator polarity 155
Regulator tests
  current 186
  voltage 186, *186*
Relay-buzzer 342, *343*
Relay
  cutout 141, *143*
    in DC generator 183, *185*
  field
    adjustment 240, *240, 241, 242*
    on alternator voltage limiter 213, *214, 215*
    test 233, *234*
Replacing battery 68, *69*
Resistance tests
  circuit 229
  starter circuit 108
Resistance unit
  ignition coil 260
Resistor
  ballast (in ign.) 301
  ignition 96
  regulator circuit 150
Retard diaphragm *315*
Reverse bias current *328*
Rotor
  assembly on alternator 194, *196*
  distributor (ign.) 272, 312, *312*
  test on alternator 247, *248*

S

SAE twenty-hour rating 43
Safety aimer *366*
Screen, aiming 362, *362, 364*
Screws, headlight adjustment *364*
Sealed beam headlights 335, *335, 336*
  replacement 355, *359*
Secondary ignition cables check 299, *300*, 301
Self-discharge of battery 43
Semi-conductors 318
Separators, battery 35, *36*
Series circuit 11, *12*
Series-parallel circuit 14, *14*
Shaft, distributor *306*
Shunt *25*, 26
Signal
  back up 339, *339*
  cornering lights 339

Signal—*continued*
  directional light 337, *338*
  emergency flasher 339
Solenoid 93, *94*
  current draw test 110, *111*
  switches 93, *94, 95*
Spark advance mechanisms 265, *266*
Spark plugs 278
  construction *278,* 279
  operation 279, *279*
Specific gravity 46, *47*
  and freezing 49, *49*
  hydrometer *46,* 47
  and state of charge 48
  temperature correction *47,* 48
  test for 54
  and tropical climates 49
Speedometer *380,* 381, *382*
Spring tension, brush 119
Stall torque test 105, *106*
Starter housing 78, *80*
Starter load test 102, *102*
Starting motor 78, *79, 88*
  circuits *82, 86,* 92
  circuit controls 97, *98*
  construction 78
    armature 80, *80*
    brushes 81
    commutator end frame 81
    drive housing 81
    field coils 78, *79*
    starter housing 78, *80*
  disassembly 112, *113*
  drives 89
    bendix (inertia) 91, *91, 93, 96*
    gear reduction *89*
    overrunning clutch 90, *90*
  operation 81
  reassembly 120
  repair 112, *113*
  tests
    circuit resistance 108
    locked resistance 107, *108*
    no load 103, *104*
    preliminary 100
    stall torque 105, *106*
    starter load 102, *102*
State of charge on battery 48
State of charge test 53
Static electricity 6
Stator
  alternator assembly 194, *196*
  3-phase Delta connection 200, *201*
  3-phase Y connection 200, *201*
  test on alternator 247, *249*
Stop lights 340, *340*
Storage battery (*see* Battery)
Sulphation in battery 75

Supply voltage test *254,* 255
Switch
  ignition 259
  neutral safety 97, *97*
  solenoid 93, *94, 95*
  starting motor 92, *96*
Switch replacement 361
Symbols
  circuit diagram *30*
  diode *324*
  zener diode *329*

T

Temperature
  compensation in DC generator 153
  effects on battery 42, *42,* 47, 48, 49, *49*
Temperature indicator 378
  gage 379, *380*
  light 378, *379*
Tension
  contact point spring 308, *308*
Test bench
  check advance 313
Tests (*see* name of specific unit to be tested)
Theft-deterrent system (horn relay-buzzer) 342, *343*
Thermostatic fuel gage 375, *375*
Timing, ignition 314, *315*
  idling 265
  initial 316
  firing order 316
  vacuum advance 269
Transistor 325, *326*
  circuits *327*
    emitter to base *327, 328*
    emitter to collector *327*
  junctions 326, *326*
Transistorized ignition system 280, *281, 282*
  circuitry *284,* 285
  contact point 281
  operating principles 286
  service 316
Transistorized regulator
  externally mounted 218, *219*
  internally mounted 220, 221, *221, 222*
Transistorized regulator service (AC) 250
  externally mounted 250
  integrated circuit *250,* 251, *251*
    testing *252, 253,* 254
Tropical climate, effects on battery 49
Trouble-shooting chart 101
  DC generator *158*
  ignition 290, 292

U

Units of electricity 8, 9

V

Vacuum advance (ign.) 269, *270, 271, 272*
Volt 9
Voltage sources 10
Voltage drop test 108, *109*
  at cable connections *110*
  in primary ignition circuit 298, *299*
  in starting motor circuit 108
Voltage limiter (regulator)
  adjustment 234, *236*
  in alternator 209, *212*, 230, *231*
  with field relay 213, *214, 215*
  in generator 148, 186, *186*
    double contact point *151*, 152, *152, 153*
Voltage setting (AC) 235, *236, 238*

Voltage supply test *254*, 255
Voltmeter *26*, 28, *28*

W-X-Y

Warranty on battery 39
Washer, windshield *345*, 346, *346, 347, 367*, 368
Water loss in battery 64, *67*, 189
Wet charge battery 75
Windshield washer *345*, 346, *346, 347, 367*, 368
Windshield wiper 343, *344*
  motor 367, *367*
Wiper, windshield 343, *344*
  motor 367, *367*
Wiring, ignition 257

Z

Zener diode 328, *329*
  symbol for *329*
Zero test of battery 44